MEXICAN FAMILY COOKING

○

Aida Gabilondo

○

FAWCETT COLUMBINE
NEW YORK

A Fawcett Columbine Book
Published by Ballantine Books
Copyright © 1986 by Aída Gabilondo
Illustrations copyright © 1986 by Laura Hartman Maestro
Silhouettes copyright © 1986 by Heather Taylor

LIBRARY OF CONGRESS CATALOGING-IN-PUBLICATION
Gabilondo, Aida.
Mexican family cooking.
1. Cookery, Mexican. I. Title.
TX716.M4G33 1986   641.5972   85-90595
ISBN: 0-449-90162-9

Text design by Beth Tondreau
Cover design by James R. Harris
Cover illustration by Heather Taylor

Manufactured in the United States of America
First Edition: July 1986
10 9 8 7 6 5 4 3 2 1

TO MY DAUGHTERS FOUR—
ZARELA, AÍDA, MARINA AND CLARISSA—
FOR HAVING MADE MY
LIFE COMPLETE

CONTENTS

MIL GRACIAS—

To my husband for his patience and loving support during the creation of this book and for his acceptance of my love affair with cooking.

To my editors, Ginny Faber, Joelle Delbourgo and Jane Mollman for their help and guidance.

To my daughter, Zarela, for carrying the torch at the end of this journey.

MEXICAN
FAMILY
COOKING

INTRODUCTION

SALT, PEPPER, AND LOVE

When I am asked about the first incident in my life that I can truly recall, I answer, "Playing cook under the huge umbrella trees that surrounded the first home I can remember." I grew up on a beautiful cattle ranch in Northern Mexico, so lovely, indeed, that it would have been the perfect setting for a Hollywood western. No doubt we had a city house too (all ranchers did), but the ranch is the one I remember.

The ranch house was rambling, with eaves—one story, sitting in the middle of fruit orchards: pear and apple trees and some peach, apricot, and plum. A tall lonely huge pecan tree grew at one end of the orchard and provided all the nuts we used during the year for baking and candy-making, and simply for eating.

My father worked very hard, of course. My maternal grandmother lived with us and ran the kitchen, and my mother ran the house. My grandmother was a very conscientious mother-in-law and I never heard any arguments, discussions, or raised voices. In fact, my father always insisted that the word mother-in-law was as lovely a word as mother in his vocabulary. We all thought that our home was the normal Mexican household—three generations living under one roof in perfect harmony.

A cattle ranch normally provides your milk, eggs (if you raise chickens), and beef, pork, and lamb. If you are industrious you may also raise rabbits and pigeons. A small vegetable garden does the rest. Then you must purchase the essential "ungrowables"—flour and sugar, coffee, tea, spices, and oil. Among what we considered luxury items were vanilla, cocoa, coconut, and various dried fruits. It was a great, rewarding life, and if it entailed hardships in some ways, we never gave them much thought.

My sisters, my younger brother, and I had a happy childhood, especially those summers spent on the family ranches in Sonora and Chihuahua. Dad bought us the best ponies money could buy, sure-footed, trained, and gaited—perfect mounts. Each of us had a monogrammed saddle, and we were trained to take care of all our gear. Picnic food from Grandmother's kitchen, tucked into our saddle bags for munching on our riding jaunts, was a treat I can still taste in memory.

I confess I was a tomboy when I was little—the marble-shooting champion of the neighborhood! I always looked disreputable, with calluses on my hands and knees. Fortunately, this phase in my life did not last long; soon I was taking singing lessons, learning grooming, and taking a more serious interest in the kitchen, previously just a warm, marvelous-smelling refuge where I could "help."

The kitchen was huge, or so I remember it with the eyes of a child. An enormous wood range stood against one wall with a big wood and kindling box beside it. The range had eight burners and a wonderful "no-fail" oven. I couldn't reach the burner lids to stoke it, so I would drop kindling into it through its small side lid that I could raise. I had a little stool that I could step on to reach the pots and pans when I wanted to stir. At this time I must have been four years old, no more than that I am sure. There was a water heater beside the stove, kept hot by stove heat, so we always had a big supply of hot water for washing dishes. Two pots were always simmering away at one end of the stove—the stock pot and the bean pot.

My grandmother was a superb cook and the kitchen was her domain. She was a tall, heavyset lady with silvery hair and china blue eyes, quiet and always calm, an ideal teacher for someone like me. She never complained of having me afoot, and never chased me out of the kitchen. Not so the maid who helped with washing pots and dishes and bringing in the wood. She would try to get rid of me by sending me on errands.

Grandmother was a loving cook: no rough stirring or pouring. She insisted that food resented being rudely handled and that finished dishes would show any mistreatment. She stirred lightly, gently folding in ingredients, tasting and adding with care, and she invariably moved pans and skillets away from high heat, preferring a simmer to a hard boil.

Years later when I started teaching cooking in my home town, I remembered her words, and when I wrote a recipe on the blackboard or dictated it to my students, I always ended the list of ingredients with the words, *"Sal, pimienta, y amor."* Salt, pepper, and love. When I first started playing with the thought of writing this book, I wanted precisely that title, but many wise people told me that salt had become a no-no and the title wouldn't do. Now it would be salt and pepper to taste, and love.

My mother, one of the most beautiful women the state of Sonora had produced, was tall, with light brown hair with red highlights in it, and lovely green eyes. She did the serving of the food, because my grandmother did not possess the skills to adorn the platters and garnish the plates. (At one time in her struggling years she had owned a boarding house, so she served all the platters boarding-house style.)

When I got into serious cooking attempts at the age of eleven or twelve, I began experimenting and collecting recipes. I scorched pans and threw out many a failure. My Waterloo was white sauce. I finally began to get good at it after throwing out at least ten thick pastelike concoctions. I suffered many discouraging catastrophes at cake-baking, but my father would say, "Doesn't it have sugar, butter, eggs, milk, and flour in it? It can't be bad," and he would crumble some of my horrible cake into a tall iced-tea glass he liked, pour some cold milk into it, and make a mush. It looked awful, but he said it was great, and he ate his cake that way until the day he died.

How do you explain a love of cooking like mine if not as a "passion" for cooking? There have been very few days in my life, except perhaps when I was ill, that I haven't done some cooking. My home has always been filled with the lovely aromas of cooking. Cinnamon and other spices often boil on the stove to give the house a welcoming scent. Cooking is to me creating, not working. And later on, on my cattle ranch inherited from my father, during windy days and wet days and snowy days, it was a blessing and true entertainment.

My daughters, all four of them, grew up imbued with this love of cooking, and all of them are great cooks. Marina, a housewife and mother in central Mexico, often produces meals as elaborate as restaurant fare. When she is on the trail of a new recipe, she tests and experiments tirelessly until she is satisfied, and then the telephone wires hum as she passes on the new idea to one or another of her sisters. Clarissa and Aída are professionals, and the eldest, Zarela, is a renowned chef.

They say you must plant a tree, write a book, or leave something else of yourself behind you when you depart this world. Well, I truly think I have done all three.

———⊙———

THOUGHTS ON MEXICAN COOKERY
FOR MY READERS

I think the cuisine of my country is one of the most exciting in the world. I cannot stress too strongly that Mexican food should not be confused with Spanish food. We have inherited much from Spain, it is true, but to the Spanish influence we have added cookery techniques and lore from our native Indians and a great overlay of original culinary thinking absolutely indigenous to Mexico.

Please do not shy away from trying the recipes in this book because you fear their pungency. All too often I hear, "I can't sample what you are preparing because I don't eat hot food." (This happened when my daughter Zarela and I prepared the Memorial Day luncheon for the Williamsburg summit meeting: The people assigned to help us in the kitchen dared not taste the finished products, or even the sauces.) Mexican food need not be too hot; the careful use of the proper spices and a judicious hand with chiles, when they are called for, can produce a dish of the utmost delicacy. Be adventurous enough to try! I believe most Americans will find that they relish fine Mexican cooking. After all, the United States is on a crest of interest in foreign and exotic gourmet food. Naturally, when I refer to Mexican food I am not thinking of the majority of so-called "Mexican" restaurants. Truly authentic and superb Mexican cooking is unfortunately the exception, not the rule, in such places. In fact, the genuine cuisine of Mexico is hard to find unless you are the guest in a Mexican home where traditional cooking is prized.

Our cuisine depends not only on unusual techniques but also on unique ingredients. However, many of these are becoming widely available in the United States. Nearly all supermarkets offer at least a minimal array of Mexican products, and most would probably be happy to stock more if they were asked. Most of the recipes in this book do not require terribly exotic ingredients, yet I beleive they retain their authenticity. My goal is to make it easy and tempting for you to embark on Mexican cookery.

I believe that attractive presentation enhances a meal immeasurably. Mexican pottery, most of it done by hand, decorated by artisans, and then baked, is beautiful—no two pieces exactly alike. Some homes still boast traditional sets of china, many of them antique, handed down from generation to generation. Whatever pretty dishes *you* possess can be mixed and matched for entrees, sauces, and condiments to give your Mexican meals a festive air. And don't forget the flowers! One of the highlights of my marketing is a trip to the flower stalls to choose my cut flowers. One would almost think the women vendors select their attire to go with their wares. Picture one in a loud magenta dress, perhaps satin, with a royal blue shawl tied carelessly around her shoulders, sitting on a tiny stool surrounded by buckets filled with a wild display of blossoms in every conceivable hue.

To my readers I say, let us join hands across the border of our countries. Just as music is a universal language, why not cooking? *Buen provecho!*

INGREDIENTS AND UTENSILS

The first section of this chapter discusses, in glossary form, various ingredients that appear in the recipes that follow, their specialized use in Mexican cookery, and where to obtain the more unusual items. The second section is devoted to the many glorious chiles that punctuate the Mexican cuisine with such verve. You will be introduced to fresh, dried, and canned chiles and the recommended methods for handling them. In the final section I have listed the items of kitchen equipment that I find most useful. Most of the ingredients and utensils discussed in this section are available from The Hilana Spice Company, 7606 Boeing Drive, Suite H, El Paso, Texas 79924. Additional sources of Mexican foods can be found at the end of this book.

INGREDIENTS

Achiote

Available in paste form, achiote, from the dark red seeds of the annatto tree, is used for coloring and flavoring food, especially in recipes from the state of Yucatán.

Avocado

The avocado sold in the United States is very, very different from the aguacates sold in Mexico, but very good and meaty just the same. The difference is in the flavor. The small thin-skinned aguacate has a slight anise flavor in its skin. It could be the poor man's butter. In fact, workmen often carry an aguacate in their lunchboxes to squeeze (yes, it's the only logical way if the aguacate is as ripe as it should be) onto corn tortillas.

Cactus

Nopales are the small pads or shoots found on the prickly pear cactus. They have a flavor similar to okra, and like okra are slightly slimy—definitely an acquired taste. Some markets carry uncooked nopales in plastic bags in the vegetable section, and you may wish to try them. The first cooking may discourage you, but throw out the first boiling water and try a second time, draining the cactus shoots when tender and leaving them to cool in a large colander. Rinse again and pat dry. However, as the fresh nopales are difficult to handle, I suggest that you buy the easily available canned product, cut into strips, or cubed and sold in jars with seasoning. Drained and refrigerated, they are wonderful as a garnish or in a salad with Pico de Gallo, and are traditionally scrambled with eggs and topped with a sauce.

Chayote

This delicately flavored, pear-shaped vegetable, a light soft green in color, appears almost daily in family menus in Mexico. It is becoming increasingly available in the produce sections of United States supermarkets. Botanically, the chayote is classified as a fruit. Years ago chayotes were covered with a thicker skin, studded with thorns, but crossbreeding has removed the thorns and made the chayote larger and meatier.

Corn Husks

Dried corn husks, used in making tamales, are available in half-pound and one-pound bags. The husks must be soaked in hot water for several minutes to soften before you use them. It is very important that the inside husk is not disturbed during the soaking, as it is filled with corn silk. Try to remove the silk carefully after soaking.

Croutons

I like to make my own, either out of small French rolls or from the baguette type of loaf made so well by bakers in Mexico City. I put several garlic cloves, peeled and slightly bruised, in a combination of salad oil and olive oil to steep for about eight hours. When the oil is deeply flavored with garlic, I slice and toast the bread, spread on a cookie sheet, in the oven until it is crisp and golden on both sides. When the slices are cool, I cover each lavishly with the garlic-flavored oil.

Garlic

An enormous amount of garlic is used in Mexican cooking. Most Mexicans like the taste of garlic but do not like to chew into any particle, no matter how minute. Therefore, most of my recipes specify mashed garlic. You may use a garlic press or a mortar and pestle. I *never* use garlic salt or dehydrated minced garlic (nor, in fact, do I use onion salt or dehydrated minced onion), and cannot recommend them.

Ground Beef

You will note that very few of these recipes call for ground beef. Hamburgers are now very popular in Mexico but they are still a fast food, eaten away from home. Ground beef is mainly used for picadillo, for meat loaf, and in meatballs (where it is combined with ground pork). It is never, but never, used in a taco.

Herbs and Spices

Naturally many of these will be familiar to you; I'll touch on the ones most commonly used in Mexican cooking. For a few, more elaboration is needed.

My daughters claim *bay leaf* is my favorite herb. Maybe so. I never seem to tire of that lovely flavor. You will find bay leaves in a great many of the recipes in this book. Even more integral to my style of cooking is *bay leaf tea.* Its preparation is child's play, but what it adds to a dish cannot be described in words.

BAY LEAF TEA

1 cup

3 or 4 bay leaves
2 cups water

Combine the bay leaves and water in a small saucepan and bring to a boil. Boil down to 1 cup, remove from heat, and allow to steep until the infusion is a deep, dark color with an intense flavor. Remove the bay leaves and use the infusion as instructed in recipes.

Fresh *cilantro* (coriander) plays a large part in Mexican cooking, and substituting parsley simply will not do. Cilantro leaves figure prominently, but often the whole sprigs, including stems, will be added to liquids boiling on the stove. Also called Chinese parsley, cilantro is available in most supermarket produce departments, and always in Oriental markets.

There are two varieties of *cinnamon*. The preferred variety here in the United States is harder and darker in color. The cinnamon sticks are dark reddish brown and harder to bend than the sticks available in Mexico. Mexican cinnamon *(canela)*, originally from Ceylon, is a light brown and very soft, easily crushed between the fingers. The flavor is milder and quite different from that found in United States spice racks. I always specify in my recipes that if Mexican cinnamon is not available, do not substitute. Just omit.

Epazote is becoming more and more popular in the northern states of Mexico; it is widely used in the south and southwest there, where one can easily find it in vegetable stalls. Its botanical name *Chenopodium ambrosioides)* is a tongue-twister—it is easier to grow it than to say it. Epazote grows wild, even in the northern United States, and requires little care. You can reconstitute dried epazote leaves by steeping them in one cup of boiling water until the water cools. The leaves will then come "back to life," soft and ready to use. Cut them with kitchen shears. If you can, by all means use the epazote tea left behind. The flavor will be out of this world.

In Mexico, *marjoram (mejorana)* is considered wild oregano. It is wonderful rubbed into pork roast or onto game.

Fresh *mint* leaves *(yerba buena*—literally, the good herb) are wonderful in salads and a must in certain soups. If you are lucky enough to have some in your garden, you will always have the best on hand, but dried mint leaves do well in soups and some salads.

Oregano is of course the most important herb in Mexican cookery. Measure the dried herb and rub it between the palms of your hands right into the food you are cooking.

Pimenton (Mexican *paprika*) is a delightful spice similar in taste to New Mexico ground red mild chile peppers. Try to find it in Mexican or Hispanic markets.

Certain herbs like mint, cilantro, sweet basil, and epazote (if you can find it) take well to quick freezing. Wash well and drain on kitchen towels. Remove stems and separate the choicest leaves into batches (I prefer small packets—about a quarter of a cup) and dry lightly between paper towels. Spread out the herbs on small sheets of aluminum foil, fold the foil gently (to avoid crushing the herbs) into an envelope shape, and place the packets in a small square plastic container in your freezer. Label!

If you always have these on hand, you won't be caught short when a wintry day finds you without the necessary herbs for a dish you want to prepare. Just open your packet, remove the amount you need, reseal the packet, and pop back into your freezer.

Jicama

A delicious white root vegetable, sweet and crisp, with the shape of a deformed turnip, the jicama is often very large, and is covered with a light brown woody skin. Jicamas make a wonderful appetizer served peeled, sliced, and eaten raw with salt, lime juice, and a light sprinkling of paprika. Though indigenous to Mexico, jicamas can be purchased all over the United States now, and are becoming more popular by the day. They keep a long time. If I find one I have missed in my vegetable bin and it looks a little sad, I wash it thoroughly, peel it, and find that the heart is still sweet and juicy. By the way, jicama bears a certain resemblance in taste to the water chestnut and makes an excellent substitute in Chinese dishes.

Lemons and Limes

Limes in Mexico are called lemons, or *limones*. But limes, not American lemons, they are. Some parts of Mexico do have a large lemon, often seedless, that somewhat resembles its American cousin. In the Huasteca Potosina, the tropical area in the otherwise desertlike land in San Luis Potosi, they are called canary lemons, a reference to their green and light yellow color. In Sonora one finds another relative of the American yellow lemon, huge, meaty, not too tart, with a very thick bright yellow skin. Lovely! There it is called royal lemon, *limon real*. Many Mexican cookbooks specify lemon juice when they mean lime juice. Here I have tried always to indicate lime juice; if I have not been definite, you may use freshly squeezed (but never bottled or artificial) lemon juice.

Maggi

A sauce not unlike teriyaki marinade, but with a more tantalizing flavor, Maggi can be obtained in large or small bottles in stores that carry Latin American foods.

Masa

Masa is the corn dough used for corn tortillas, tamales, and many other dishes. It is made from dried white corn kernels cooked in a large amount of water with lime. After the skins are loosened, the kernels are washed and rubbed until the skins are removed. At this state the corn is called *nixtamal;* it is then ground to make masa. Instant masa is called dried corn flour, and it is available (notably a Quaker product) in American supermarkets in bags of various sizes, often labeled *masa harina.* Mixed with water, this flour makes a passable masa. Since I believe that the majority of my readers will probably not be able to buy masa in their communities, I recommend the use of this instant dried corn flour.

Mole

Mole, a lovely multichile sauce with traces of chocolate and sugar, can be obtained in stores that sell Mexican foods. It may be called *mole poblano* paste. If you do not find it, why not suggest to your grocer that he add it to his Mexican food section?

Piloncillo

This unrefined pure cane sugar in the shape of hard cones, either large or small, is used in many Mexican dessert dishes, and to sweeten coffee and gruels. You may have difficulty locating it (your best bet would be a Mexican food market), so when it is specified in this book, an alternative is given.

Pine Nuts

Health food stores usually carry pine nuts. Be sure to check the taste for freshness; they turn rancid easily (this can also be true of the shelled pine nuts found in jars on supermarket shelves). Pine nuts are difficult to shell.

Plantain

The large plantains *(platano macho)* found in Oriental markets should be purchased when dark in color to assure ripeness and sweet flavor. They are wonderful with rice dishes, and sautéed in butter and sprinkled with sugar, they make a fine dessert or snack.

Pumpkinseeds

Hulled pumpkinseeds *(pepitas)*, either salted or unsalted, are most often found in health food stores. They are a must in Pipian—the pumpkinseed sauce highlighted by the addition of pure red chile powder which is outstanding over poached chicken pieces.

Tomatillos

Firm, usually small, green tomatoes, tomatillos have a paperlike husk that must be removed. (Do not let the "green" throw you; they are at their peak precisely when they are a lovely deep green color.) Tomatillos have an acid flavor and make excellent sauces, but should always be slightly sweetened with a small amount of granulated sugar to cut the acidity. The canned variety is great for sauces, or you may use the prepared tomatillo sauce, canned, salted, and slightly seasoned, called Mexican green hot sauce or *salsa verde* in some of the recipes.

Keep your special pantry shelf well stocked with the canned and packaged products specified in this book, particularly the basics. Then, with the aid of treasures in your refrigerator and freezer, and the happy addition of whatever is temptingly fresh in your local market, you will be prepared to cook a Mexican meal any time the spirit moves you.

CHILES

Now we come to the most important part of any Mexican cookbook, the kinds of chiles to use—dry or the fresh green ones, large or small, sweet or pungent. You must have heard, I am sure, that there are enormous varieties of chiles in Mexico, probably well over sixty. However, set your mind at rest. Only a very few will be called for in the recipes here, and they will be easily available in your local supermarket, in specialty shops, or where Latin foods are sold.

I would like to dispel the myth that Mexican cooks use an overwhelming amount of chiles in their cooking. Chiles are always used to enhance the

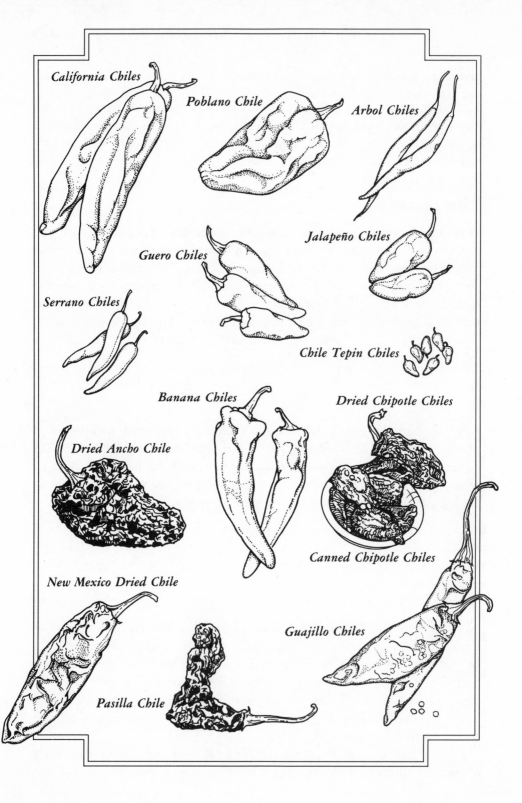

California Chiles

Poblano Chile

Arbol Chiles

Jalapeño Chiles

Guero Chiles

Serrano Chiles

Chile Tepin Chiles

Banana Chiles

Dried Chipotle Chiles

Dried Ancho Chile

Canned Chipotle Chiles

New Mexico Dried Chile

Guajillo Chiles

Pasilla Chile

flavor of dishes, not overpower them. Stem and seed chiles before using and taste them carefully with the tip of your tongue. If they seem too hot, use the tips only and save the stem ends for a hotter sauce to place on the table. When working with chiles, be they fresh or dried, take care to protect your hands: wash them frequently and be very careful not to rub your eyes or face. One last general comment: Throughout this book the Mexican spellings, chile and chiles, are used in preference to the anglicized chili and chilies.

Fresh Chiles

Banana chiles, large, meaty, and not hot, are pale yellow and lovely to look at. They are great pickled, and as a garnish. They are sometimes called wax chiles in American cookery.

California or *Anaheim,* my favorites, are pale green, long and slender with a rounded tip and a very mild flavor. If you have guests who are afraid of pungent Mexican dishes, stick to California chiles and you will be safe. They can be found in nearly all supermarkets, but are not available all year long. I normally buy fifteen or twenty pounds at the peak of the season when the price goes down, blister them, and freeze them, wrapped.

The *guero,* a small, light yellow, waxy pepper, is similar to a banana pepper but very hot, with a flavor all its own. When chopped and used with tomatoes in scrambled eggs, the guero is a delight, and it is wonderful in tomatillo-based sauces, and in pickling. To my mind, gueros do not keep as well as do serranos and jalapeños.

Fresh, dark green, lovely *jalapeños* are America's favorite. Tantalizing in taste, the meaty jalapeño is excellent in all recipes calling for a pungent pepper. It is most often used raw, without peeling. Above everything, it keeps almost indefinitely. Simply wipe clean and dry and store in the vegetable drawer of your refrigerator.

Poblano chiles, heart-shaped and dark green, are natives of the state of Puebla. Very meaty, with an extremely thin skin, the poblano can range from mild to very hot in flavor. Do taste them and set aside the fiery ones for a sauce; the milder ones are ideal for stuffing, especially with meat mixtures.

The *serrano,* smaller and slimmer than a jalapeño and very hot, is excellent in Pico de Gallo and almost all the uncooked sauces. A small serrano will go a long way. They will keep indefinitely, unwashed but wiped clean and stored in your refrigerator. Use first the ones whose green hue is beginning to show signs of ripening to yellow and red.

Handling Fresh Chiles

Such chiles as poblanos or Californias should be firm and meaty. Prick them with a fork to prevent them from bursting if they become dangerously inflated during broiling. Place them on a hot griddle and turn them from time to time with the prongs of a fork or an ice pick until their skins are blistered on all sides.

Now, picking them up carefully with tongs, drop them into a paper bag and close it tightly over them, or better yet, wrap them in an old damp dish towel. Set aside for at least 30 minutes.

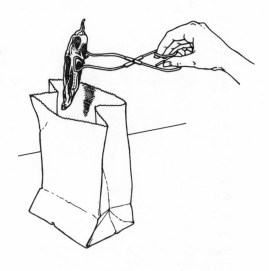

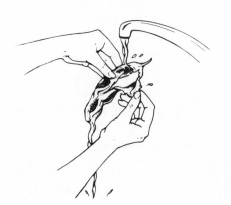

This will permit them to steam, loosening the skin, which will then peel off easily, especially under cold running water.

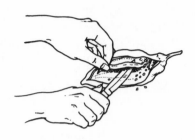

Slit each chile along the side, not tampering with the stem or top ridge. Wash out the seeds and core thoroughly and remove as many of the veins as you can without tearing the chile too much. Drain and dry with paper towels. Then cut into strips or chop as the recipe directs. By smelling and tasting cautiously with the tip of your tongue you should be able to judge how hot the chiles are. Beware of a few violent ones if you are dealing with poblanos. These may be left to soak in cold, mildly salted water for half an hour to moderate their fire.

If the pepper must remain firm, not limp, and retain its lovely color, I prefer to use another method to prepare chiles for peeling: deep-frying in hot oil. This quick technique renders the chiles bright in color, very firm, and with a fresh taste. Though you may be dismayed at the amount of vegetable oil required, do not despair—you can strain it and use it again for the same purpose. Heat the oil very hot, immerse the chiles (if they are not completely dry they will spit and sputter, so guard against being burned), and watch until they blister all over. Remove with a slotted spoon to paper towels, and peel when they are cool enough to handle.

If you must, you may use the broiler in your oven. I do not recommend it as highly, for the chiles will become a brownish green in color, very limp, and will have a "cooked" flavor. However, if you want to try it, place the chiles on a baking sheet a few inches below the broiler. When the skin on the heat-exposed side is well blistered, turn once and only once, to blister the other side. Then proceed as for the griddle method.

The type of stove you have will to some extent determine which method you use. The electric range will not do for the griddle technique—the griddle becomes so hot that it could damage the top of the stove. If you have an electric stove, you will have to use the oven broiler or deep-fry the chiles.

The gas range is fine for all methods, even including blistering the peppers over an open flame—but be sure you use a long-handled fork for safety.

Jalapenos and serranos may also be charred on a griddle, but you can chop them raw, with the skins on, too. Gueros are great broiled on the griddle, then skinned, stemmed, and chopped seeds and all. (Most of the recipes in this book call for the use of fresh jalapenos and serranos unpeeled and chopped raw.)

Dry Chiles

When I was a youngster, dry chile day in the fall was a great occasion. We would sit around a large new washtub on small stools and stem the chiles, shake them, scrape them inside a bit with a small paring knife, and shake again. Then the chiles were placed carefully in a large open black metal roaster and baked in the oven, under my grandmother's supervision, until they were crisp and lightly browned. She watched them closely (and trusted no one else with that job) to be sure they did not burn. When cool, the chiles were ground into a powder in a food mill, jars were filled and labeled, and the precious powder was stored in a dark corner of the basement to be used throughout the year. Lovely smell, and what a flavor!

Ancho, the favorite among the dried red chiles, is quite large, a lovely red brown color, and two to three inches long. It is a wide, meaty pepper with a thin skin and a very slight bitter taste that grows on you. The ancho is actually a chile poblano ripened on the vine and sun-dried. By all means, try them. They are expensive because they are sold by weight, and are heavy, but three will go a long way. They usually come three to a small plastic bag, and may be wrongly labeled *pasilla.*

Arbol chiles will be found in very small ½- or 1 oz. bags at your spice counter and will probably be labeled "jap peppers." They are wonderful boiled and puréed with tomatoes and garlic for a cooked sauce.

The *chile tepin,* pronounced *chiltepin* when I was growing up, is an angry little red ball the size of a poorly grown Spanish peanut. In my opinion it has no special delightful flavor, but I have known many people who would really walk a mile for a handful. Chiltepins grow wild in the hills of Sonora, doing well with the little rainfall the Lord allows them. They are harvested by hand when they are red and about to fall from the large bushes, but also may be harvested green and pickled in small bottles in a vinegar-flavored brine. The chiltepin is now considered a luxury, and is sold in supermarkets in small plastic bags, twenty or thirty to a bag. I understand that a somewhat longer version, more like an egg than a small round ball, is now grown and harvested in Texas.

While I recommend that you stick to the canned pickled variety, dry *chipotles,* if properly treated, can impart a glorious smoky taste without too much fire to your broths or sauces. Chipotles are actually ripe jalapeño chiles that have been dried and then smoked. They are golden brown, with a very wrinkled skin, and very, very hot. If you decide to try them, you must use the chipotle whole, without breaking its skin in any way, much less attempting to remove the head and seeds, which would naturally release the fire within. They are great, but one to a sauce is plenty. If you find them at your spice counter, they will come three or four to a small bag.

Guajillo chiles are similar to dried red chile pods. I like to keep a few on hand to use in *ajillo* dishes, using the highly garlic-flavored oil sauce.

New Mexico dried red chile pods are my choice for mild red sauces for enchiladas, tamale fillings, and sauced meat dishes. They may be purchased in plastic bags labeled to show whether the chile pods are mild *(dulce)*, medium hot *(mediano)*, or hot *(picoso)*. I recommend that you buy the mild, the only one that can be used comfortably. California dried chile pods, quite plentiful on the West Coast, are about the same as the New Mexico pods, and are delightful.

Pasillas, not to be confused with anchos, dry to a dark blackish red color. Sweet and pungent, they are good combined with anchos in a paste, then used in a sauce.

Pure powdered red chile is made from New Mexico dried chile pods or from a similar variety grown in Arizona. Please note the word "pure." This chile powder has nothing added, and is completely different from any prepared product with the commercial name "chili powder," which comes with spices and seasonings in it. The pure powder is a great condiment; it is an essential ingredient in the Mexican sausage, chorizo, and may also be substituted for red chile paste.

Handling Dry Chiles

In the northern part of Mexico dried red chiles are not toasted on a griddle. Instead they are turned once or twice in mildly hot oil in a small skillet. They must be very carefully watched lest they overbrown and become bitter. (You can brown them in their whole, natural state if you like; I prefer to do them stemmed and seeded.) Once browned, they are boiled and made into a strained sauce either lightly or heavily flavored with garlic. Cooked in a light roux, they may be further seasoned with oregano and salted to taste. Follow the browning and boiling procedures outlined above for ancho, New Mexico, Arizona, and California dried red chiles.

Jap chiles or chiles de arbol (included here in one or two sauces) are just washed and stemmed.

Canned Chiles

These are now available in many sizes and varieties, so you should be able to find just the ones you want and need. You must be sure to take note of the "heat level" illustrated on the cans, from mild to very hot.

California peppers are perhaps the best of the lot. Normally labeled "peeled green chiles," they are canned either whole or chopped in four-ounce and ten-ounce cans. The "heat scale" will always read "mild." Canned green chiles will often have bits of black charred skin left on them. Be sure to pick them over, but do not rinse.

Pickled chipotles are available in several can sizes; the small one will normally contain four or five chiles. Their smoky flavor is terrific, but they are potent and should never be taken too much for granted. Rarely would a recipe call for more than one. I open a small can and usually purée the entire contents with a cup of water, fill a jar with this concoction, and store it in the refrigerator to have on hand. Then I measure out the purée by the teaspoon, tasting until the correct degree of pungency is reached. Strained into sauces, this purée is great. For a garnish, I simply serve the whole pickled chipotles in a small bowl—but I always warn my guests! Pickled chipotles are rather difficult to find in United States supermarkets, but if you ask your grocer to stock them, I am sure he will.

Jalapeños come canned both plain and pickled. They will always be bright red on the "heat" scale, and you must be careful not to confuse them with milder chiles. Normally available in four-ounce cans, the *plain jalapeños* come whole or diced, the latter saving you time and burned fingers. They are canned with salt and citric acid, and perhaps calcium chloride, but no spices, vinegar, or pickling liquid of any kind. The *pickled jalapeños* are another thing altogether—they come whole, in round slices, or in slivers or strips. Some have pickled carrot slices added, and a few garlic cloves, plus spices. Beware, the pickling liquid is hot. Most common are the green jalapeños, but the red jalapeño strips are a novel and colorful garnish if you can locate a store that sells them. Green or red, strips are a more frugal purchase, since you are not paying for seeds and stems. Jalapeños come in cans of all sizes, even up to a gallon.

Rajas de chiles are strips of peeled roasted green chiles, usually poblanos or Californias. However, all companies that offer pickled chiles in one form or another can a special type of strip cut from the pickled jalapeño. This is a wonderful product, milder because the chiles have been stemmed and seeded.

Serranos are pickled in the same manner as jalapeños, but come in cans of smaller sizes. They are less expensive and make a good accompaniment to sandwiches—a perfect treat in picnic basket or lunchbox. Serranos are also great with refried beans with corn chips. In my home, pickled serranos always, but always, are served with sautéed liver or kidneys in any form.

I have never found serrano chiles canned whole without pickling liquid. However, if a recipe calls for serranos and you haven't any fresh ones, you may substitute one of the unpickled canned jalapeños mentioned above.

UTENSILS

For the most part, Mexican cookery can be managed nicely with the regular utensils found in an American housewife's kitchen. It is very helpful to have duplicates of certain essential pieces of equipment, and if, as I hope, you become serious about this cuisine, you will want to purchase the one or two specialized items listed below.

Blenders

I keep two blenders busy. I have one that is pungent with the scent of garlic and chiles, so you know what I use that one for. The other is for purées, desserts, and so forth.

Dutch Ovens

Again, more than one will be useful. I have three. Of course you want the kind that can be used on top of the stove as well as in the oven, so that you can do preliminary browning or sautéing and then assemble the remaining ingredients and bake in the same casserole.

Electric Mixer

Mine has attachments, but you can manage perfectly well with a simple one.

Food Mill

Mine is the old-fashioned kind, and among other things I use it to grind spices and prepare jerky (dried beef strips). There are a number of simple, lightweight models on the market with interchangeable plates with holes of various sizes. These are particularly handy when you want purées with more texture than is possible to achieve in a blender.

Griddle

For tortillas, and for blistering chiles, nothing can take the place of the heavy, cast iron griddle. The Teflon-coated type is also handy. I recommend that you have one of each.

Meat Grinder

I like my separate, small grinder even though I have a meat-grinding attachment on my electric mixer.

Mortar and Pestle

While I usually mash my garlic right on the chopping board with my old-fashioned wooden meat masher, the mortar and pestle is a godsend when I'm in a hurry. The garlic cloves don't seem to get away from me. You will find lots of other uses for it, too.

Pressure Cooker

I have two, one large and one small. Nothing beats a pressure cooker for swift, moist cooking of such items as beef tongue or tripe that would take hours of simmering otherwise.

Skillets

Naturally, you have several skillets of various sizes in your kitchen. I recommend that at least one or two of them be Teflon-coated.

Strainers

I have three or four strainers and use them constantly—the small, very fine one for straining teas and infusions and the others, from medium to very large, for sauces and the blanching of vegetables.

Tortilla Press

Besides being essential in the making of tortillas, a tortilla press comes in handy for flattening the balls of dough for turnovers and empanadas, as well as for gorditas and other small, thick dough patties. Some models are very heavy and not rustproof. I don't care for these. I prefer a lighter aluminum model in a 6-inch size.

Wooden Spoons

My favorites! Wonderfully gentle on the linings of your pots and pans, especially those of Teflon, assorted wooden spoons with long handles that never overheat are a must, I think.

BASIC
TECHNIQUES

COOKING HINTS

The traditional cooking techniques of the many cuisines of Mexico can be quite involved as far as the old family recipes are concerned. But in this book you will find home cooking at its simplest. Even the most elaborate dishes, such as tamales, are easy to make once you get a feel for things, and all the recipes are based on the fundamental cooking techniques that every good cook knows. My years of cooking have taught me a few tricks of the trade, however, and I would like to share with my readers some special tips that will help give your cooking an authentic Mexican flavor.

Always *fry, sauté* or *stir-fry* in very hot fat, and always use lard, vegetable oil, vegetable shortening, or bacon grease. Olive oil and butter are not much used in Mexican cooking. My favorite cooking fat is bacon grease; nothing compares to it for flavor. I am sure this will be a welcome piece of news. So many housewives have an abundance of bacon grease on hand, and this is a great way to use it up. Bacon grease is essential for frying kidneys or liver, and it also imparts a delightful flavor to pork chops. Except when frying, cook over *low to medium heat. Stirring* is best done lovingly and, whenever possible, with a wooden spoon. In a Mexican kitchen, you will find wooden spoons in a variety of shapes and sizes, most often hand carved.

When *poaching* or *boiling* a chicken or meat, do not use an overabundance of water. Place the chicken or meat in a pot large enough to hold it comfortably, add water just to cover, season well with salt and pepper, and cook over medium heat until tender. Save the broth to use in soups, stews, and rice dishes, and always as the liquid in tamale dough.

To *thicken* sauces or gravies, always use a light-colored roux. A conventional blend of all-purpose flour and water will do the job, but if you have pre-toasted the flour or cooked it first in butter or shortening the taste will be much better and your sauces and stews will have a delightful nutty flavor. To this day, I remember my grandmother toasting her flour in the oven, stirring it often to keep it a light golden color. When cooked, it was placed in a glass jar with a tight-fitting lid and stored in the refrigerator.

Tortillas . . . the word itself does not refer only to corn tortillas. All the northern states of Mexico make tortillas using wheat flour. Corn tortillas are made in the middle and central states, down to the southernmost tip of Mexico. This chapter includes a great foolproof recipe for wheat-flour tortillas, and I urge you to learn how to make both kinds. There is nothing like homemade tortillas for taste.

Tamal dough must be made with whipped lard or solid vegetable shortening, never with cooking oil. (By the way, *tamal* is singular. The word that is familiar to American cooks, *tamales,* is the plural form.) The filling for the tamales should always be used at room temperature, never hot or warm. The liquid you use in the dough, whether it is the broth from chicken or pork, must also be cooled and strained. I like to let the broth chill in the refrigerator before I use it. That way the fat rises to the surface and may be removed easily. Store broth in the refrigerator until ready to use, as it sours easily. (Freeze for longer storage.)

When making tamales, make sure that the corn husks

have been well softened in hot water before attempting to separate them. Remove them from the water one by one, and discard as much of the corn silk as you can without opening. Rinse once or twice to make sure all the corn silk is out. Many a time a guest, as well as his hostess, has been embarrassed as a tamale was left uneaten because a string of corn silk was mistaken for human hair.

But don't let all this talk scare you. Making tamales is a wonderful experience, and is definitely a feather in your cap as a cook. Once you have made them you will want to do it again.

TORTILLAS

Every cook has his own way of doing things. I come from Sonora, and Sonorans are not known as corn lovers because we grow an abundance of wheat. Thus I perfected my skill at the making of wheat-flour tortillas earlier than I mastered corn tortillas. However, I assure you that if you follow the procedures outlined here, you will produce excellent (if not perfectly shaped) tortillas of either kind, and the varieties of the corn tortilla, very quickly.

While I do urge you to try making your own tortillas—they are really unsurpassed when fresh from your griddle —you can certainly rely on the store-bought type for many of the recipes in later chapters in this book. If you live in a fairly large city, you may be able to buy freshly made corn-flour and wheat-flour tortillas, and you almost surely can buy frozen ones. If you use the latter, take them out of the freezer and let them thaw for 20 to 30 minutes so you can separate them. Place them in a plastic bag in the top of a double boiler with simmering water in the bottom. Rotate them, top to bottom, and keep checking lest they get too soft. In a microwave oven, defrosting is even simpler. I just put the tortillas in a plastic bag, a few at a time, and heat them a few seconds, testing as I go.

CORN TORTILLAS
Tortillas de Maiz
————⊙————

In Mexico, corn tortillas are always made with fresh corn masa. Since masa is not readily available in the United States, I have used the instant corn flour, called masa harina, in this recipe. It is a more than satisfactory substitute. Quaker Masa Harina is available in most U.S. supermarkets.

————⊙————

16 small tortillas

2 cups instant corn flour (masa harina)
1⅓ cups warm water

EQUIPMENT
2 sandwich-size plastic bags (6¾ by 8¼ inches)
A tortilla press

Heat griddle (preferably Teflon) over medium flame and have ready.

Mix corn flour (masa harina) and warm water together to form a soft dough. Pinch off pieces of dough about the size of a Ping-Pong ball. Dampen hands and roll ball around in the palms of your hands to smooth it. Keep dough covered with damp towel or in a plastic bag to prevent it from drying.

Open tortilla press and lay a plastic bag on bottom half. Place a ball of dough a little off center, more toward the hinge side.

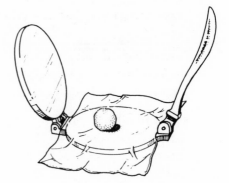

Cover with second plastic bag and press with palm of hand first, to flatten ball slightly.

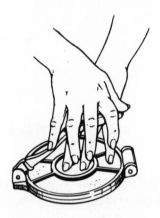

Close and press firmly, then open. Peel top plastic bag off, dampen hands, and lift up the plastic bag with tortilla resting on it.

Now transfer tortilla, dough side down, to your hand.

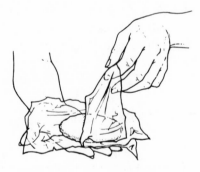

With your free hand, carefully peel the bag off the dough.

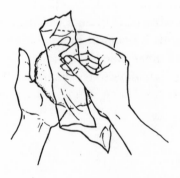

Note of warning: If the dough stays rather thick and has a grainy uneven edge all around the tortilla, it is too dry. Add more warm water and mix again.

If dough does not peel away easily from plastic bags, or if it sticks to your hand, it is too wet. Add a little more flour. Always keep hands damp by dipping in water before handling dough. Place gently on the hot griddle and cook, turning once only, as you would pancakes. This should take about two minutes.

TOSTADAS

8 tostadas

1 cup vegetable oil for frying
8 corn tortillas

Heat the oil to about 350° in a 8-inch skillet. Slip a corn tortilla into the hot oil and press it down into the hot oil immediately with a hot metal pancake turner to keep it from bubbling up. Continue to press down while frying, and turn over with tongs to fry other side. Tortilla must fry flat at all times. Do not allow it to curl. Drain between paper towels.

TACO SHELLS

——⊙——

16 taco shells

1 cup oil for frying
16 corn tortillas

Heat the oil to about 350° in a large
skillet. Grasp a corn tortilla in tongs
and dip it in the hot oil on both sides.
This is done to soften the tortilla.

Continuing to hold tortilla with
tongs, fold it in half and fry it,
holding on to it, until it is crisp.
Never allow the ends of the tortilla
to touch. Remember the shell must
fry open at all times so that the
filling can be easily spooned in.

Drain on paper towels.

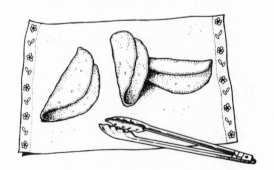

CORN-FLOUR TURNOVERS
BAKED ON A GRIDDLE
Quesadillas

———⊙———

8 turnovers

1 cup instant corn flour (masa harina)
2 tablespoons wheat flour
4 tablespoons oil
¾ cup warm water or a little less, to make a manageable dough

Have griddle ready, preheated to about the setting you would use for cooking pancakes.

In a large bowl mix all ingredients. Form dough into 8 balls the size of a Ping-Pong ball, and cover with damp cloth to keep them from drying out.

Flatten each ball between 2 small plastic bags in your regular corn tortilla press, as described on pages 33–34. Bake on hot griddle but do not allow to brown. Tortillas must be pliant and white.

Note: Tortillas for quesadillas should be turned only once.

———⊙———

WHEAT-FLOUR TORTILLAS
Tortillas de Harina

—⊙—

In the northern states of Mexico, tortillas are made with wheat flour. Corn flour is not used. Toasted in the oven, buttered and sprinkled with grated cheese and a bit of ground red chile powder, flour tortillas make wonderful appetizers. A more elaborate version might include a pizza-style topping of green chile strips and cheese. Mouth-watering! Follow instructions to the letter, and there is no reason why you can't roll out a luscious, almost round flour tortilla.

—⊙—

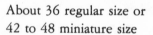

About 36 regular size or
42 to 48 miniature size

6 cups all-purpose flour
1 teaspoon baking powder
2 teaspoons salt
1 heaping cup vegetable shortening
2 cups warm water, or a little more

Mix dry ingredients (it is not necessary to sift them), work in shortening with your hands until you get the consistency of oatmeal, and then pour in the lukewarm water all at once. Mix well and knead for 2 or 3 minutes. Dough should be moist but manageable—a little drier than biscuit dough. Coat with a little oil or more soft shortening and put into a plastic bag for 20 minutes until dough is soft.

Take a large piece of dough and squeeze out a portion about the size of a Ping-Pong ball.

Roll the ball around in the palms of your hands until smooth. (It is best to prepare half the dough in balls while you keep the remaining half in the plastic bag so it won't dry out.)

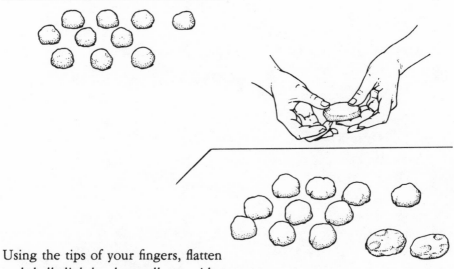

Using the tips of your fingers, flatten each ball slightly, then roll out with a rolling pin to the size of a saucer.

(Instructions continue)

Heat your griddle hot, and cook the tortillas like flapjacks until they are cooked through and have developed brown spots. Do not allow to scorch— lower heat as necessary to maintain an even temperature. The tortilla will puff up slightly as it cooks. Once you have turned a tortilla and completed the cooking cycle on both sides, press down with your spatula for about 30 seconds or more on all edges of the round so that you produce a flat, golden disk, crisp and tasty.

Do this on both sides.

Cool on a clean dish towel.

You may now store them wrapped by the dozen in squares of aluminum foil. They freeze well.

Note: Of course the yield will depend on the size of the balls. If you make walnut-sized balls, the results will be beautiful: miniature tortillas the size of a demitasse saucer. These are a delight folded in half and filled with crabmeat hash, or shredded pork, beef or chicken (poached first), shredded mozzarella cheese and strips of green chile. A real treat that you'll never find on any restaurant menu!

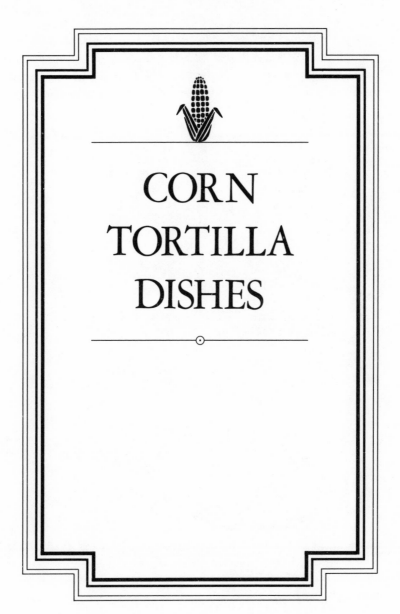

CORN TORTILLA DISHES

When one thinks of Mexican cooking, what immediately comes to mind are the delightful corn-based dishes, more often than not prepared with or accompanied by a chile-based sauce. Corn has been a mainstay of our cooking since, and assuredly prior to, first recorded time. By the time of the birth of the city of Tenochtitlán, Aztec capital and cultural center, corn was considered a sacred plant. Prized for its nutritional value, accessibility, and versatility, it represented, to prehispanic cultures, a *modus vivendi.*

Ah! the magic of corn! Like the gods, corn is capable of adopting many forms. The metamorphosis begins when the dried corn is boiled with lime. This has a double purpose —the skin is removed and the corn is fortified with calcium. When corn is washed and ground, the carnival begins.

The corn becomes a tortilla, the basis of so many of our foods. This in turn becomes a taco, quesadilla, enchilada, or tostada. The *masa* can be made into plump *sopes* and *gorditas,* succulent *tamales,* or a nourishing drink called *atole,* or even a delicious chile and masa soup, *chileatole.*

Or the lime-treated cooked kernels can be skinned and washed under cold running water and left whole to be cooked until they burst to become *pozole* (hominy). In the state of Jalisco pozole is combined with pork and chicken; in Sonora it is married to pork and beef, with beans added.

This Mexican hominy is also cooked with cut-up pieces of tripe to become the ever-popular *menudo.*

But corn is also eaten on the cob, bathed in butter and sprinkled with lime juice and chile powder, and of course it is used in soups, casseroles, and fresh corn tamales.

ROLLED ENCHILADAS WITH CHEESE
Enchiladas de Queso

——⊙——

6 servings

    12 corn tortillas
    ½ cup oil
     4 cups Basic Red Chile Sauce (page 285), heated
     2 cups shredded mozzarella cheese
     1 cup chopped green onions

Heat oil in skillet. Using tongs, quickly dip each tortilla into hot oil for a few seconds and place on a large cookie sheet.

When all the tortillas have been dipped in the hot oil, cover the bottom of a 13 × 9 × 2-inch baking dish with warm sauce. Fill one fried tortilla at a time with 1 tablespoon sauce and 1 tablespoon cheese and green onions, mixed. Roll, and arrange seam-side down on top of the sauce in the baking dish. Crowd as many as you can in dish, but have one layer only. Spoon sauce on top to cover, sprinkle with remaining cheese and onion mixture, and bake in a 350° oven for 10 or 15 minutes.

Garnishes: Shred one head of lettuce and mix with ½ cup sliced radishes. Season with ¼ cup vinegar, and salt and pepper to taste.

——⊙——

GREEN ENCHILADAS
Enchiladas Verdes

——⊙——

6 servings for dinner;
12 as luncheon dish

  2 cups Green Sauce (see below)
  2 cups shredded poached chicken breast
  ½ cup oil
  12 corn tortillas
  1 pint sour cream
  Salt
  ½ teaspoon finely mashed garlic
  ¼ cup milk
  12 strips Monterey Jack cheese
  Grated Parmesan cheese

Prepare sauce and set aside. Poach chicken breast in well-seasoned water to cover, cool in its own broth, and shred. Set aside.

Heat oil in small skillet. With tongs, carefully place the corn tortillas, one at a time, in hot oil to soften for 5 seconds. Turn each tortilla over quickly and soften other side for 2 seconds. Drain on a plate, keeping all the softened tortillas together ready for stuffing and rolling.

Flavor sour cream with salt to taste and mashed garlic, and then thin with ¼ cup milk. If you wish, add 1 tablespoon instant chicken bouillon.

Fill bottom of a 13 × 9 × 2-inch Pyrex baking pan with a thin layer of sauce. Fill each softened tortilla with 1 generous tablespoon shredded chicken, 1 cheese strip, and 1 tablespoon green sauce. Roll and place seam-side down in sauce in baking dish. Crowd enchiladas in dish but arrange one layer only. Cover with more sauce and then spoon thinned sour cream over all. Sprinkle evenly with Parmesan cheese. Bake in a 350° oven for 12 minutes, or until heated through.

GREEN SAUCE
  1 pound tomatillos, peeled
  2 garlic cloves
  1 cup cilantro leaves
  ½ cup sliced onion
  2 tablespoons oil
  Salt
  1 teaspoon sugar

Remove paper-like husks and boil tomatillos in 3 cups water until tender. Allow to cool slightly and place in blender container with 2 cups of cooking water, add garlic cloves, cilantro leaves, and onion slices. Purée until smooth and creamy. Pour into 2 tablespoons hot oil in medium-sized saucepan, add salt to taste and sugar, and simmer for 5 minutes.

Note: If you are in a hurry, or cannot obtain tomatillos, you may use the canned Mexican green hot sauce made with tomatillos. I use two 7-ounce cans, rinsing out each can with an ounce of water, so I have 2 cups of the sauce. Then I proceed with the recipe, simply reducing the salt.

———⊙———

FRIED TORTILLA STRIPS WITH RED SAUCE AND CHEESE
Chilaquiles
———⊙———

This is a wonderful way to use up leftover corn tortillas. It makes a breakfast partner for scrambled eggs and is good for a quick lunch if served with Refried Beans.

———⊙———

4 servings

10 corn tortillas
½ cup oil for frying
2 cups Basic Red Chile Sauce (page 285)
¼ cup finely chopped white onion
2 cups shredded Jack cheese or white Cheddar

With kitchen shears, cut tortillas into thin short strips. Pour oil ¼-inch deep into a large skillet and heat to 350°. Fry tortilla strips until crisp and golden. Drain on paper towels.

Arrange fried tortilla strips in a round baking dish and add half the sauce. Sprinkle with the chopped white onion, and then pour on the rest of the sauce to cover. Sprinkle shredded cheese on top and bake in a 325° oven until heated through and cheese has melted. Serve garnished with shredded lettuce tossed with a simple vinegar and oil dressing.

TOSTADAS WITH SAUSAGE AND POTATOES
Tostadas de Chorizo con Papas

———⊙———

8 tostadas

8 Tostadas (page 35)
1 cup homemade Refried Beans (page 236)
½ cup sautéed chorizo
1 cup boiled cubed potatoes
  Finely shredded lettuce and sliced radish salad seasoned with a little
    vinegar and salt
  Grated Parmesan cheese and shredded mozzarella cheese, mixed

Make tostadas and drain them on paper towels.

Spread each tostada with a very thin layer of the refried beans, then spoon on small amount of chorizo and potato, mixed. Garnish with shredded lettuce salad and sprinkle cheese on top. Serve with one or several fresh salsas such as Fresh Sauce (page 287), Liquid Sauce (page 294), Home-style Sauce (page 290), and Green Green Sauce (page 299).

Note: This is an excellent way to use up leftover meatloaf. Just crumble and use as you would the chorizo and potato mixture.

———⊙———

GARDEN TOSTADAS
Tostadas Jardineras

———☉———

8 tostadas

2 cups shredded lettuce
1 cup unpeeled chopped ripe tomato
¼ cup chopped green onions (both white and green parts)
½ cup sliced radishes
¼ cup cilantro leaves
1 recipe Garlic Vinaigrette (page 275)
2 cups Guacamole (see below)
8 Tostadas (page 35)
1 cup shredded mozzarella cheese
4 tablespoons grated Parmesan cheese
Salt and pepper

Make a relish-type salad with the lettuce, tomatoes, chopped green onions, radishes, and cilantro. Toss with 4 tablespoons vinaigrette. Add salt and pepper if you think necessary.

Prepare the Guacamole.

Spread 2 tablespoons Guacamole on each tostada. Cover with lettuce salad and sprinkle lavishly with a mixture of the two cheeses.

Serve topped with chopped stuffed green olives and slices of fresh mushrooms.

GUACAMOLE
3 ripe avocados
¾ cup peeled chopped tomatoes
½ cup chopped onions
Lime juice
Salt

Mash avocados on a platter, fold in chopped vegetables, and season with a little lime juice and salt to taste.

Note: If you have enough Garlic Vinaigrette on hand, there's no need to make it. If not, make a batch, use the ¼ cup specified here, and refrigerate the rest.

CRISP-FRIED TACOS
Tacos Doraditos

————⊙————

12 tacos or 6 servings

2 pounds flank steak
Salt and pepper
2 tablespoons oil
½ cup finely chopped onion
1 tablespoon mashed garlic
12 corn tortillas (page 33)
Oil for frying
Shredded lettuce, chopped peeled tomatoes, and chopped green
onions for garnish
Shredded mozzarella or Monterey Jack cheese mixed with grated
Parmesan

Place steak in large saucepan. Cover with water, add salt and pepper, and bring to a boil. Reduce heat and simmer, covered, for 1 hour or until well done. Allow to cool in its own broth. Drain. Cut meat into medium-sized pieces across the grain; this makes shredding much easier. Shred and set aside.

Heat 2 tablespoons oil in a dutch oven and sauté chopped onion, but do not allow to brown. Stir in the shredded meat and add the mashed garlic. Taste for seasoning. Meat should be moist but with no liquid visible.

Soften tortillas and fill each with 2 tablespoons meat mixture. Fold and fasten with toothpicks.

When all of the tortillas are filled, pour the oil into a large skillet to about a depth of ¼ inch. Heat oil and fry filled tacos until crisp and light golden in color. Be sure to drain them well between paper towels. Remove toothpicks and push in a little bit of the garnish. Then sprinkle with additional shredded lettuce, chopped peeled tomatoes, chopped green onions, and the shredded cheeses.

Have a small platter of Refried Beans (page 236) at table, and a bowl of Guacamole (page 49), and of course, the salsas—Fresh Sauce (page 287), Liquid Sauce (page 294), Home-style Sauce (page 290), and Green Green Sauce (page 299). Liquid Sauce keeps indefinitely and is always good on tacos.

————⊙————

CHICKEN TACOS
Tacos de Pollo
————⊙————

Tacos do not appear daily on the tables of Mexicans. Judging from the eating habits of my household, I would say about once a week would be normal. They are often made to use up leftover tortillas and leftover meat.

————⊙————

12 tacos

1 2½- to 3-pound chicken cut into serving pieces
   Salt and pepper
4 garlic cloves, mashed
2 tablespoons chopped onion
3 tablespoons chopped peeled ripe tomato
1 tablespoon vegetable oil
12 taco shells (page 36)
   Shredded lettuce
   Grated Parmesan cheese
   Sour cream thinned with a little fresh milk
   Salsas

Place the chicken pieces in a small kettle or large saucepan and add water to cover, salt and pepper, and mashed garlic cloves. Bring to the boil and partly cover. Simmer for 35 to 40 minutes. Let chicken cool in its own broth. When cool, remove from saucepan and take off skin. Shred chicken meat and set aside.

Sauté 2 tablespoons chopped onion and 3 tablespoons chopped peeled ripe tomato in 1 tablespoon oil, and add salt and pepper to taste. Add shredded chicken and cook 1 minute. Use this as filling for tacos.

Prepare taco shells according to the recipe on page 36. Fill them with 2 tablespoons of prepared chicken. Garnish with shredded lettuce and a teaspoonful of thinned sour cream and top with a sprinkle of Parmesan cheese. Serve with a choice of sauces. Be sure that at least one of them has dry oregano leaves in it to enhance the flavor of the chicken. Good choices would be those listed for Crisp-fried Tacos (page 50) with the addition of Sauce for the Children (page 293).

————⊙————

TUNA TACOS
Tacos de Atun

——⊙——

8 tacos

1 6½-ounce can tuna
1 cup chopped unpeeled ripe tomatoes
¼ cup chopped green onions (much of the green added, please)
¼ cup chopped cilantro leaves
1 tablespoon chopped seeded fresh jalapeño
1 teaspoon freshly-squeezed lime juice
   Salt and pepper
   Pico de Gallo Sauce (page 298)
8 taco shells (page 36), freshly made
   Shredded lettuce
   Grated Parmesan cheese mixed with 1 cup shredded Jack cheese

Shred drained canned tuna. Add tomatoes, green onions, cilantro, chopped jalapeño chile, lime juice, and salt and pepper. Mix well and place in a covered bowl in the refrigerator to chill. Make the Pico de Gallo sauce. Chill.

Prepare taco shells and drain them on paper towels.

Fill taco shells with 2 tablespoons tuna mixture, garnish with lettuce, and sprinkle with grated cheese mixture. Pass the sauce.

This is a salad taco, so do not serve beans with it. However, Guacamole (page 49) is in order, and a Warm Zucchini Salad (page 259).

——⊙——

FIESTA TACOS
Tacos Festivos

————⊙————

If you neglected to buy meat or chicken for a taco filling but have tortillas on hand, try this ham and cheese appetizer variation often served at the luxury hotel at the Ixtapan de la Sal Spa.

————⊙————

24 tacos

24 fresh 5-inch corn tortillas
½ pound Jack cheese (if thicker slices are desired, get 1 pound)
6 slices boiled ham
1 cup vegetable oil or more for deep-frying
 Guacamole (page 49)
 Salsas
 Shredded lettuce or grated cabbage
 Chopped unpeeled ripe tomato
 Sliced radishes
 Garlic Vinaigrette (page 275)

Soften tortillas by placing them in a plastic bag and heating in a microwave oven for 30 seconds. Or put them in the top of a double boiler, covered, over boiling water. If you are in a hurry, turn them once on a hot griddle, fill immediately, and fold.

Cut 24 slivers of cheese and get four strips of ham out of each slice of ham. Fill each softened corn tortilla with one strip of ham and one strip of cheese. Fold each and hold together with a wooden toothpick.

Heat 1-inch of oil in deep 6- or 8-inch skillet. Fry filled tacos until golden and crisp. (Cheese melts and oozes out; keep changing the oil and wiping out the skillet.) Drain on paper towels. Remove toothpicks and let each person garnish their own.

Using condiment dishes or pottery bowls, place the following garnishes in center of table or buffet or bar top: Guacamole (page 49), Sauce for the Children (page 293) and Liquid Sauce (page 294), and a salad of shredded lettuce, tomatoes, and radishes in Garlic Vinaigrette.

These tacos may be made ahead of time and frozen. Then deep-fry when you need them. Refried Beans (page 236) are great to eat with crisp corn tortilla chips as an added treat. If you have a hungry crowd on your hands why not offer a mug full of Gazpacho (page 95) as a first course while you're frying the tacos?

GRILLED CHEESE AND CHILE TORTILLAS
Quesadillas con Chile Verde

———⊙———

The classic quesadilla is normally made with a filling of zucchini blossoms, but green chiles are easier to come by and delightful, and a perfect combination with cheese.

———⊙———

8 quesadillas

8 flour tortillas (page 39)
1 4-ounce can diced green chiles
3 tablespoons chopped onion
5 tablespoons oil, or more
Salt
Epazote leaves or dill weed
½ cup grated or finely cubed Jack cheese
Sauce of your choice

Prepare quesadillas. Keep griddle hot or heat 2 to 3 tablespoons oil in a large skillet.

To make filling, sauté diced green chiles and chopped onion in 2 tablespoons oil. Salt to taste, and add epazote leaves. There is no substitute for epazote, but I have sometimes sprinkled on a bit of dill weed and it is great. You might want to choose a sauce with oregano in it.

Fill tortillas with 1 heaping tablespoonful of filling and 1 tablespoon grated or finely cubed Jack cheese. Fold filled tortillas and continue to cook on griddle, sprinkling 1 teaspoon oil over each. Press down lightly with a pancake turner. The turnovers must be golden in color and look slightly toasted. (I prefer to continue the cooking in a large Teflon skillet with 2 or 3 tablespoons corn oil. They look nicer and cook evenly.) Serve with a green salad and Mexican Red Rice (page 215). By all means put a few slices of ripe avocado in your salad if available. As to your choice of a salsa, suit yourself and make do with what you have in your pantry and refrigerator.

Note: For weight-watchers, less oil may be used. Figure on 2 quesadillas per person for hungry guests.

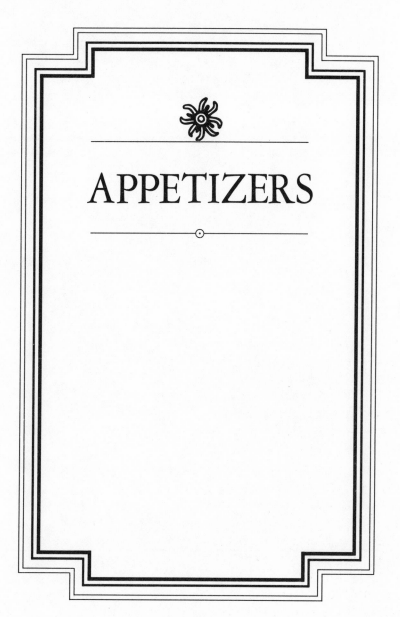

APPETIZERS

A favorite way to entertain in Mexico on Saturday or Sunday afternoon is to invite guests over to *botanear*. The word *botana* is used in Mexican slang to describe a person who is fun to be with or has a delicious sense of humor. So if you ask friends and family to *botanear,* it could be said that you are also asking them to have fun. A staggering assortment of appetizers is assembled and served with ice cold beer, margaritas, or other drinks. Not surprisingly, this enormous repast often takes the place of lunch!

Any of the recipes in this chapter would make exciting additions to a cocktail party menu. Most of them invite experimentation. You can, for example, substitute salmon for the tuna in Tuna with Fresh Chile Relish. Add a slice of boiled ham to a griddle-cooked Quesadilla for a light lunch. Sauté leftover chicken or roast beef with garlic and onions and use to stuff your Gorditas. Use whatever shellfish may be available in place of the fish fillets in White Ceviche.

Many of these dishes can be readily mastered on your first attempt. However, I urge you to practice a bit, using your family as critics, before you plan to offer some of the more complex preparations, like Miniature Tamales or Pinched Filled Patties, to guests.

NACHOS

———⊙———

Nachos have caught on like fire! I don't know where they originated but I do know that one of the best restaurants in Juarez, Chihuahua, across the border from El Paso, Texas, used to serve them about forty years ago.

The secret of the good nacho is to eat it hot from the broiler. They don't keep well; they become soggy.

———⊙———

4 dozen

12 corn tortillas
 Oil for deep-frying
 Salt
 3 cups shredded longhorn or Jack cheese
48 slices mild pickled jalapeño chiles

Cut tortillas into fourths with kitchen shears. Pour oil into a large skillet and heat to 350°. Slip 4 to 6 tortilla chips into the hot oil and fry until crisp and a light golden color. Drain on paper towels and sprinkle with salt as you would french fries.

Lay chips on a large baking sheet and place 1 tablespoon of grated or shredded longhorn cheese or Jack cheese on each corn chip, and garnish with a slice of mild pickled jalapeño chile. Place under the broiler until cheese melts. Serve at once. Have plenty on hand; you'll never have enough!

Note: It is best to fry all the corn chips and remove hot oil from stove. Strain into a grease pot and save for another day. I always keep my nacho oil and my green chile frying oil separate. This is economical, and you always have some oil on hand. (Always strain oil before storing away.)

———⊙———

FRIED TORTILLA CHIPS
Totopos

———☉———

This is the most popular Mexican snack in the United States, of that I am sure. The beauty of making your own chips is that if you have corn tortillas in your freezer and feel that they have been there too long, you can use them up in totopos. Fry them in the cold stage, but take into consideration that every time you put a few into the hot oil the temperature is lowered and it's pretty difficult to have each batch come out the same.

———☉———

4 dozen

12 corn tortillas
Oil for deep-frying
Salt

With a sharp kitchen knife or with kitchen shears cut tortillas in fourths. Pour oil 2 or 3 inches deep in large skillet and heat to medium high temperature. Fry tortilla pieces a few at a time until crisp and light golden in color. Drain on paper towels and sprinkle with salt from a shaker. Set in large bowl if to be eaten immediately, or they may be stored in an airtight container.

Strain oil and keep to use again.

Note: A salt-water wash works well but takes a little more time. To use one, dissolve 8 teaspoons of salt in 1 cup of water. Brush tortilla pieces with salt-water wash, set aside, heat oil, and deep-fry. The wash may also be sprayed on crisply fried tortilla chips, but be sure to spray very lightly.

———☉———

CORN-FLOUR PATTIES
Gorditas

————☉————

This is a lovely snack but it has to be served freshly made. I think it's a great idea to have your guests sit near or around your kitchen work area where they can chat and have their drinks while you make the gorditas. Let each guest garnish his own. Figure on three per guest, at least, but don't be surprised if they eat six or more.

————☉————

24 gorditas

  2 cups instant corn flour (masa harina)
  4 tablespoons all-purpose flour
  ½ teaspoon baking powder
  ½ teaspoon salt
1½ cups warm water
    Oil for frying
  1 cup shredded Jack cheese mixed with 2 tablespoons Parmesan
  2 cups shredded cabbage
    Salsa Liquida (page 298)
    Additional grated Parmesan cheese

Mix flours, baking powder, and salt, and add the warm water. You may need a little more warm water to make a moist, smooth dough. Make balls the size of a walnut, a few at a time, and keep the dough in a plastic bag to prevent it from drying out.

Moisten a cloth napkin or tea towel and spread out on a flat surface. Roll each ball of dough in moistened palm of your hand until smooth, lay on the damp towel, cover with a plastic bag, and press down with your hand to flatten to the size of a silver dollar. To shape the patty, flatten again with a small can

or flat-bottomed glass into a perfectly smooth circle 2 to 2½ inches in diameter. It should be about ¼ inch thick. Peel the plastic bag off the top, then lay the tortilla in your hand and peel off the damp cloth.

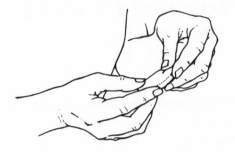

Smooth any rough edges with your fingers and the tortilla is ready to fry.

Slide the patties into the hot oil and fry until they are a light golden brown and slightly crisp on top, about 1 minute on each side.

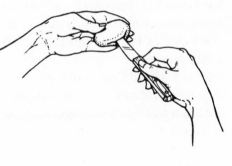

Drain on paper towels and make a slit on the side as soon as they have cooled enough to handle.

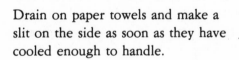

Push about 1 teaspoon of shredded cheese through the slit, garnish with shredded cabbage, and sprinkle with some sauce and Parmesan cheese. These do not keep well; they must be eaten immediately.

MINIATURE CORN-FLOUR TURNOVERS
Quesadillas Miniatura

———⊙———

10 or 12 quesadillas

1 cup instant corn flour (masa harina)
2 tablespoons all-purpose flour
1 teaspoon baking powder
½ teaspoon salt
⅔ cup warm water
1 cup shredded Jack cheese or white Cheddar
1 4-ounce can chopped green chiles
Oil for frying

Combine dry ingredients in a medium-sized bowl. Mix well, and add the warm water all at once. You may need to add a tablespoon or two more, as you will need a moist, soft dough. Blend thoroughly.

Place dough in a plastic bag and pinch off small pieces the size of a walnut. Roll pieces of masa in the palms of your hands, being sure to moisten your hands often. Dampen a small napkin or tea towel and spread out on a flat surface. Place the small balls of dough on the tea towel and cover with a plastic bag or even a small piece of plastic. Press with the palm of your hand to flatten the dough balls and then shape by pressing with a small flat-bottomed can. This will flatten each ball to a 3-inch circle. Remove plastic.

Heat oil to 350° in a small skillet. Place ½ teaspoon of shredded cheese and 2 pieces of green chile on one half of the patty. Now peel the tea towel from bottom half and fold dough over to cover the filling. Press edges of dough together. Peel turnover from tea towel, and slip it into the hot oil. Fry until crisp and light golden in color. Drain. Serve immediately.

———⊙———

MINIATURE TAMALES
Tamales Miniatura
————⊙————

Making tamales no matter what size is a laborious enterprise. Once you have mastered the art, you feel a sense of accomplishment equal to none other in the culinary arts. The finished product is breathtaking. These tamales show off beautifully in a Mexican pottery dish that will accommodate their shape and coloring. You should provide a lined colorful basket or another larger pottery dish for the husks. Many a stranger to our kind of food has been very embarrassed when he was later told that he should have removed the husks before attempting to eat the tamales.

————⊙————

20 to 24 tamales

        2 cups instant corn flour (masa harina)
        1 teaspoon baking powder
        1 teaspoon salt
     1¼ cups warm water
        ⅔ cup vegetable shortening
20 to 24 small corn husks
        1 cup shredded Monterey Jack or mozzarella cheese
        1 4-ounce can chopped green chiles

Mix dry ingredients and pour in the warm water to make a moist dough. Beat shortening until creamy and fluffy and mix with the dough. It must be of spreading consistency, so you may have to add a little more warm water. (I always make a test tamal by pressing 1 tablespoon of the prepared dough in a dampened corn husk and folding it over. I cook it on top of the stove in a small heavy cast-iron skillet. When the husk chars on one side I flip it over and cook the other side. If the husk peels off the "masa," it has the right amount of shortening.) Taste for salt.

Soak the outer corn husks in hot water. (I never use the inside husks because they are full of the corn silk and they get all over everything.) When the husks are pliable, rinse under warm running water and set in a colander to drain.

Hold a husk in the palm of your hand and spoon in about 1 tablespoon of dough. Place a teaspoon of shredded cheese and 1 or 2 pieces of canned green chiles on top of the dough. Fold as instructed on pages 329–30, and steam. I like to use a rack and just place it in a dutch oven with 2 cups of water. Be sure to stack the tamales with open ends up. Cover them with a damp napkin, and pour the water in carefully around the sides so that it does not wet the stacked tamales. Steam 1 hour, covered.

PINCHED FILLED PATTIES
Sopes
———⊙———

These snacks are made in different sizes. The small size that I recommend here is special because it is a two- or three-bite snack—it never gets soggy, never gets cold—it's just right.

The instructions in the recipe specify that you fry the patty. That is the correct way to make them if the tortillas have been made ahead of time. However if you are making them and eating them hot off the griddle, just pour ½ teaspoon of hot oil over the patty, fill, and dribble the green or red salsa over it. Allow no less than three per guest; best to count on six per guest.

———⊙———

12 sopes

1½ cups instant corn flour (masa harina)
¾ cups warm water
Oil for frying
Filling (see below)
Fresh Sauce, (page 287)
Green Green Sauce, (page 299)
Shredded lettuce
Grated Parmesan cheese

Preheat a griddle, preferably Teflon, and keep hot over medium heat.

Mix instant corn flour with warm water in a small bowl. Add more water if necessary to make a moist, smooth dough. Place dough in a plastic bag. Pinch off pieces of dough the size of a walnut, roll in the palms of your hands until smooth, then place dough between two small plastic bags and press down with the palm of the hand to flatten to a thick patty about 2½ inches in diameter.

Peel off top plastic bag and then bottom bag, and bake patties on the hot griddle, turning once only. Set aside.

When all patties are baked, moisten tips of fingers with cold water and pinch around edge of each patty to shape into a tart to be filled.

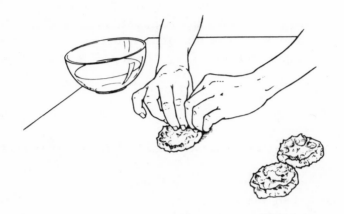

Heat oil in a skillet and fry the patties for 30 seconds, just to heat through but not brown. Fill with shredded chicken mixture, add 1 teaspoon either sauce, garnish with shredded lettuce, and sprinkle with grated Parmesan cheese. Pass extra sauce at table; some people like their sopes overflowing with sauce.

FILLING
2 chicken breasts, poached in well-seasoned water to cover
¼ cup finely chopped green onion
½ cup finely chopped peeled tomatoes
1 teaspoon mashed garlic
    Salt and pepper
1 tablespoon oil

Mix all ingredients except oil and stir-fry 2 minutes in 8-inch skillet coated with the oil. Cool.

———⊙———

WHITE CEVICHE
Ceviche Blanco

———⊙———

The first time I tasted White Ceviche I fell in love with it because frankly all the other ceviches are too tart for my liking. It should be served on crisp corn tostadas and if you make your own corn chips at home be sure and cut your corn tortillas into large chips. I prefer homemade mayonnaise and I omit the lemon juice from the recipe for this dish.

———⊙———

24 servings as appetizer

2 cups finely chopped raw fish fillets (meaty, white fish, such as scrod, cod, etc.)
½ cup lime juice, freshly squeezed and strained
1 cup carrot strips (see below)
1 cup peeled chopped ripe tomatoes
½ cup chopped green onions
⅓ cup chopped fresh cilantro leaves
1 tablespoon olive oil
2 tablespoons white vinegar
   Salt and pepper
¼ cup ice water
½ cup mayonnaise

Marinate chopped raw fish in lime juice for 1 hour. Drain and dry on paper towels.

Boil carrots in salted water until crisp-tender, and peel under cold running water. Cut into thin short strips.

Combine all vegetables with oil and vinegar. Add salt and pepper to taste, and ice water. Fold chopped fish into vegetable mixture. Cover and place in refrigerator to meld the flavors.

Before serving, drain mixture and add ½ cup mayonnaise. Serve on corn-chips and cover with chopped lettuce.

———⊙———

GREEN CEVICHE
Ceviche Verde

————⊙————

There are many schools of thought regarding the making of ceviche of any color or any fish. My theory is that you have to drain all of the lemon or lime juice thoroughly once you have marinated the small seafood or fish pieces. Too much tartness spoils a flavor for me. This is a terrific appetizer, more a dip than a fish and vegetable relish type of thing.

————⊙————

4 to 5 cups

1 pound fish fillets (scrod, cod, etc.), chopped
¼ cup lime juice
¼ pound tomatillos
1 ripe avocado
1 clove garlic
  Salt and pepper
1 teaspoon sugar
1 cup peeled chopped tomatoes
½ cup chopped green onions
1 small fresh crisp hot green jalapeño chile,
  seeded and chopped
1 teaspoon crushed oregano leaves
  Chopped cilantro

Marinate chopped fish in lime juice for 1 hour. Drain and dry with paper towels. Remove dry outer skin from tomatillos. Place tomatillos in blender and purée with peeled, chopped avocado and garlic. If too thick add 2 tablespoons ice water. Add salt to taste, and sugar.

Chop tomatoes, green onions, and green chile. Add salt and pepper. Sprinkle with oregano leaves. Stir in marinated, drained, chopped fish.

Combine avocado mixture with fish mixture. Place in a bowl suitable for a dip and surround with large corn chips. Sprinkle chopped cilantro on ceviche dip just before serving.

————⊙————

FRANKFURTER CEVICHE
Ceviche de Salchichas
o Salchichon

————⊙————

The meat-packing plants in Mexico have been pushing their sausage-type products by distributing easy and economical recipes. I ran across one of them in my grocery bag the other day. Since I was short on most of the ingredients I normally have stashed away for emergencies, I made this frankfurter ceviche. It was delightful. Good on toast, on corn chips, or on crackers. *Buen provecho!*

————⊙————

3 cups

    2 cups thinly sliced or chopped frankfurters
    1 cup chopped peeled ripe tomatoes
    ½ cup chopped white onion
    1 jalapeño, seeded and chopped
    ¼ cup chopped cilantro leaves
      Salt and pepper
    ⅛ cup freshly squeezed lime juice or fresh lemon juice

Mix all of the above ingredients and place in a bowl in the refrigerator to chill. Drain off excess lime or lemon juice before serving.

————⊙————

FRIED CORN-FLOUR TURNOVERS
Quesadillas

————⊙————

1 dozen 4½-inch
turnovers

    1½ cups corn flour
     2 tablespoons all-purpose flour
     ½ teaspoon baking powder
     ½ teaspoon salt
     ¾ cup warm water or a little more
    12 strips Monterey Jack cheese
       Canned chopped green chiles
       Oil for frying

Combine dry ingredients in a bowl. Add warm water and mix by hand until dough forms into a ball (you may need one or two extra tablespoons of water). Place in plastic bag so that dough will not dry.

Shape dough to form 12 balls the size of a Ping-Pong ball. Cover dough balls with moistened dish towel to keep them from drying. Press out each ball according to tortilla-making instructions (page 33) and place on dish towel. Fill each with a strip of Jack cheese and a teaspoonful of chopped canned chiles and fold to shape like a turnover. Press edges with tines of fork to seal.

Heat oil to a depth of ½ inch in a large skillet. Fry turnovers about 2 minutes on each side, or until golden brown. Drain on paper towels and serve immediately with Liquid Sauce (page 294) on the side, and cold beer. *Maravilloso!*

————⊙————

CHEESE CRISPS
Tostadas de Tortillas de Harina

————⊙————

This is a snack to place in the center of a coffee table, picnic table, or the top of a home bar. You break off a bite-sized piece and indulge. If you have a crowd, keep the tostadas coming. They are that good. I put a shaker filled with ground red chile (no spices) within reach because it adds that certain touch when the tostadas come to the table, the cheese melted and sizzling. Wonderful with beer!

————⊙————   4 tostadas

    4 8-inch Wheat-flour Tortillas (see note)
       Melted butter
    2 cups shredded longhorn cheese
       Mexican paprika

Place tortillas on a cookie sheet in a 350° oven and bake until light golden in color and crisp. Take out of the oven and brush with melted butter. Sprinkle with shredded cheese and return to oven until cheese melts. Serve topped with a mixture of:

    1 cup chopped peeled ripe tomatoes
    ½ cup chopped green onion
    ¼ cup chopped cilantro leaves
    1 tablespoon chopped fresh jalapeño (optional)
       Salt to taste

Sprinkle on paprika before serving.

Note: Use flour tortillas from the supermarket. I always keep 1 or 2 dozen in the freezer for my easy "Mexican pizzas."

SEAFOOD COCKTAIL
Campechana

———⊙———

In some parts of Mexico the word *campechana* means a blend or mixture—two kinds of something, be it food, a combination of beverages, or gasoline. Yes, gasoline. You will see the words Extra and Nova on respective pumps, meaning leaded and unleaded. Since most customers believe that one is definitely better than the other, they will buy a mixture—maybe half of the leaded and half of the other. Why this reasoning? I don't know, but they will say, "Don't you think my car is working better with the *campechana* of gasoline that I put into the tank?"

So it goes with the Campechana Seafood Cocktail. The normal combination is half oysters and half shrimp, and if there are no oysters perhaps a combination of poached fish cut into small cubes, and chopped shrimp. It's a delight. The sauce is often half tomato juice and half cocktail sauce or catsup. This variation of the cocktail sauce is great because that very sweet catsup is tastier if diluted with juice.

If you are brave enough to venture into the eateries in the large *mercado* in the city of Guadalajara you will be pleasantly surprised to see clean stalls selling various combinations in their cocktails, but you have to watch the vendors because they do go overboard with the limes. If you order a large cocktail they will prepare it in the regular old-fashioned glasses used for ice cream sodas here in the States—seafood, then some chopped green onions, then a measure of cold court bouillon the shrimp or fish were poached in, and the juice of half a lime or more, and then they fill the glass with sauce. Wonderful!

———⊙———

6 to 8 servings

1 pound medium-sized shrimp
1 pint oysters
2 cups cocktail sauce or catsup
1 cup tomato juice
Freshly squeezed juice of 1 small lime or to taste
Salt and pepper
Dash or more of Tabasco sauce

½ cup finely chopped scallions (optional)
½ teaspoon finely mashed garlic
1 ounce dry red wine

To cook shrimp: Combine 4 cups of water, 1 tablespoon salt, 2 tablespoons vinegar, and 2 bay leaves in small saucepan and boil. Add the fresh or frozen shrimp, in shells, and heat again to boiling. Cook about 1 to 3 minutes and drain, but save the liquid and strain. Keep in refrigerator until later. Peel shrimp and remove the vein that runs down the back. Cool and cut up into bite-sized pieces.

Drain the oysters and save the liquid. If you are going to substitute or to add fish, poach the fish fillets and allow to cool in their own cooking broth, drain, and cut up into bite-sized pieces. Set aside.

Prepare sauce by combining last 8 ingredients and allow to set for at least 30 minutes. Add the reserved oyster liquid and ½ cup of the reserved bouillon the shrimp were cooked in. Taste for flavor and correct seasoning.

Combine prepared seafood with the amount of sauce you normally use. Serve cold and garnish with a slice of peeled ripe avocado.

————⊙————

AVOCADO DIP WITH COTTAGE CHEESE
Guacamole con Cuajada

————⊙————

Necessity is the mother of invention. A friend who ran a very successful restaurant in my home town had ordered a case of ripe avocados to make guacamole for a businessmen's luncheon. When the crate of avocados was opened only about half of them were ripe enough to be peeled and mashed for guacamole. No time to spare —how to make a whole recipe from half a recipe? In the refrigerator were two quart containers of creamed cottage cheese that had just been delivered. Let's try a bit mixed in with some of the guacamole. Eureka! A gold mine—marvelous taste, lovely texture. Thus was this recipe born. It was such a terrific hit that it was always afterward made thus.

————⊙————

3½ cups

2 medium-sized ripe avocados
1 cup small-curd creamed cottage cheese
½ cup chopped peeled ripe tomatoes
2 teaspoons chopped green onion
  Salt
¼ cup chopped cilantro leaves

Peel and mash avocados. (I prefer to mash them in a large platter; it seems easier than doing so in a bowl, and I don't approve of puréeing them in a blender.) Mash cottage cheese and add to avocado, blending completely. Add chopped tomatoes, green onion, and salt to taste. Add cilantro leaves at the end.

Serve as an appetizer with corn chips or crudité vegetables. I love to serve this on chopped lettuce on a salad plate as a first course. Garnishes could be slices of cucumber, bell pepper, and a cherry tomato. It is so light and delicious and you could add more cottage cheese.

————⊙————

WHEAT-FLOUR TORTILLAS WITH CHEESE
Quesadillas de Tortillas de Harina

———⊙———

This is a wonderful snack. If you taste a small piece just once you are hooked for life. Good—because this is a super way to use up leftover flour tortillas. Please serve while fresh and hot.

Want to add a not-too-traditional touch? Keep a small bottle of good old Tabasco sauce on hand; it's so good sprinkled on top lavishly or carefully—suit yourself.

———⊙———

8 quesadillas

8 6-inch wheat-flour tortillas (page 38)
  Melted butter
2 cups shredded longhorn cheese
1 4-ounce can chopped green chiles

Heat flour tortillas slightly. Butter lightly. Spread half of the tortilla with cheese, add a few pieces of the chopped green chiles, fold over, and cook on a hot griddle. Press down on the "turnover" while grilling, as if you were making grilled cheese sandwiches.

If you prefer, you may spread the open tortillas with shredded cheese, add bits of chile, and bake in a 350° oven until cheese melts and tortillas brown lightly.

Either way, they are lovely in color and taste. The "turnover" model may be eaten with the fingers, perhaps after dipping in a favorite sauce.

———⊙———

AVOCADO DIP WITH CHILE
Guacamole con Chile

———⊙———

This is a lovely dip—not too spicy; just right. I like to mash the avocados in a large platter with a fork. I do not subscribe to the notion that the avocados and the rest of the ingredients should be puréed in the blender. To me, this renders the mixture too smooth, too artificial, and not at all traditional. It tastes and looks like a commercial blend of some sort.

———⊙———

2 cups

2 large ripe avocados
1 teaspoon mashed garlic plus ¼ cup ice water to make an infusion
1 cup chopped peeled ripe tomatoes
½ cup finely minced onion
1 tablespoon freshly squeezed lime juice
1 fresh jalapeño chile, seeded and chopped
½ teaspoon salt
¼ cup chopped cilantro leaves

Peel avocados and mash them in a large platter. Add strained garlic infusion and remainder of ingredients. Correct seasoning. Serve immediately with corn chips or slices of jicama.

———⊙———

GREEN CHILE AND CHEESE
Chile con Queso

────⟨○⟩────

The recipes for Chile con Queso are like the formulas for dry martinis. I once read a short essay to the effect that if you were lost at the North Pole, the one sure way to be rescued was to take the pack from your back, kneel in the snow, and get out your gin or vodka and your dry vermouth and a jar. Before you have even started to mix, someone will come up and say, "Making martinis, eh? That's not the way I make them. . . ." He'll make better martinis than you possibly could but who cares. Your rescuer is kneeling right there in the snow with you. So goes it with Chile con Queso. So many recipes, and so many of them terrific!

────⟨○⟩────

2 to 3 cups

½ cup sliced onion
2 tablespoons vegetable oil
1 4-ounce can mild chopped green chiles
1 small can evaporated milk diluted with 1 cup of warm water
  Salt and pepper
1 pound Monterey Jack cheese or Wisconsin white Cheddar, cubed

Sauté onion in hot oil in a deep saucepan. Do not allow onion to brown; it should be just barely wilted. Add the chopped canned chiles (be sure to remove any blackened peel often found in this type of canned pepper). Add diluted canned milk and season with salt and pepper to taste. Bring to a simmer; do not allow to come to a boil.

Place cubed cheese in a serving bowl. Pour hot chile and milk mixture over cheese. Allow to set 2 or 3 minutes before ladling into small cereal bowls. Serve as a side dish to eat with grilled steak strips, corn tortillas, and cole slaw.

AS A DIP

Do not dilute canned milk. Correct seasoning. Serve in a chafing dish or over a candle warmer. Use corn tortilla chips.

────⟨○⟩────

CREAM CHEESE AND GREEN CHILE DIP
Botana de Queso Crema y Rajas
———⊙———

I love this dip, and made with canned chopped green chiles it's tasty, economical, and easy to make. When using canned, chopped, green chiles it is most important that you check all the pieces as small charred chile skins adhere to them and this will spoil the looks of the finished product and also discourage a squeamish person from eating it.

———⊙———

2½ cups

1 8-ounce package pasteurized cream cheese
½ cup mayonnaise
1 cup sour cream
2 4-ounce cans chopped green chiles
Salt

Soften cream cheese at room temperature for at least an hour. Mash in large platter and add mayonnaise and sour cream slowly, a tablespoon at a time. Fold in chopped green chiles and season with salt.

Serve with fresh raw zucchini sticks, slices of jicama, or corn chips. This is also great as a sandwich filling, and wonderful on toasted bagels.

———⊙———

TUNA WITH FRESH CHILE RELISH
Atun con Pico de Gallo

———⊙———

This is one of those last-minute recipes that will come to mind if you stand in front of your pantry and survey just what you happen to have on hand. If there is a can of tuna and you have the makings of the Pico de Gallo, you are all set. Mix the relish first, and allow it to stand for a few minutes. Garnish the finished dish with ripe olives, sliced radishes, carrot curls, whatever will add color and substance.

———⊙———

2½ to 3 cups

1 6½-ounce can chunk light tuna packed in oil
1 cup peeled chopped ripe tomatoes
1 cup chopped white onion
1 seeded chopped jalapeño chile
Juice of ½ lime
Salt and pepper
½ cup chopped fresh cilantro leaves

Break up canned tuna in small pieces. Do not drain oil. Arrange on small platter and smother with Pico de Gallo relish made by combining all remaining ingredients.

Serve with fresh corn chips, on crackers, or in miniature flour tortillas. This would even be good in a fresh, warm, small French roll.

SOUPS

S oup is taken very seriously in Mexico. Mexican men feel they haven't eaten if they do not start their noon meal with a bowl of some extra-special concoction. My father had his own special deep soup bowl that would hold two generous portions, and his own large heavy soup spoon. All his daughters would join in the soup preparation—peeling, slicing, simmering.

Mexican soups are as diverse as its many regions. There are wonderful sauce creams, rich broths, exotic mixtures using avocados or squash blossoms, nourishing dried legume purées, and the rich, full-bodied, stewlike soups such as Cocido. This often constitutes a meal in itself when accompanied by a basketful of freshly made corn tortillas and piquant salsa. And from the northern state of Sonora comes the unusual taste of Menudo, a tripe soup with hominy. This is the traditional pick-me-up after a night out.

When I was a girl, dances were always stag, and, like Scarlett O'Hara, young ladies did not eat much before going to a dance. That way you showed off a flat tummy and could stand up straight and gracefully and dance like an angel. But then when the ball was over, everyone, but everyone, met at the menuderias, delightful modest all-night cafes that served Menudo. Over a bowl or two of the potent soup we discussed who had danced with whom, so-and-so's gown, who was engaged, and so on. We lingered on over the last cup of coffee and the last warming drop of our Menudo.

RICH HOMEMADE CHICKEN BROTH
Caldo de Pollo (Casero)

If I were directing a cooking school this recipe would probably be one of the first I would teach. It is most important because it serves as a base for so many soups and other dishes. Do make this broth. You probably have a recipe just as good, but if you plan to use it in Mexican preparations remember to omit celery. This flavor is not Mexican and gives other dishes for which you might use the broth a flavor foreign to the Mexican cuisine.

I always like to strain the broth and then cool it rapidly in the freezer so that the grease will coagulate on top, to be easily removed later.

2 quarts

- 1 boiling or stewing chicken, giblets and all
- 2 ripe tomatoes, peeled and cut in half (do not use canned)
  Salt
- 1 tablespoon peppercorns
- 1 tablespoon mashed garlic

Cut up chicken and add giblets and any wing tips, necks, and backs that you might have in your freezer. It is important that all of the chicken grease goes into the pot. The idea is to produce a rich thick broth.

Place chicken and extra parts in a large soup pot and add 12 cups of hot water. Add tomatoes, salt, peppercorns, and garlic. Bring to a rolling boil, uncovered, and skim the foam, if any. Lower heat and cover. Cook at a simmer, with cover slightly ajar, for about 2 hours, or until the legs of the chicken feel tender. If you cook the chicken whole, it will be done when the legs of the fowl move quite easily when bent. If necessary, add hot water. You want at least 8 cups of rich stock at the end of the cooking process.

Strain soup, pushing tomatoes through strainer with the back of spoon. Taste for strength and correct seasoning.

Serve in bowls as is or add shredded chicken meat and garnish with chopped green onions and cilantro leaves. Or use in other soup recipes that follow.

VERMICELLI IN CHICKEN BROTH
Sopa de Fideo con Caldo

————⊙————

8 servings

      8 tablespoons salad oil
      4 ounces vermicelli twists or thin noodles
      2 tablespoons lard
      ½ cup chopped onions
      1 cup chopped tomatoes
      8 cups well-seasoned homemade chicken broth
      1 teaspoon mashed garlic
6 or 8 sprigs cilantro
        Salt and pepper
      2 cups shredded Monterey Jack cheese mixed with 4 tablespoons
        grated Parmesan cheese

Heat oil in a large skillet and brown the vermicelli twists on both sides, being careful not to break them. They should be a light golden color. Drain on paper towels. Set aside.

Heat 2 tablespoons lard in a dutch oven and sauté the onions and the chopped tomatoes, stirring over medium heat, for about 2 minutes. Pour in the chicken broth and the mashed garlic. Add the cilantro sprigs and test for taste. Add salt and pepper if needed. Add drained vermicelli, bring to the boil, cover, and then lower heat and cook at a simmer until pasta is tender, usually about 20 or 25 minutes.

Pour into heated soup plates and pass the shredded cheese. Delightful with flour tortilla crisps.

Note: It is well to remove the cilantro sprigs before taking the soup to table.

————⊙————

TORTILLA SOUP
Sopa de Tortilla

———⊙———

Tortilla soup is best made with homemade broth. It is very tasty and very Mexican in flavor. If unexpected guests arrive, cut up a few extra tortillas and add a cup of cooked frozen peas and carrots and a little more broth. This will take care of two or three more people.

———⊙———

6 to 8 servings

8 corn tortillas
1 cup oil for frying
2 tablespoons vegetable oil
½ cup chopped white onion
1 cup peeled and chopped ripe tomatoes
6 to 8 cups degreased homemade chicken broth
6 to 8 cilantro sprigs
½ cup shredded mozzarella cheese

With kitchen shears cut corn tortillas into narrow short strips. Heat 1 cup oil in 10-inch skillet and deep-fry the tortilla strips until crisp. Drain on paper towels.

Heat 2 tablespoons oil in dutch oven and sauté the chopped onion for 1 minute, stirring over medium heat; do not brown. Add the chopped tomatoes and cook 1 minute. Add soup stock, correct seasoning, add the cilantro sprigs, cover, and simmer for 10 minutes. Remove cilantro.

Place a handful of crisp tortilla strips in colorful Mexican clay soup bowls and fill with hot broth. Add a tablespoonful of shredded mozzarella cheese.

———⊙———

TLALPA-STYLE SOUP
Caldo Tlalpeño

———⊙———

This recipe is best made with clarified homemade chicken stock but you can make it with canned chicken broth if you are careful to use it almost the way it comes out of the can. If it is diluted too much you do not get the flavor you sought. I place the condiments in small pottery dishes as I do very often when I serve curry.

————————⊙————————

8 servings

8 cups highly seasoned chicken broth
2 cooked chicken breasts, skinned and shredded
6 sprigs cilantro
1 cup canned garbanzos (chickpeas), skins removed
1 ripe avocado
  Chipotle Chile Sauce (below)
  Slices or wedges of fresh green lime

In large soup pot or dutch oven, heat the chicken broth and taste for seasoning. Add shredded cooked chicken breasts and 6 sprigs of cilantro. Bring to the boil and simmer, covered, for 5 minutes or until chicken meat is heated through and flavors meld. Remove cilantro sprigs.

Spoon 8 to 10 chickpeas into heated soup plates, add 2 tablespoons or less shredded chicken, and fill each bowl with ⅔ cup of hot broth.

Garnish with chopped avocado (avocado should be peeled and chopped just before serving).

Pass the Chipotle Chile Sauce. Remember that 2 or 3 drops from the serving spoon will enhance your Caldo Tlalpeño and give it that lovely smoked flavor. If you are hooked on the taste of fresh green limes, squeeze a few drops into your soup. *Buen provecho.*

FAST AND EASY CANNED
CHIPOTLE CHILE SAUCE

1 cup

½ cup canned chipotle chiles (smallest is a 100-gram can)
½ cup cold water
1 teaspoon instant chicken bouillon granules

Place all ingredients in blender container and purée to liquefy. Strain and rinse out blender container with additional ⅓ cup water. This makes 1 cup of the hottest chile sauce you will ever taste.

ZUCCHINI BLOSSOM SOUP
Sopa de Flor de Calabaza

———⊙———

So good, so unusual, so satisfying—but sometimes so difficult to find the fresh or the canned blossoms. If you do find the ingredients, I assure you the search will be worth your while. Some people insist that this is an acquired taste. Maybe so, but it doesn't take too long to acquire it.

See the note at the bottom of the recipe. Dried epazote leaves are now available in the United States and this is one ingredient that may *not* be substituted.

———⊙———

8 servings

1 small zucchini, finely chopped
¼ cup butter
2 tablespoons oil
¼ cup chopped onion
½ cup peeled chopped tomatoes
2 cans zucchini blossoms, drained, or 2 bunches fresh
8 cups well-seasoned homemade chicken broth
1 teaspoon mashed garlic
1 4-ounce can chopped green chiles
8 dried epazote leaves (see note)
   Salt and pepper
2 cups shredded mozzarella or Monterey Jack cheese

Finely chop zucchini and set aside.

In dutch oven, heat 4 tablespoons butter with 2 tablespoons oil. Sauté chopped zucchini for 2 minutes and add chopped onion and chopped tomatoes. Stir-fry 2 minutes. Add the zucchini blossoms and cook for 1 minute, stirring often. Pour in the chicken broth and add mashed garlic and canned chopped green chiles. Add infusion of epazote (see note). Bring to a boil, lower heat, and simmer 10 minutes. Check seasoning, adding salt and pepper if necessary.

Serve in bowls and pass the Fast and Easy Canned Chipotle Chile Sauce (page 85). Just the tip of a teaspoonful of it will highlight your soup. Garnish each serving with 1 tablespoon of shredded mozzarella or Monterey Jack cheese.

Note: I personally always make an infusion of the dried epazote leaves, allowing them to float in 1 cup of hot water and brewing them for 5 minutes; do not boil. Then cut leaves in 2 or 3 pieces with kitchen shears and pour them into the broth, water and all. If leaves are too small, leave whole. When serving, be sure to place 1 epazote leaf in each soup bowl.

———⊙———

FARM SOUP
Sopa Milpa Verde

This soup has a melodious ring to its Mexican name. The word *milpa* could aptly be translated as farm, but most likely a truck garden type of farm where produce is raised and sold.

The adjective always follows the noun in Spanish except in poetic expressions. Hence we would say *Casa Blanca* (House White) for the residence of the United States president. And in this title, farm green instead of green farm.

———⊙———

6 to 8 servings

1 10-ounce package frozen shoepeg corn in butter sauce
1 cup chopped zucchini
6 cups chicken broth
   Trace of fresh sliced small green serrano or fresh jalapeño chile (optional)
1 fresh green California chile, blistered in hot oil, seeded, and chopped
3 or 4 dried epazote leaves
   Salt and pepper
1 cup shredded mozzarella cheese

Cook corn according to package directions and set aside. Blanch chopped zucchini and drain.

Heat chicken broth in large soup pot and add cooked corn, including its sauce, and blanched zucchini. Add remainder of ingredients except shredded cheese and bring to the boil.

Serve in warmed soup bowls and sprinkle each serving lavishly with cheese.

For a wonderful accompaniment, place small flour tortillas on baking sheet and toast in a hot oven. When crisp, butter lavishly, and before bringing to the table sprinkle them with Mexican paprika *(pimenton)* or ground pure New Mexico chile powder.

SUPREME CREAM OF ARTICHOKES
Crema de Alcachofas Suprema

———⊙———

I first tasted this soup because my hostess insisted. She had asked us out to lunch to my favorite restaurant in Mexico City, San Angel Inn. The head waiter laced the soup with dry sherry and sprinkled it with fresh black pepper from a huge pepper mill. It was absolutely the best soup I had ever eaten and it is still in first place in my book of memories. It can be made ahead of time if you are cooking up a storm in your kitchen. Be sure and keep everything chilled until you are ready to heat and serve it.

If you must use canned artichoke hearts, be sure you avoid those that say clearly that they are canned with citric acid added. These are too tart and will not give you the flavor you are looking for. I insist that the only perfect soup will be produced if you use the frozen artichokes or the hearts from boiled fresh artichokes.

———⊙———

8 servings

¼ cup butter
¼ cup flour
8 cups well-seasoned chicken broth
1 cup evaporated milk or heavy cream
  Salt and white pepper
1 package frozen artichoke hearts
½ teaspoon nutmeg
  Dry sherry
  Garlic croutons

In dutch oven, heat butter and add flour. Cook, stirring often, for 2 minutes. Do not brown. Slowly add two cups broth and the evaporated milk or cream. Cook until smooth, stirring often. Add remainder of broth and season to taste.

Cook frozen artichoke hearts in plenty of salted water according to package instructions. Allow to cool in their cooking liquid and purée in blender with 1 or 2 cups of their cooking broth.

Strain puréed artichokes into chicken stock mixture and bring to the boil. Lower heat and cook at a simmer for 5 minutes, stirring often. Add nutmeg, correct seasoning, and serve laced with dry sherry and topped with freshly made garlic croutons.

SUPREME CREAMED BEAN SOUP
Crema Suprema de Frijol

———⊙———

This soup could be considered a one-dish meal. It is heavy and tasty and leaves you with no cravings at all, especially if you have been served plenty of fresh garlic flavored croutons and a piece of cheese or a cheese board on the side. I like to drop pieces of croutons right into the soup and push them down into the broth. This soup is a winter soup, of that there is no doubt; one would hardly crave it on a sweltering summer day.

———⊙———

8 large servings

   1   cup pinto or pink beans, soaked overnight,
       or 1 16-ounce can refried beans
   4   tablespoons butter
  ½   cup coarsely chopped green onions
  ½   cup chopped tomatoes
   1   poblano or California chile, blistered in hot oil, seeded and chopped
   1   tablespoon cornstarch mixed with ¼ cup cold water
   4   cups chicken broth, canned or homemade

Cook fresh beans in 6 cups salted water until mushy. Cool. Purée with all their cooking liquid until creamy and smooth. If you use canned refried beans, purée them in blender with 2 cups water.

Heat butter in small skillet and sauté onions and chopped tomatoes until mushy. Add chopped green chile.

Combine all ingredients including cornstarch mixture and chicken broth in large soup pot and bring to the boil. Simmer over low heat for 3 minutes, stirring constantly, as cornstarch mixture is the thickening agent and must not settle in bottom of kettle. Taste and correct seasoning.

Serve in a soup tureen and pass the garlic-flavored homemade croutons, or better still, serve the Mexican way with a handful of thin corn tortilla strips that have been deep-fried until golden and crisp.

———⊙———

CREAM OF CAULIFLOWER SOUP
Crema de Coliflor

My mother-in-law could really show off when she served this glamorous soup at one of her glorious meals. I have modified it a little, using less butter, but it still tastes like hers, only not as rich.

10 servings

2 cups puréed cooked cauliflower
2 teaspoons freshly squeezed lemon juice
3 cups cauliflower cooking liquid
4 tablespoons butter
2 tablespoons flour
1 small can evaporated milk
Salt and pepper
6 cups chicken broth
6 or 8 cauliflorets to garnish each soup plate (optional)
Grated Parmesan cheese

Wash cauliflower, remove leaves, and cut out core. Wash head under cold running water to remove any particles of soil. In a deep saucepan place base of head in about 3 inches of boiling salted water. Add 2 teaspoons fresh lemon juice. Cover and cook until crisp-tender, about 20 to 25 minutes depending on size of cauliflower. Drain, but save the cooking liquid, measured into a 1-quart container.

Purée one-half of the cauliflower head with 2 cups of reserved liquid. Set aside. Reserve other half to cut into florets to garnish soup bowls.

In a medium skillet melt the butter and brown the flour very lightly, as we want a light-colored sauce. Add the small can of milk diluted with 1 cup reserved cauliflower liquid. Cook, stirring constantly, until thick and creamy. Taste, and if necessary add salt and pepper to taste.

In dutch oven or large soup pot combine puréed cauliflower, chicken broth, and white sauce and cook until the mixture comes to the boil. Serve in bowls, garnished with florets and sprinkled with grated Parmesan.

CREAMED EGGPLANT SOUP
Crema de Berenjena

————⊙————

Eggplant is one of my favorite vegetables and this particular discovery of a creamed soup made with it made me very happy. The eggplants grown in Mexico are often bitter and not always too good so it takes quite a bit of laboratory work to produce the egg plant purée that must go into the making of this soup. But in the States this is simple. So, you lucky cooks, try this soup—you will enjoy it and make it over and over again if you are an eggplant lover.

————⊙————

10 servings

1 eggplant weighing at least 1 pound
¼ cup chopped white onion
1 teaspoon mashed garlic
6 cups thin chicken broth, fresh or canned
1 cup medium white sauce (2 tablespoons butter and 2 tablespoons
    flour to 1 cup milk)
    Salt and freshly ground pepper
½ teaspoon ground cumin
    Croutons made by frying cubes of French rolls in oil
4 tablespoons snipped parsley leaves

Wash and peel eggplant. Cut into wedges and cook in 2 cups salted water for 12 minutes. Set aside. When cool, drain and purée with onions and garlic, and stir into chicken broth.

Make white sauce and strain into soup pot until completely combined with eggplant mixture. Season with salt and pepper and add cumin. Bring to the boil, lower heat, and simmer for 10 minutes.

Serve with freshly made croutons and garnish with snipped parsley leaves. A little sprinkle of grated Parmesan cheese and a few drops of fresh green lime add a delightful touch.

————⊙————

FRESH MUSHROOM SOUP
Caldo de Hongos Frescos

———⊙———

This is a clear soup and should be flavored heavily with jap chiles; that is, allow them to season the soup and perhaps remove them later on as they are very pungent. This is a great soup to serve in cups or in mugs. Leave the pot ready to just heat and serve if you are going out to a football game and know you will need to be warmed from the tummy out when you come in. Good, easy to make, and low in calories.

———⊙———

6 to 8 servings

½ pound fresh mushrooms
4 cups canned chicken broth
2 cups water
6 dried epazote leaves
1 teaspoon salt
2 arbol chiles (dried red miniature jap chiles), optional

Wash mushrooms and slice. Place stems in soup pot with the chicken broth and bring to the boil. Simmer 2 minutes and set aside.

Heat the 2 cups of water, float the epazote leaves on top, and brew until water turns green and is flavorful. Remove the leaves carefully and snip with kitchen shears. Return to the flavored tea water.

Combine the epazote tea and the hot chicken broth. Add the mushroom slices and salt and simmer 10 minutes.

The dried chiles are optional. You might try adding them to the soup the last 2 minutes of the cooking time; then remove or simply season with a pinch of cayenne and see what happens.

Serve with garlic bread.

Note: This clear soup is usually very pungent and spicy. It would be a shame to serve it too mild. I suggest you try it with the jap chiles, being careful not to bruise or crack them—they must remain whole. Remove them before serving the soup.

———⊙———

CREAM OF AVOCADO SOUP
Crema de Aguacate

———⊙———

8 servings

1 large avocado, peeled and cut into quarters
2 cups light cream or half and half
4 cups chicken broth
1 tablespoon freshly squeezed lime juice
1 clove garlic, finely mashed
1 cup cilantro leaves
  Salt and white pepper
1 cup commercial sour cream
  Finely chopped parsley leaves, for garnish

Place avocado in blender and add light cream, broth, lime juice, garlic, and cilantro leaves. Blend until smooth. Pour into a large bowl, cover, and chill. Before serving, season with salt and white pepper. Serve in chilled mugs or soup bowls, topped with a dollop of sour cream sprinkled with chopped parsley.

Note: I like to blend the mixture in batches so that the blender blades do not stick and the mixture does not overflow. Be sure the avocado is ripe and that any dark spots are removed. If you are in doubt about the adequacy of its size, use 2 or 3 medium avocados instead.

———⊙———

COLD AVOCADO SOUP
Sopa de Aguacate

This soup is probably the most beautiful looking soup in the world. Texture and color are perfect and flavor is excellent but must be blended carefully, tasted, and reseasoned. Ripe avocados are bland so your stock and the rest of the ingredients have to be highly seasoned to offset the lightness of the flavors.

Canned chicken broth is fine, but do taste and do not dilute as much as the recipe instructs until you are sure it is intensely flavored.

6 to 8 servings

    3 large ripe avocados
    1 cup heavy cream
   ½ teaspoon mashed garlic
    6 cups chicken broth (use 3 14½-ounce cans
          and add water to measure 6 cups)
   ½ cup sour cream
    2 tablespoons dry sherry

Chill soup plates or consommé cups.

Peel avocados and mash with a fork in a large chilled platter.

Season heavy cream with mashed garlic. Add seasoned cream to mashed avocados slowly and combine thoroughly.

Chill chicken broth in serving bowl or tureen and stir in the mashed creamed avocado. Correct seasoning. Add salt if needed.

Stir sherry into sour cream.

Serve soup with a dollop of sherried sour cream sprinkled with Mexican paprika. Pass the garlic croutons, and perhaps fresh lime wedges.

CREAM OF CANTALOUPE SOUP
Crema de Melon

8 to 10 servings

1 medium-sized ripe cantaloupe
4 cups canned chicken broth, or your own homemade
2 egg yolks
1 quart light cream or half and half
½ cup granulated sugar
1 teaspoon vanilla
½ teaspoon salt

Peel and seed cantaloupe and cut into large pieces suitable for puréeing in blender. Purée with 2 cups of the broth and the 2 egg yolks. Strain into a large container. Whip remainder of ingredients in blender until frothy. Stir into cantaloupe mixture and correct seasoning.

Serve in ice cold mugs or small cold soup bowls and float a slice of strawberry on top of each portion. Keep the soup refrigerated up until the moment of serving, as it must be served very, very cold. It does not keep well.

GAZPACHO

Serving cold soups is not too common in Mexico. I personally like gazpacho and on a hot sultry day especially in our tropical climates it is refreshing. The recipe given here has undertones of Mexican spicing whereas the Spanish version is mild and tasty.

4 to 6 servings

1 quart canned tomato juice
¼ cup olive oil
¼ cup wine vinegar
1 teaspoon pickling liquid from canned jalapeños
Salt and pepper
1 teaspoon mashed garlic
2 cups canned chicken broth
½ teaspoon oregano

Combine first 6 ingredients in blender container and liquefy. Strain into chilled soup tureen.

(Recipe continues)

On a lazy susan arrange your condiments in small glass dishes.

Add 2 cups canned chicken broth to chilled soup in tureen. Taste for seasoning. Sprinkle with oregano.

Chill soup plates or large mugs. Place 2 ice cubes in each and fill with gazpacho. Garnish with condiments of your choice. Serve with homemade croutons or hot garlic bread.

CONDIMENTS

1 cucumber, peeled, halved, seeds scraped out, and chopped
1 ripe avocado, peeled, seeded, and chopped
  (do this just before serving)
  Green onions, tops and bulbs chopped
  Wedges of fresh green limes
  Hard-boiled eggs, shelled and chopped
  Pickled jalapeño peppers, rinsed, stemmed, seeded, and chopped
  Croutons made by frying sliced French rolls in hot oil and draining

---

WHITE GAZPACHO
Gazpacho Blanco

8 servings

6 cups canned chicken broth
1 ripe avocado
1 cup plain yogurt
1 cup cucumber, peeled, seeded and chopped
  Salt and pepper to taste

Place all ingredients in a blender or food processor and purée until creamy.

Serve cold, in chilled soup bowls. Garnish with a dollop of sour cream and chopped parsley.

CHEESE AND POTATO CHOWDER
Caldo de Queso con Papas

The years that I lived on our cattle ranch were, to say the least, lean years. I always kept a few goodies hidden at the back of my pantry shelves—a few small cans of green chiles and small cans of evaporated milk. When unexpected guests arrived, my hidden loot saved the day.

4 generous servings

    4 potatoes
    Salt
    1 white onion, chopped
    2 tablespoons vegetable oil
    1 large ripe tomato, peeled and chopped,
        or two large canned tomatoes
    1 small can chopped green chiles
    1 small can evaporated milk
    1 pound Wisconsin white Cheddar or similar cheese, cubed

Peel and cube the potatoes and cook in 6 cups well-salted water for about 15 minutes. Be sure to check often. Potatoes must stay crisp-tender, otherwise they will disintegrate before they are brought to the table in the soup.

While potatoes are cooking, sauté chopped onions in oil in a large deep kettle or dutch oven. Do not allow onions to brown, just wilt them. Add chopped tomatoes and chopped canned chiles. Stir over medium heat for 2 or 3 minutes. Set aside.

As soon as the potatoes have cooked, add them to kettle with their cooking liquid and correct seasoning. Add small can of evaporated milk and bring to a simmer. Do not allow to boil.

Drop half the cheese cubes into the soup. Place the remainder of the cheese in individual soup bowls, 4 or more cubes to each. Ladle the steaming hot soup on top. As you serve, be sure to stir well so that all bowls have some of each ingredient.

This soup is excellent with crisp toasted flour tortillas brought hot and well buttered to the table. Serve one or two per person on a bread and butter plate.

LENTIL SOUP
Sopa de Lentejas

———⊙———

Lentils in Mexico are very tiny and very hard to pick over and clean
. . . but since this soup is a favorite, served often during the Lenten
season, we cooks learn to clean and sort them—with our reading
glasses on!

———⊙———

6 to 8 servings

    2 cups lentils
    2 teaspoons salt
    ½ teaspoon freshly ground pepper
    1 tablespoon mashed garlic
    2 bay leaves
    4 tablespoons vegetable oil
    ⅓ cup chopped onions
    1 cup chopped peeled tomatoes
    ½ teaspoon cumin
    Croutons (see below)

Rinse lentils. Drain and place in a large soup pot. Add 8 cups of water, salt
and pepper, garlic, and bay leaves. Cover and simmer for 1½ hours or until
cooked and mushy.

In small skillet, heat 4 tablespoons oil and sauté onions and chopped
tomatoes. Add to soup pot and simmer, stirring often, for 5 minutes. Add
cumin, taste for seasoning, and remove bay leaves. Add 2 cups hot water if
mixture is too thick.

CROUTONS

In ½ cup oil fry slices of small French rolls until golden and crisp. Drain these
croutons and sprinkle with grated Parmesan cheese. Cool.

———⊙———

SPLIT PEA SOUP
Sopa de Chicharo Seco

This one soup above all soups was a favorite when I was a little girl. My grandmother made it often and she always flavored it with a ham hock or perhaps a knuckle bone, and even a wiener or two. We ate it with fresh French bread that I brought back from the nearby bakery every day.

I had forgotten about split pea soup until I traveled years later to Holland and tasted it; I ate it often served with a bottle of Dutch beer—the best.

8 servings

  1 pound green split peas
  1 ripe tomato, peeled and cut into wedges
  1 cup chopped onion
  1 teaspoon mashed garlic
  1 bay leaf
  1 teaspoon salt
  ½ teaspoon pepper
  2 14½-ounce cans chicken broth
    Canned Vienna sausages

Combine peas in 6 cups of water with tomato, onion, garlic, bay leaf, salt, and pepper. Cover pot and cook for 1 to 1½ hours, stirring occasionally. When cooked, add 2 cans of chicken broth. Taste for seasoning. Soup must be consistency of heavy cream.

Rinse some canned Vienna sausages and slice. Put 3 or 4 sausage slices in each bowl before filling with soup.

Serve with garlic toast or hot French bread and herbed butter (see below).

HERBED BUTTER

Soften ½ cup butter at room temperature. Mash with a fork in a small platter and add ¼ teaspoon either crushed oregano, crushed basil, or tarragon. Or make the three kinds and place in small Mexican clay dishes on the table.

MEXICAN FISH SOUP
Caldo Michi

This is a modified version of the recipe as you will have surmised by my calling for bottled clam juice. It is important that you taste before seasoning because clam juice is oversalted. Do not overcook either the pieces of fish or the assembled dish. If the type of fish you have selected does not require too much time, simmer only 2 or 3 minutes instead of 5 minutes. I am very fond of bottled clam juice because I find it works beautifully wherever fish broth is called for.

---

6 to 8 servings

1 cup finely chopped white onion
1 cup peeled and chopped ripe tomatoes
1 pint bottle of clam juice
1 teaspoon mashed garlic
1 bay leaf
Salt and pepper
1 pound of fish fillets
4 tablespoons oil
¼ cup coriander leaves

In a dutch oven sauté chopped onions and chopped tomatoes. Cook 2 minutes, stirring often. Add 6 cups water mixed with the clam juice. Stir in mashed garlic and bay leaf and season with salt and pepper. Bring to the boil and lower heat to simmer.

Salt and pepper the fish fillets and cut into bite-sized pieces. Heat 4 tablespoons oil and sauté the fish pieces for 2 minutes, turning once only. Fish must not brown or get crisp.

Slide each piece of fish from a slotted spoon into the simmering fish broth and cover. Cook at a simmer for 5 minutes or until fish flakes easily. Taste for seasoning. Ladle into soup bowls and garnish with snipped coriander leaves. Serve with wedges of freshly cut limes.

Note: If using frozen fish, you save time by not thawing the fish. Remove the package from the freezer and let stand 15 minutes at room temperature. Unwrap the fish and cut the block into 3 or 4 pieces. Tightly wrap any pieces that you are not going to use and return to the freezer. In this case do not sauté, just poach the frozen fish and add to simmering fish broth.

If you have fresh fish scraps and a fresh fish head, you may wish to make your own fish broth. If so, follow any recipe of your choice for a court bouillon omitting any spirits you might usually add. Boil 15 minutes and strain. Forget about the clam juice and the water; just be sure you have 8 cups of well-seasoned fish broth and proceed with the recipe.

———⊙———

TRIPE AND HOMINY SOUP FROM SONORA
Menudo de Sonora
———⊙———

In northern Mexico and along the American border it has long been the custom on weekends to look for this delightful take-out dish. Someone from home is always sent out with a brightly colored covered pot to bring fresh Menudo for supper or for breakfast the next morning. With the soup you are given small portions of the garnishes to serve with it.

Menudo is not just a soup, it is a national institution. Even as far back as three or four generations, it was as important socially as it was in the culinary world. Many think it is an acquired taste. I believe most people who sample it like it. Try it and see.

———⊙———

6 to 8 servings

3 to 4 pounds tripe (be sure to include 1 piece of honeycomb)
6 or more garlic cloves, bruised but not peeled
1 teaspoon peppercorns
Salt
1 28-ounce can white hominy
6 to 8 cilantro sprigs
4 to 6 green onions, cut into thirds

Rinse tripe under cold running water and cut large pieces into 1-inch squares (you will need a sharp butcher knife). Place tripe in a large soup pot with 4 quarts of hot water, garlic, peppercorns, and salt to taste. Bring to the boil and skim foam if necessary. (If not too much foam comes to the surface, don't bother.) Reduce heat and cook at a simmer for 2 or 3 hours or until tripe is tender. Broth will have boiled down.

Add canned hominy, liquid and all. Cook 15 minutes longer. Add 6 to 8 cilantro sprigs and 4 to 6 green onions, each cut into 3 pieces. Cook at a simmer 15 minutes more. Taste and correct seasoning if necessary.

With a slotted spoon try to remove most of the garlic, the cilantro sprigs, the green onion pieces, and as many of the peppercorns as possible. This is easier when the tripe soup is poured into the heated soup tureen, as the peppercorns normally sink to the bottom of the soup pot. Bring tureen to the table.

Serve in heated soup bowls with about equal amounts of hominy and tripe pieces and a generous amount of the hot broth in each portion. In some sections of the state of Chihuahua, a tablespoonful of mild red chile sauce is added. This is a welcome embellishment, both flavorful and colorful. Garnishes may include chopped cilantro leaves, oregano, and ground red chile or Mexican paprika. Maybe lime wedges. And always chopped onions.

Note: This is a hearty soup. If you prefer a lighter version, prepare the recipe a day ahead and place soup in the refrigerator overnight. Next day skim the chilled layer of fat off the top and then reheat the soup. Its flavor will be the same, but the calories will be greatly reduced.

MEXICAN BOILED DINNER
Cocido

————⊙————

Cocido is the king of Mexican soups and is most definitely a one-dish meal. I have eaten a New England boiled dinner and I think it is similar. Most of the hostesses I know have special colorful large pottery bowls in which to serve their Cocido and Menudo (tripe soup).

————⊙————   8 to 10 servings

    3 pounds lean beef short ribs
    2 pounds beef stew meat cut in 2-inch pieces
    2 pounds shank bones (you need marrow bones)
      Salt and pepper
    1 tablespoon mashed garlic
    2 peeled ripe tomatoes cut in fourths
6 or 8 cilantro sprigs
    3 ears of corn, cut in thirds or in 4 small pieces
    2 zucchini, cut into thirds, stems removed
    2 large carrots, peeled and cut into thick slices
2 or 3 turnips, peeled and cut in fourths
    1 small head of green cabbage, about 1½ pounds, cut into wedges
    2 medium-sized potatoes, peeled and cut into large pieces

TO COOK MEAT:

Wash pieces of meat and bones in cold water and place in a very large soup pot. Add 2 quarts water, salt and pepper, garlic, and peeled tomatoes. Bring to the boil. Lower heat and skim foam from surface. Partially cover and cook at a simmer for 1 hour. Taste broth for seasoning and correct if necessary. Strain broth into a large saucepan. Set aside and save. This is the broth that will go into the soup plates.

As you will note, the meat isn't tender yet, so to it add 4 or 6 cups of water or to barely cover, add salt to taste, and cover. Bring to the boil, lower the heat, and cook at a simmer until tender, 1 more hour or longer.

TO COOK VEGETABLES:

Parboil all vegetables separately in mildly salted water, except the potatoes. All must be crisp tender. Peel and quarter the potatoes and leave in cold water to cover so that they won't discolor.

(Recipe continues)

FINAL COOKING:

Drain the hot cooked meat. Heat the reserved soup stock. Add the cilantro sprigs.

I like to use a large turkey roaster for this final step. Arrange the meat and vegetables in the roaster and add the potatoes. Pour the hot soup stock over all. The meat pieces and vegetables should be well covered. Set on the stove and turn up the heat. Bring to a simmer and cook for a few minutes until the potatoes are cooked. Test potatoes with one prong of a two-pronged fork. They should be cooked until tender in the center. If they are overcooked they will be mushy.

TO ASSEMBLE:

In each large heated soup bowl, place 1 piece of meat, 2 or 3 pieces of the vegetables, and then ladle in the broth, about 1 cup or more to the bowl. Arrange any leftover vegetables and meat on a large platter and bring to the table.

Serve with a choice of sauces, including one made with fresh tomatoes, onions, and green chiles like the Fresh Sauce, page 287, or the Home-style Sauce, page 290, and one without chiles for those on a blander diet. Other accompaniments are hot flour tortillas or flour tortilla chips, or better still, hot, buttered small French rolls fresh from the bakery. A cheese board is a must. Garnishes could be lime wedges, chopped cilantro leaves, and chopped green onions.

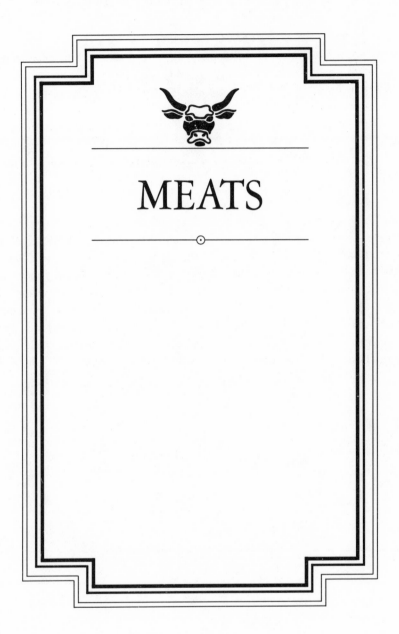

MEATS

The cattle-producing states of the north—Chihuahua, Sonora, Sinaloa, Durango, Nuevo Leon and Coahuila— provide Mexico with most of the beef it consumes. However, due to faulty transportation systems and the great distances that need to be covered, the further south one goes in the country, the less beef one finds in regional cooking. What beef is available is quickly procured by first-class restaurants that cater to the international tourist trade. Less choice cuts are sold in local butcher shops to be made into tacos, guisos or stews, or butterflied for carne asada, a thin steak usually grilled over mesquite and served with roasted chile strips, avocado slices, and piles of fresh corn tortillas. The meat stalls in the markets, or *mercados* are independent. That is to say, each butcher has his specialty —pork, beef, or poultry, for instance. This is a very competitive business so it stands to reason that the proprietors give excellent service and are exceptionally agreeable because they want to keep their customers happy. In their accommodating way, they will remove surplus fat, butterfly a loin for you, cut extra-thick pork chops and make a stuffing pocket in them—you name it and they happily comply. My own friendly butcher is Abel Rodriguez at Stall 8 in the Coyoacan market. He even saves me the trimmings from pork chops so I can make cracklings.

Most of my life was spent on cattle ranches in the states of Sonora and Chihuahua, and beef was a way of life. Most of our days revolved around one aspect or another of cattle growing, from branding to selling, and occasionally one animal was sacrificed for our personal use. My parents' ranch foreman knew which choice cuts should go to the big house when a steer was slaughtered: the tenderloins, at least half of the liver, the kidneys and some short ribs, and at least four very large choice beef roasts, plus shoulder meat for hamburger. All this was chilled, wrapped, labeled, and placed in the freezer. The rest was portioned out to the workers.

The head is usually oven-roasted or wrapped in a gunny sack and barbecued in a pit, often heavily scented with garlic and oregano. On the ranch this was usually served to the ranch hands or *vaqueros* who prized its meat. They would make wonderful burritos with freshly made flour tortillas and a fresh chile sauce. But this delicacy is not limited to the north; it is also very popular in Guadalajara, Jalisco, where small restaurants around the Mercado de San Juan de Dios specialize in beef-head tacos made with fresh corn tortillas and a cilantro-flavored chile sauce. They are a favorite snack of late party-goers who finish off a night listening to mariachis in the nearby Plaza de Los Mariachis and then walk to their favorite restaurant for their tacos.

Caldillo, a specialty of the states of Durango and Chihuahua, is a delicious stew made with beef chunks, peas and/or potatoes, and chile strips or cubes. In Durango, one also finds wonderful barbecued short ribs. The state of Sonora is known for its dishes made with machaca, beef jerky. For breakfast, it is combined with green chile and eggs.

Further south, the preferred meat is pork, perhaps due to its greater availability. It is often combined with fruits and chiles or nut-based sauces to make exotic stews or roasts. Guadalajara is known for its tender pork cubes often glazed with orange juice and always served with chile sauce and the ubiquitous corn tortilla. In Yucatán, one finds suckling pig rubbed with a mixture of achiote, a paste made with powdered annato seeds and spices, and the juice of sour oranges, wrapped in banana leaves, and cooked in a pit, a hole in the ground.

Lamb and goat are also popular, especially in the north where they are often served *al pastor,* shepherd's style. This translates into a rotisserie and is a familiar sight in fairs or food stalls. They are also frequently barbecued in a pit and served with salsa borracha, a sauce made with aged cheese, pulque (sap juices of the maguey), and ancho chile.

PORK CHOPS WITH GREEN CHILE
Chuletas de Puerco con Chile Verde

————⊙————

This is a good backyard dish and may be made successfully in a giant wok. It is relaxing to assemble and I am sure if you practice once or twice you will be an expert and can show off in front of guests while wok-cooking the chops.

————⊙————

4 servings

1 teaspoon salt
½ teaspoon black pepper
8 ½-inch thick loin pork chops, trimmed of fat
¼ cup flour
2 tablespoons lard
2 cups canned tomatoes
1 cup chopped canned green Anaheim chiles
½ cup chopped onion
½ teaspoon crushed oregano leaves

Season and dredge chops with flour. Heat lard in skillet, and brown both sides of chops lightly. Add remainder of ingredients. Cover and simmer until tender, about 30 minutes. I suggest that you serve these with a baked potato and sliced ripe tomatoes with a sprinkling of capers and a mild garlic-flavored vinaigrette.

Note: Figure 2 chops per person if they are small. Any mild canned green chile will do.

————⊙————

PORK CHOPS
WITH GREEN TOMATO SAUCE
Chuletas de Puerco con Salsa de Tomatillos

———⊙———

This is fast and easy to make and quite delicious. It may be made with leftover pork roast as well. This sauce is definitely on the sour side and requires the addition of sugar to lower the acid flavor of the tomatillo sauce. Add the right amount of sugar according to your taste.

———⊙———

4 servings

1 teaspoon salt
½ teaspoon black pepper
8 pork chops
¼ cup flour
2 tablespoons lard or shortening
1 cup chicken stock
1 7-ounce can Mexican green hot sauce (tomatillo)
1 teaspoon sugar
½ cup chopped onions
½ teaspoon oregano
1 cup sour cream
2 tablespoons milk
2 mashed garlic buds

Salt and pepper the chops lightly, dredge them in flour, and brown them in hot lard or shortening very lightly, turning once only. Add stock, hot sauce, sugar, onions, and oregano, cover, and cook over medium heat until tender, about 30 minutes.

Mix sour cream with milk and garlic, add to chops, and simmer 5 minutes. Correct seasoning. Serve with steamed rice or mashed potatoes.

———⊙———

SAVORY PORK STEW, PUEBLA STYLE
Tinga Poblana

————⊙————

Tingas originated in the state of Puebla. To my mind this is a true example of what resulted from the melding of the two cuisines, the Indian and the Spanish. The first tinga might have been made with venison or wild boar, and the first combination of herbs and spices must also have been a mixture of the native-grown and those brought from Spain.

A tinga is actually a stew. The version here omits the chorizo often called for, because I believe that when chorizo is used it tends to dominate and the taste of the sauce is almost entirely lost.

————⊙————

12 servings

    3 pounds boneless pork, in two or three pieces
    ¼ cup fresh mint leaves or 1 tablespoon dried mint leaves
    2 whole chicken breasts, boned and cut into 4 or 6 pieces
    2 tablespoons lard or oil
    1 onion, finely chopped
    2 cups unpeeled chopped tomatoes
    4 garlic cloves, mashed
    ½ teaspoon dried marjoram
    ½ teaspoon ground cumin
    2 ancho chiles
    1 teaspoon sugar
    1 tablespoon vinegar
      Salt and pepper

Boil pork and mint in well-seasoned water to cover until tender, about one hour. Add chicken for last 15 minutes of cooking time. Drain, and reserve stock. Place pork and chicken in a casserole and keep warm. When meat is cool enough to handle cut into bite-sized pieces.

Heat oil in skillet and sauté the onion and tomatoes for 10 minutes. Add garlic and herbs.

Boil the red ancho chiles 20 minutes after removing the tops and seeds. Drain and purée in blender with 1 cup reserved stock; add sugar and vinegar.

Strain purée into the sauce and boil for 10 minutes. Correct seasoning and pour over meat and chicken. Simmer until sauce is thick.

Serve with white rice. Refried Beans (page 236) go well with this dish.

ORANGE-FLAVORED ROAST PORK
Asado de Puerco al Orange

———⊙———

Pork is without a doubt the first choice in all the cuisines of Mexico. Our pork is good, safe, lean, and almost always tender. Often the young porkers are brought to market for meat while the larger animals, fattened for the production of bacon, ham, and lard, are kept longer at the hog farms.

This orange-flavored roast is so good, and it may be fixed ahead of time and later reheated.

———⊙———

6 servings

1 3- to 4-pound pork loin blade roast
6 garlic cloves
1 teaspoon salt
1 cup orange juice
1 cup water
  Peel from one orange, cut in slivers
1 bay leaf
  Juice from small can of pickled chipotle chiles

Stud roast with garlic cloves cut in half lengthwise, by inserting the tip of a knife into the meat and pushing the garlic into a meat pocket as you remove the knife. Cut about 12 evenly spaced pockets on meat's surface. Rub roast with salt.

Place meat on a rack in a shallow roasting pan. Pour 1 cup orange juice and 1 cup water into pan and add orange peel and bay leaf. Insert a meat thermometer. Roast, covered at first, in a 325° oven for 2½ hours or until meat thermometer registers 170°. After roast has been in the oven about 1 hour, remove it, baste, and drain juices into a small saucepan. Set juices aside for later and return meat, *uncovered,* to oven and continue roasting until done. Place on a platter and carve at table.

In the meantime, place juices in freezer to hasten coagulation of grease on meat drippings. Remove grease, taste, correct seasoning, and add the pickling juice from one small can of pickled chipotle chiles. Go easy. Add half a teaspoon at a time so it won't be too pungent, and if necessary dilute with the fresh juice of another orange. Serve in a sauceboat and pass to the daring.

This meat dish goes beautifully with steamed buttered rice and cranberry relish. Serve with garlic bread. Spinach salad would be lovely.

ROAST LEG OF PORK IN MILK
Asado de Puerco en Leche

———⊙———

The first time I saw my friend Ileana fix this dish in her home in Guadalajara, I couldn't imagine what would happen to that enormous amount of milk. I discovered that the meat juices seem to curdle the milk and it begins to evaporate. You must watch this and as soon as the milk thickens and curdles, remove the pan from the oven. Then proceed as the recipe directs. I like to serve the pork already sliced.

———⊙———

8 servings

1 5- to 6-pound round of pork
6 to 8 garlic cloves
2 to 4 quarts of milk
1 teaspoon peppercorns
4 bay leaves
1 tablespoon salt
Puréed chipotle chiles

Have butcher trim your roast of fat. With a small sharp knife, make 6 to 8 incisions in the meat and into each cut insert a sliver or a whole garlic clove. Place meat in a deep pot and pour in cold milk to almost cover. Add peppercorns, bay leaves, and salt. Marinate overnight.

The next day heat oven to 300° and place meat, covered, in oven. Bake for 2 hours. Remove from the oven and take roast out of milk sauce. Wrap meat in heavy foil and return to oven in another pan to continue roasting. Cover.

Cool curdled milk sauce and strain. Taste for seasoning. Flavor half of the sauce with a small amount of puréed chipotle chiles and leave the rest plain.

Check meat for doneness during the next hour. Uncover last 30 minutes and allow to brown. Do not overcook; meat must slice without shredding. Carve at table or slice and arrange in a platter with some of the plain sauce. Serve chipotle sauce in a separate sauceboat. Wonderful with a rice pilaf, guacamole, and a tossed green salad. Corn tortillas are good for this meat dish, but it is outstanding with hot French rolls.

———⊙———

PORK LOIN WITH PRUNE SAUCE
Asado de Puerco con Salsa de Ciruela Pasa

———⊙———

This is indeed a party dish, and I am sure it must be classified as modern Mexican cooking in every sense of the phrase. It's different and a great new flavor. I first encountered this when it was served by some friends of my youngest daughter at a birthday luncheon. I am silently critical of these modern innovations but I liked it so well that I thought it might be a welcome addition even though not "traditional."

———⊙———

8 servings

  1 tablespoon prepared mustard
  3 pounds pork loin or other pork roast
  1 large ripe tomato, chopped
  ½ cup chopped onion
  3 tablespoons lard or shortening
  3 cups water
  1 tablespoon chicken bouillon granules
    Salt and pepper
10 cloves
  2 cups Coca-Cola
  ½ pound prunes plus whole prunes for garnish
  2 teaspoons granulated sugar
    Lemon slices

Smear mustard all over pork roast and place meat in roasting pan.

In skillet sauté tomato and onions in lard or shortening. Add water mixed with chicken granules, salt, pepper, and cloves. Pour over roast in roaster.

Cover and cook on top of stove for 45 minutes. Uncover and add Coca-Cola, ½ pound prunes, and sugar. Bake, covered, in 350° oven until roast is tender and sauce thickens, about 1½ hours, basting often.

Cut into slices and garnish with steamed whole prunes and thin lemon slices. I think this dish needs a salad, preferably a spinach salad with garlic-flavored dressing. Hot bread, please!

———⊙———

PORK YUCATAN STYLE—
A MODERN VERSION
Cochinita Pibil

―――⊙―――

The traditional way of preparing Cochinita Pibil is quite out of the question if you live in a small apartment or far from the source of banana leaves. I first ate this modified version at a friend's ranch in the state of Jalisco. It was absolutely wonderful. Do try it.

Yucatán is an ideal place to visit, astonishing you with its unparalleled beauty and diversity of scenery. Mérida, the capital city, is known throughout Mexico as *la ciudad blanca,* the white city. On a recent trip there, the hotel dining room served one special garnish —Onions Yucatán Style (page 540). They were correct to do it. These are a must with this dish.

―――⊙―――

10 servings

1 cup fresh orange juice
1 tablespoon white vinegar
2 tablespoons achiote paste (comes packaged in
    2-ounce boxes, ready to use)
2 tablespoons mashed garlic
   Salt
5 pounds pork (ask the butcher for either pork butt or, better still, 2
    thick round steaks and a few short ribs, but be sure steaks are cut
    into large pieces)

Prepare marinade of the orange juice, the vinegar, achiote paste, garlic, and salt to taste. Mix all ingredients well and rub into the meat. Marinate the pieces of pork for at least one hour.

Line a roaster with heavy foil and arrange the marinated pork in it, covering pork with any leftover marinade. Seal the meat by wrapping foil tightly around it. Cover and bake in a preheated 300° oven for 2 or 3 hours. Check often and turn pieces of meat in their own juice. Roasting time varies according to toughness of meat.

This is primarily a "soft taco filling." Chop meat into small cubes and discard any fatty parts. Serve with a basketful of freshly made corn tortillas, spoon meat into them, and roll. Eat at once, garnished with pickled onions. Great with beer.

ROAST LEG OF LAMB WITH GARLIC
Pierna de Carnero al Ajo

This is one of those meat dishes that cannot go wrong. There is no way that you can make a mistake with it. Undercooked or over-cooked, it's still good.

The spring lambs we raised on our ranch were what holiday menus were made of. A week before a big holiday celebration my four daughters would have a choice, filet mignon, ham, roast beef, or leg of lamb with various sauces on the side. They would put the choices on slips of paper and draw one out. Leg of lamb was always it. For years this went on. One day, being curious, I opened up all four folded slips and found they all said "lamb."

8 servings

    1 5- to 6-pound leg of lamb
    4 large garlic cloves
1½ teaspoons salt
½ teaspoon coarsely ground pepper
    1 cup Bay Leaf Tea (page 11)
¼ cup white vinegar

With a small sharp knife, make 6 or 8 incisions in the meat and into each cut insert a sliver of garlic. Rub with salt and pepper. Roast in a preheated moderately slow oven (300° to 325°) for 30 minutes to the pound, well covered.

Baste meat frequently during the last hour of roasting with 1 cup of Bay Leaf Tea mixed with ¼ cup white vinegar, but drain juices out of roasting pan first. Place juices in refrigerator so that grease will rise to the top and coagulate.

Remove grease from drippings and make a gravy with pan drippings and 2 cups water. Thicken with 2 tablespoons cornstarch mixed with ¼ cup cold water, taste for seasoning, and add salt to taste. If there is any basting liquid in pan, add it to gravy, and if fat rises to the top of the gravy be sure to skim it off before taking to the table.

Carve at the table and offer a mint sauce. This is a gala dish; homemade rolls are in order. A zucchini and corn casserole is great, and a tossed green salad, a must. Wine would be perfect, and for a hot summer afternoon a frosty pitcher of sangria.

MEXICAN STEAKS
Chuletas a la Mexicana

———⊙———

On the cook's day off my mother loved to fix these steaks for us and the grandchildren when we were visiting. These strips are wonderful eating, and great rolled in tortillas, but they can become formal the minute you serve them with a hot buttered vegetable and a fancy salad. (If you use a more expensive cut than chuck, there is no need to tenderize.)

———⊙———

8 servings

3 pounds chuck steak cut into strips and tenderized
½ cup salad oil
3 cups peeled and chopped ripe tomatoes
1 cup chopped green onions
2 cups sliced bell peppers
1 fresh green jalapeño pepper, seeded and chopped
2 cups peeled sliced potatoes
  Salt and pepper
1 cup water
4 garlic cloves, mashed

Salt and pepper steak strips and pan-fry lightly to desired degree of doneness in oil in skillet, turning once only. Place in baking casserole and set aside.

In same skillet add more oil as needed and sauté vegetables. Add salt and pepper, water, and garlic and simmer for 5 minutes. Take care not to overcook the potatoes. Check seasoning and pour over the meat. Bake a few minutes to heat through.

Serve with a tossed salad and perhaps green beans prepared in your favorite way. No additional starch is needed—the potatoes take care of that.

———⊙———

STEAK STEW FROM CHIHUAHUA
Caldillo de Chihuahua

————⊙————

Chihuahua, the largest state in Mexico and second in production of beef, is also rich in mining and farming, and the principal Mexican producer of peaches and apples. This dish is a favorite with almost all the American tourists who visit in the border towns of Chihuahua. Surprisingly, it is also available in many small American restaurants in the towns and cities along the Texas-Chihuahua border, and very good it is—quite authentic in flavor and presentation. If a menu prices it at a high level you can be sure you are getting Caldillo made with expensive steak meat; if it is priced low you are getting the dish made with stewing beef.

————⊙————

6 servings

    2 pounds beef chuck steak (slash edges to avoid curling)
    4 cups water
    1 teaspoon crushed garlic
      Salt and pepper
    4 tablespoons oil
    ½ cup finely chopped onion
    1 cup chopped peeled ripe tomatoes
    ¼ teaspoon crushed oregano leaves
    1 cup frozen peas and carrots, blanched
    1 medium potato, peeled and cubed

Cut steak into 4 large pieces. Place in a dutch oven and cover with water. Add crushed garlic and salt and pepper. Cover and simmer for 1 hour. Allow meat to cool in its own broth. Drain meat and save broth. Chop meat into small cubes, discarding fatty tissue. If broth does not measure 3 cups, add water.

Heat oil in a large saucepan and sauté chopped onion and chopped tomatoes over medium heat, stirring often. Add reserved meat broth and oregano. Add cubed cooked beef and bring mixture to a boil. Correct seasoning. Cook for about 5 minutes or until tasty. You should have at least 3 cups of broth plus the meat.

Add the peas and carrots and the cubed potato. Return to stove and cook until potato is tender. Serve in small soup bowls. Garnish with a fresh salsa and serve with some freshly made small flour tortillas on the side (page 38).

Variation: Add 1 4-ounce can of chopped green chiles. The transformation they work on the original Caldillo is amazing.

SMOTHERED STEAK STRIPS
Bisteks Encebollados

———⊙———

Butchering beef on some of the northern cattle ranches in Mexico is still done with very primitive methods. But somehow or other the beef has a wonderful flavor. The cuts are all the same as if you were purchasing your meat supply from a reliable city butcher.

When I first started as a ranch housewife I ordered a butchering guide from the Montgomery Ward catalog. It was a very valuable companion, let me tell you. I was able to direct the butchering and cutting of the special meat selections, which would in turn be wrapped, labeled, and frozen in a large Kenmore freezer (my trusty helper for twenty years). I would cut up about ten pounds or more of these steak strips because they were miracle packages when I was in a hurry. They thawed fast and could be prepared in numerous ways. These smothered steak strips were my favorites.

———⊙———

4 to 6 servings

Salt and pepper
2½ to 3 pounds round steak, cut into strips
½ cup flour
¼ cup oil
Sufficient thinly sliced white onions to smother meat
½ teaspoon oregano leaves

Salt and pepper steak strips and roll in the flour. Heat oil in skillet and brown meat lightly, turning once only. Place in baking dish and set aside.

In same skillet, adding more oil if needed, sauté sliced onions until soft but not brown, add oregano leaves, and pour over meat. Cover and bake in moderate oven for 10 minutes. Delightful served garnished with pickled canned jalapeño pepper strips and with toasted garlic bread.

———⊙———

MINCED STEAK BURRITOS
Burritos de Chuleta

———⊙———

This is a beautiful filling, but expensive. You may use a cheaper cut but it won't be the same. The steak may be broiled in your backyard like any other steak, but have a chopping board handy and a sharp knife to do the mincing. This is the pan-fried version.

———⊙———

Filling for 4 to 6 burritos

1 large top sirloin steak weighing 1 pound or more
  Salt and pepper
2 tablespoons oil
4 to 6 flour tortillas
  Grandmother's Fresh Chile Sauce (page 288)

First cut steak around the edges to keep it from curling, and sprinkle with salt and pepper to taste. Heat oil in large skillet and pan-fry the steak. Cook steak to desired degree, turning once only. Remove from skillet; save pan juices. Place meat on cutting board and cut into small pieces with a sharp knife. Return to pan and stir well so that meat will pick up the juices. Keep meat warm but do not cook further.

Heat griddle and warm tortillas until soft, but do not allow them to get crisp. Fill centers with 2 to 4 tablespoons meat pieces, fold sides over, and roll. This will enclose filling completely. Serve immediately or tortillas will become soggy. When ready to eat, open up and add salsa, then reroll. A crisp tossed cabbage salad with a bit of carrot and bell pepper added is grand with these.

———⊙———

BEEF WITH GREEN CHILE
Carne con Chile Verde

———⊙———

This is a fine dish for those who are cooking the Mexican way for the first time, easy and economical and also good for leftovers. In small containers it freezes well and you will always have your perfect burrito filling ready to thaw and heat.

———⊙———

2 cups of filling;
2–3 main course servings

1 pound lean beef round
4 cups water
1 teaspoon salt
   A pinch of pepper
2 garlic cloves, mashed
½ cup chopped onion
2 tablespoons pure pork lard or salad oil
½ cup peeled chopped ripe tomato
4 fresh California green peppers, broiled or pan-fried in hot oil and
   then peeled, seeded, and chopped or use 1 4-ounce can

In a large saucepan, cook beef in large pieces with water, salt, pepper, and garlic for one hour, or until tender and well done. Allow to cool in own broth. When cool, drain stock and set aside. Chop beef into small pieces.

In 10-inch frying pan sauté onion in hot lard, stirring constantly. Do not allow to brown. Add chopped tomato, chopped green chiles, and 1 cup of reserved broth. Bring to a simmer and cook for 3 minutes. Add chopped cooked beef and correct seasoning. Allow to cook for 5 minutes or until some of the liquid boils down.

Serve as a filling for burritos. This also makes a nice main course. Good with a baked potato and a fresh green salad. (This recipe is easy to double, if you want to serve more than three.) Eat with flour tortillas, corn tortillas, or hot garlic bread.

Tip: Beef round is the perfect cut to buy because it is waste free. If you like fat beef, choose a steak that is thick and has some fat around it; if not, choose the leanest you can find. Whichever you do buy, it is always best to remove the fatty edge once it has cooled in its own broth. I like to cut the steak in about 4 large pieces, as this will keep the meat from curling while cooking.

MEXICAN ROAST BEEF
Asado de Res Mexicano

————⊙————

The cattle ranges in northern Mexico are similar to those in New Mexico, Arizona, and Texas. The grasses that grow there in profusion are high in protein and ideal feed for grazing cattle. Though there is much wild sage in Texas, it is more abundant in Chihuahua and some parts of Sonora. A strange phenomenon occurs. As you broil a steak from one of the steers that have roamed these rangelands, especially in an outdoor barbecue grill, the lovely smell of wild sage assaults the nostrils, and it is often difficult to convince your guests that you did not marinate your steaks—that all they have on them is salt and pepper.

This recipe for Mexican roast beef is unusual because of the garlic used in its preparation. It is delicious served cold with sour cream and horseradish—if you have any leftovers to serve cold!

> 4 pounds beef tenderloin
> 8 garlic cloves
> 1 teaspoon salt
> 1 teaspoon black pepper

Cut about 12 evenly spaced pockets on meat's surface. Stud roast with garlic cloves cut in half lengthwise, by inserting the tip of a knife into the meat and pushing the garlic into the meat pocket as you remove the knife. Rub roast with salt.

Place on rack in shallow open roasting pan. Pour 2 cups water into pan around roast and insert meat thermometer so tip is in center of thickest part of meat. Roast at 300° about 20 minutes per pound, basting occasionally, or until thermometer registers 140°. Allow meat to stand 15 minutes in a warm place. Remember that meat continues to cook after removal from the oven.

Serve with diluted pan juices thickened with 1 or 2 tablespoons flour stirred into ½ cup cold water. Allow gravy to boil until it loses the raw flavor of the flour. Correct seasoning and add pepper. Thin with water if too thick and strain into gravy boat.

Delightful served with hot corn tortillas and a fresh pungent salsa, but be sure to carve into thin strips as this presentation is an open invitation to "roll your own" taco. Top with salsa and serve with your own version of mashed potatoes and a fresh green salad. The gravy with the garlic flavor is sensational with mashed potatoes.

ROAST FILET MIGNON
Filete al Horno
————⊙————

My handsome brother, who is considered one of Mexico's foremost authorities on the cattle industry, started showing his inclination for the business he would inherit at a very young age. All of us at one time or another in our young lives played at being ranchers and owning great herds of cattle. On the ranch, you would find carcasses of dead cattle lying on the ground. The bones, white from having been washed and dried by rain and the sun, supplied our herds. We used the backbones. The largest were the bulls, the medium, the mother cows, and the smallest, our baby calves. My kid brother always drew his personal brand, a bar H bar, on his toy herd. This roast beef recipe, which is a Fiesta dish in his home, is out of this world.

> 3 or 4 pounds beef tenderloin
> 6 garlic cloves
> Salt and pepper
> 6 tablespoons oil

Remove skin, fat, and ligament from underside of beef with a sharp knife. With a small sharp knife, make 6 or 8 incisions all along the top of the tenderloin. Into each cut insert a sliver of garlic. Rub meat with salt and pepper.

Heat oil in a large skillet and brown tenderloin on all sides. Wrap in a piece of heavy broiling foil and place it in a small roasting pan, without water. Bake in a 300° oven 30 to 35 minutes per pound. Save all of the pan juices, taste for seasoning, and serve well heated in a sauceboat.

I like this roast served with hot flour tortillas—like a very fancy barbecue! Corn on the cob and cole slaw would be good additions.

————⊙————

MEXICAN POT ROAST
Tapado de Res Mexicano

———⊙———

This is a plain homespun dish, nothing fancy but quite delicious, and it may be served many ways. I prefer it cooked atop the stove in a thick cast iron dutch oven but it is easier, faster, and less messy in the oven.

My grandmother was a whiz at cooking this pot roast, but she always added large pieces of peeled carrots and some large chunks of peeled potatoes a few minutes before serving time. She always parboiled the carrots because she contended that they sweetened her sauce, and I think she was right.

———⊙———

6 servings

3 tablespoons pork lard
2½ to 3 pounds beef round steak
4 garlic buds, finely mashed
3 unpeeled ripe tomatoes, chopped
2 onions, cut into thick slices
1 teaspoon salt
1 teaspoon cracked black pepper
2 bay leaves
2½ cups hot water

Heat lard in a heavy dutch oven (cast iron is best). Cut through the fatty round on the steak and brown it on both sides. Add all remaining ingredients and water. Transfer to a covered baking dish and bake at 350° until tender, approximately 1½ hours. Or cook covered, on top of stove over medium heat, basting often, for the same length of time.

I like pickled serranos or the favorite jalapeños as a garnish. For a change of pace, I cut the jalapeños in half, dig out the seeds, rinse and pat dry, and fill with cream cheese sprinkled with paprika.

———⊙———

RED CHILE CON CARNE
Carne con Chile Colorado

———⊙———

This is a very tasty concoction that freezes well and can be very versatile. In a pinch it might be used for a tamal filling, or for burritos if drained a bit first.

I have tried making this dish in an overnight slow cooker at very low heat and it was perfect. I like a teaspoon of ground cumin stirred in at one time or another, but suit yourself.

———⊙———

6 servings

2 pounds lean beef or pork, or half of each, cut into
    medium-sized pieces
7 ancho chiles or 10 New Mexico mild red chiles
4 garlic cloves, peeled
½ cup pork lard
¼ cup flour
1½ teaspoons salt
1 teaspoon dried oregano leaves

Boil the meat in well-seasoned water to cover until tender. Drain the meat, saving all the broth, and cube it. Set aside in some of the broth.

Remove tops and seeds from the red chiles and boil in salted water for 10 or 15 minutes. Cool and purée in blender with 1 or 2 cups reserved meat broth and 4 garlic buds. Strain. You should have 4 cups.

Pan-fry the meat in ¼ cup lard, and set aside. In remainder of lard brown the flour until golden brown and add the strained chile purée. Cook until sauce thickens, season with salt to taste, add oregano leaves, and boil 10 more minutes until thick.

Add sauce to meat just to barely cover, and cook a few minutes stirring constantly. (If you have any red chile sauce to spare, save to make red enchiladas.) If Chile con Carne is too dry, add a little of the reserved broth until right consistency is reached.

Serve with fresh flour tortillas and a bowl of any crisp salad on the side. Beans in any shape or form are a must. For that matter some Mexican Red Rice (page 215) would also be just perfect.

———⊙———

GREEN CHILE CON CARNE
Carne con Chile Verde

———☉———

When I make this dish I always double the recipe. It freezes well, and it isn't a bad idea to have a few pints of it on hand. Remember, this can also be used as a filling in crisp taco shells if well drained or cooked until some of the liquid is boiled down. Another advantage is that you may use rump or round or some other cut as long as you pick over the cooled cooked meat to eliminate fatty tissues and tendons.

———☉———

6–8 servings

2 to 3 pounds lean beef, cut in large pieces
2 tablespoons pork lard
2 tablespoons flour
1 cup chopped onions
4 chopped ripe tomatoes or
   2 cups Italian-style canned tomatoes
2 4-ounce cans chopped mild green chiles
4 garlic cloves, minced
1½ teaspoons salt
¼ cup chopped cilantro leaves
½ teaspoon black pepper

Boil meat in well-seasoned water to cover until tender. Let cool in its own broth. When cool chop meat into medium-sized cubes and reserve broth.

In hot lard brown flour until golden. Add chopped onions and sauté for 3 minutes. Add tomatoes, green chiles, and minced garlic buds, season with salt, and add the cilantro leaves. Add enough broth to make a thin sauce. Correct seasoning before adding the cubed meat, and add more broth if needed. Simmer until the stew is thick.

Good as a filling for burritos and tostadas and also as a main dish. I often serve this with a rice dish, buttered yellow squash, and a cucumber salad on the side.

———☉———

MEXICAN MEAT LOAF
Albondigon

———⊙———

This is a superb meat dish. If you like, you may substitute for the cracker crumbs 1 cup of masa harina (the corn flour used for tortillas) mixed with ¾ cup warm water. This soft dough must be kneaded into the ground meat mixture and will produce a perfect consistency for slicing once the meat loaf has been cooked. It also gives you an authentic Mexican flavor emanating from the combination of the corn flour and meat juices.

———⊙———

6 servings

2 pounds lean ground beef
1 cup ground cracker crumbs (you will need about 18)
1 beaten egg
1 tablespoon vinegar
2 garlic cloves, finely puréed
2 chopped green onions, tops only
1 teaspoon salt
½ teaspoon black pepper
1 teaspoon sweet paprika
4 slices bacon

Combine all ingredients except bacon and mix thoroughly. Turn into a Pyrex loaf pan that has been lined with the bacon slices. Bake in a 350° oven for 1½ hours. I like to cover the loaf pan with heavy foil for part of the baking time. Remove from the oven, drain off the bacon grease, and let stand for 10 or 15 minutes. Serve from loaf pan with freshly made Guacamole (page 49) and Red Rice (page 215).

———⊙———

MEATBALLS IN CHIPOTLE SAUCE
Albondigas al Chipotle

————⊙————

This particular recipe is definitely a winner. When you order it in a restaurant, in Mexico City especially, the dish that will normally appear before you consists of two large meatballs in a fair amount of the sauce, and you will be served Red Rice on the side. This is an ideal way to serve it at home also, because if the sauce is too hot the rice will make it just about right. Made very small, these meatballs are a perfect appetizer.

————⊙————

8 servings

1 pound lean ground pork butt
1 pound lean ground beef
1 large egg
1 cup corn flour (masa harina) mixed with ¾ cup warm water
4 garlic cloves, finely mashed
Salt and pepper
3 pounds very ripe unpeeled tomatoes, or 2 28-ounce cans Italian-style tomatoes
5 garlic cloves
4 tablespoons vegetable oil
½ cup chopped onion
2 tablespoons instant chicken bouillon granules
1 teaspoon ground cumin
3 canned chipotle chiles, puréed in blender with 1 cup cold water

Mix pork, beef, egg, masa harina and water mixture, and 4 finely mashed garlic cloves. Knead well, adding about 1 teaspoon salt and ½ teaspoon black pepper as you knead. Set aside.

Purée the tomatoes with 5 garlic cloves and strain, pushing mixture through sieve or large strainer with the back of a wooden spoon until only the seeds are left. Set aside.

Heat oil in a dutch oven or deep kettle that has a tight-fitting lid and sauté the chopped onion over medium heat, stirring, for 2 minutes. Do not brown. Add strained tomato purée and cook, covered, over medium heat about 5 minutes, stirring often. Add the bouillon granules and the cumin. Cook 2 more minutes. Correct seasoning—it may require more salt, but add sparingly. Now regulate the heat to keep the sauce at a simmer (you should have about 6 to 8 cups of sauce; if not, add water or pure tomato juice). Strain puréed chipotle chiles into sauce a teaspoon at a time, and taste as you stir. This is very important, as chipotles are treacherous. Add the cumin and stir.

To shape meatballs, moisten hands and squeeze out enough meat mixture to form balls the size of Ping-Pong balls. Roll each one in the moistened palm of your hand and drop them into the simmering sauce. Raise the heat and bring sauce back to boiling. Cover and cook the meatballs without stirring for 3 minutes. Lower the heat to a simmer and continue cooking for 30 minutes. With a spatula, turn the meatballs once while cooking, using caution so as not to break them.

Don't count on 8 servings! I have had guests ask for second helpings and even thirds. If you do not have corn tortillas on hand, try hot buttered corn bread or corn muffins (not the sweet ones, though). White rice goes well, and so does Green Rice (page 215). Guacamole (page 49), of course, and a crisp green salad with a tart dressing.

——————⊙——————

FANCY PICADILLO
Picadillo Festivo

—⊙—

Picadillo is one of those dishes that is great to prepare for a large group of people. Once assembled, it will keep until you are ready to serve. I prefer the hot flour tortillas with it but some very good sandwiches can be made with this filling. You need fresh French rolls, small if available. Remove the top and dig out some of the soft inside and discard. Fill with the picadillo, add some fresh salsa, some shredded lettuce, and some guacamole, replace top, squeeze to melt all the ingredients, and start eating at the open end.

—⊙—

Enough filling for 8 burritos
or 8 chiles or bell peppers

1 pound ground pork
1 pound lean ground beef
2 tablespoons lard
   Salt and pepper
2 onions, finely chopped
4 garlic cloves, mashed
3 medium-sized ripe tomatoes, peeled and chopped
3 canned pickled jalapeños, seeded and sliced
1 teaspoon Mexican cinnamon (canela), finely ground
½ teaspoon ground cloves
¼ cup slivered almonds
1 tablespoon sugar
1 tablespoon vinegar
1 cup canned chicken broth (optional)

Brown meat in lard in a large skillet until no longer pink. Add salt and pepper. Add remaining ingredients except chicken broth and cook, covered, for 30 minutes. If needed add 1 cup canned chicken broth to prevent meat from sticking to bottom of skillet. Correct seasoning. This is a good filling for burritos and the accepted filling for Chiles en Nogada (page 321), the stuffed poblano chiles with a nut-based sauce and a pomegranate seed garnish. And to give American stuffed bell peppers a Mexican twist, why not stuff them with Fancy Picadillo; they taste great. May be served with a tossed green salad and garlic bread, hot and oozing with butter.

MEXICAN HASH
Picadillo

⊙

This is a fast and tasty dish and could be made with regular inexpensive hamburger meat if you drain the fat that the meat generates as it browns. It's great with corn tortillas but better still with hot flour tortillas oozing with butter. This is a good snack to be eaten at the beach if you have a place to heat the meat in a skillet and a place to warm the tortillas.

⊙

4 servings

1 tablespoon lard
1 pound ground round or other lean beef
2 tablespoons oil
1 onion, finely chopped
1 potato, peeled and diced
1 ripe fresh tomato, diced
1 teaspoon salt
½ teaspoon pepper
1 teaspoon Mexican cinnamon (canela)
½ teaspoon ground cloves
2 garlic cloves, finely chopped
½ cup seedless golden raisins
¼ cup sliced stuffed green olives
½ cup water

Heat lard and add meat. Cook, stirring constantly, until no longer pink. Set aside. Drain grease if any settles around meat.

In 2 tablespoons oil fry onion, potato, tomato, and seasonings. Cook 5 minutes and add to meat. Add rest of ingredients. Mix well and correct seasoning. Cover and cook over medium heat 10 minutes.

Serve as a filling for burritos or as a main dish accompanied by a green vegetable and a salad.

⊙

SPECIAL SMOTHERED LIVER
Higado de Res Especial

——⊙——

There were many great cooks on both sides of my family. I am lucky enough to have cooked with most of them, even one or two generations removed. This liver recipe was personally taught to me by one of my father's aunts. She was married to an American gentleman, and when I use that term I mean a gentle man. My uncle Bob, who came from pioneer Texas stock, was well known and respected all over the parts of Arizona and Mexico where I grew up. My dad used to say that he was tops as an appraiser of beef on the hoof. He married my aunt Josephine long before I was born. My aunt's mother-in-law used to fix liver this way and I have converted many a liver hater with precisely this recipe.

——⊙——

8 servings

8 ½-inch slices of liver, preferably calves' liver
1 quart boiling water
1 tablespoon vinegar
2 tablespoons Worcestershire sauce
4 garlic cloves, finely mashed
  Salt and pepper
  Flour as needed
  Bacon grease or oil

Place slices of liver in a large bowl and pour boiling water over them. Allow liver to blanch. When grayish in color, remove from hot water and remove skin from edges of the slices. Marinate in mixture of vinegar, Worcestershire, garlic, salt, and pepper for at least 30 minutes.

Remove liver from marinade and roll in flour. Brown in hot fat, then reduce heat and cook over low heat for 10 minutes. Avoid overcooking. Turn once only.

Serve with fried onions and crisp bacon slices, with pickled serrano peppers on the side if available. If not, pickled canned jalapeño chiles are a must.

——⊙——

OXTAIL STEW
Guiso de Cola de Res

————⊙————

This used to be an inexpensive dish. Not so today. At the ranch when we butchered I would clean, cut, and wrap each oxtail and then freeze them until I had enough for a stew. All the family were fond of them and one was not enough. This is a finger food. It is difficult to get the juicy meat tidbits out from between the bones so you have to get up to rinse your fingers as soon as you finish eating.

————⊙————

4 to 6 servings

    2 disjointed oxtails, trimmed of excess fat
    2 quarts well-seasoned water, or more if needed
    4 garlic cloves, mashed
    2 bay leaves
    ½ teaspoons peppercorns
      Salt
    1 medium onion with a few whole cloves stuck into it

Cover oxtail pieces with water and add remaining ingredients. Cover and simmer 3 hours until tender. Let cool in its own broth. Save broth. I degrease it and use it to make Onion Soup.

Remove oxtail pieces and brown in hot fat. Serve with a fresh hot salsa and fresh corn tortillas. This is an excellent finger food and is delightful with french fries.

An excellent variation: Simmer the stewed oxtail bits for 10 minutes in the red chile sauce that we use in Red Chile con Carne (page 126), and sprinkle with slightly browned sesame seeds (easily browned in butter in a small skillet over medium heat).

————⊙————

SWEETBREADS ANITA
Mollejas Anita

———⊙———

Strange as it might seem, I had very little contact with the woman whose name I use in this recipe. A sister-in-law of mine married to a colorful Spanish gentleman passed it on to me. Anita was his sister. Follow instructions carefully and clean the sweetbreads properly. The flavor of the finished dish is excellent.

———⊙———

6 servings

2 pounds sweetbreads
8 tablespoons butter
4 tablespoons flour
½ cup finely chopped green onion
¼ cup finely chopped fresh parsley
1 can beef bouillon diluted with 2 cups water
   Salt and pepper
   Dry sherry as needed

Drop sweetbreads into boiling salted water. Simmer over low heat for about 30 minutes. Drain. Plunge into cold water and remove membranes. Chop into very small cubes the size of marbles.

Melt butter in skillet and brown the sweetbreads to a golden color, stirring constantly. You may find it necessary to scrape the bottom of the pan, as the juice sticks and you will need the rich flavor of the particles that have stuck to the pan.

Once the sweetbreads are sautéed, add the flour and continue cooking until the flour is a light brown color. Add the chopped onion and chopped parsley and stir for 5 minutes, scraping often. Now add the diluted bouillon all at once, lower the flame, and cook for about 5 or 10 minutes until you have a smooth sauce. Correct seasoning—careful with the salt unless you used unsalted butter. Add some freshly ground pepper and your dry sherry before serving.

I serve this on toasted garlic bread as a creamy filled sandwich, but you may serve it as an entrée with yellow rice and buttered peas and carrots. For a salad, never lettuce—spinach or watercress would be perfect.

———⊙———

FRIED KIDNEYS WITH SHERRY AND ONIONS
Rinones Encebollados al Jerez

————⊙————

If you do not care for kidneys I would venture to say that it is probably the smell that upsets you. I wish you would dare to make some kidneys my way. The soaking in milk and this marinade makes all the difference in the world. Be sure you use beef kidneys always; never pork.

————⊙————

6 servings

2 beef kidneys
2 cups milk
Marinade (see below)
Flour
½ cup oil
2 cups sliced white onions
Salt and pepper
¼ cup dry sherry
Pickled red jalapeño strips for garnish

Wash beef kidneys, remove outer membrane, and split through center lengthwise, or slice thickly. Remove fat and white tissue. Soak in cold milk for about an hour. While kidneys are soaking, prepare marinade.

Drain kidneys and marinate for 30 minutes. Drain. Roll in flour and pan-fry 15 minutes in hot oil. Place on hot platter.

Sauté onions in butter until golden in color and soft, add salt and pepper to taste, and add sherry. Heat through and smother fried kidneys with onion mixture. Garnish with jalapeño strips or whole pickled jalapeños.

MARINADE
2 tablespoons Worcestershire sauce
1 tablespoon lemon juice
1 tablespoon vinegar
Salt and pepper

Note: Kidneys may also be sliced, but not too thinly, as slices tend to dry while cooking.

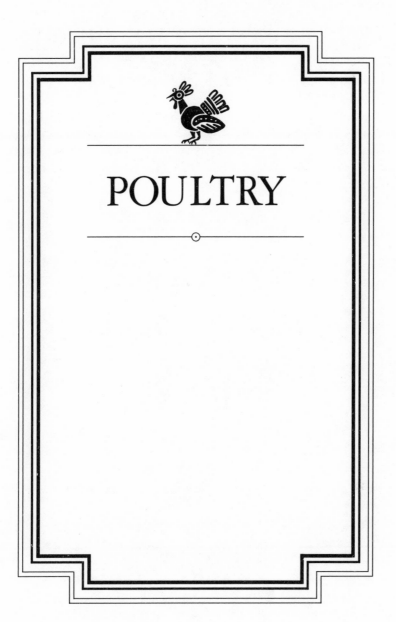

POULTRY

C hicken, and to a much smaller degree, turkey and duck, are tremendously popular in Mexico. In rural areas, even the poorest farmer keeps his chickens in his yard to provide him with eggs and to convert into a tasty stew such as Mexican-style Chicken or Chicken Breasts Veracruz Style. Leftovers, if any, become tacos or enchiladas, sopes or gorditas, burritos or tostadas.

Poultry in general and chicken in particular have a great affinity for our varied and wonderful moles and pipianes. Two notable examples are the Chicken Fricassee in Green Pumpkinseed Sauce and the well-known, traditional Mole Poblano (Chicken in Chile and Chocolate Sauce). This particular mole is usually an all day affair and, when done the old-fashioned way, reserved for special occasions. For everyday use, the Mexican housewife will buy her mole pastes in the *mercados,* or markets. These may be black, red, dark or light brown, yellow or green, the color determined by the ingredients contained. As more and more women leave the household for the work place, commercial preparations are becoming increasingly popular and most are quite good. Here, I present a way of making mole the easy way.

Chicken and chile are natural mates and all sorts of imaginative combinations are available. One good example is Chicken in Adobo Sauce. Even the simplest poached or baked chicken is magically transformed when combined with tangy tomatillo sauce, especially when rolled in a freshly made corn tortilla or piled on a crisp tostada.

There are stands in the markets in Mexico, especially in the larger cities, that sell only chicken. The owner has an enormous pair of shears that he handles like a magician. He will cut the fowl the way you wish, bone the breasts, pound them for you—you name it. It is normal to give him or his helper a small tip. They will always give you the head and the feet. I take them because it is customary to do so, but I must confess I've never used them. Frankly, I don't know what to do with them. If I cooked them, I'm sure I wouldn't even taste them.

CHICKEN AND RICE
Arroz con Pollo

————☉————

When I am asked what I would recommend for a large family gathering or reunion, I invariably choose Chicken and Rice. For quantity cooking chicken breasts would be too expensive; I would choose whole chickens cut up into individual pieces, about eight pieces to the chicken (use winglets only, not the tips), one chicken per recipe. The recipe can be doubled if you use a large dutch oven or roaster, and you can cook it (tightly covered) in the oven successfully. The dish will be fine set aside for fifteen minutes after cooking but it loses its delightful flavor if you have to reheat it, especially if you add extra liquid to do so.

————☉————

4 servings

2 whole chicken breasts
1 quart water seasoned with salt, bay leaf, and peppercorns
1 cup long grain rice
4 tablespoons salad oil
2 cups chicken stock
1 cup chopped tomatoes
½ cup chopped onions
4 garlic cloves, finely mashed
Salt and pepper
½ cup bell pepper slices

Poach chicken breasts in seasoned water for about 15 minutes, and allow to cool in their own broth. Set aside.

Sauté rice in salad oil until golden in color, then add 2 cups chicken stock, tomatoes, onions, garlic, and salt and pepper to taste. Bring to a boil. Lower heat.

Cut poached chicken breasts into bite-sized pieces and arrange, with sliced bell pepper, on top of boiling rice to form an agreeable pattern. Cover and cook over very low heat for 35 minutes. Serve in platter with hot corn tortillas and guacamole. Cucumbers with yogurt or cottage cheese go well with this rice and chicken dish.

————☉————

CHICKEN IN ADOBO SAUCE
Pollo en Adobo

When I make adobo sauce I always double this recipe because it keeps well and freezes beautifully. It is a good sauce to have on hand for emergency dishes in the Mexican style. Chicken in Adobo Sauce can be made ahead of time and reheated before serving.

As a girl, visiting friends, I would gasp at the sight of my friends' fathers seated at the head of the table with a large bib on. Once this sauce hits the shirt front, goodbye shirt. That stain will not come out!

8 servings

2 2½ pound broiler-fryers, cut up into serving pieces
4 ancho chiles or 6 New Mexico chiles
6 garlic cloves
2 tablespoons vinegar
1 teaspoon sugar
  Salt and pepper
2 tablespoons chile seeds

Poach your chicken in well-seasoned water until tender. (However, we don't want the meat falling off the bones.) Cool in its own broth.

Remove tops and seeds (save seeds) from chiles and boil chiles in salted water 15 minutes. Cool and purée in blender with 1 cup reserved chicken broth and garlic. Strain. Add vinegar, sugar, crushed oregano leaves, and salt and pepper. Correct seasoning. Chile paste must have a pungent taste.

Place your drained chicken pieces in a baking dish, spread chile paste on top, cover with a sheet of heavy foil, and bake in the oven for 30 minutes at 350°. Uncover and sprinkle a few chile pod seeds on top. Good served with hot flour tortillas, boiled beans, or Refried Beans (page 236).

MEXICAN-STYLE CHICKEN
Pollo a la Mexicana

————☉————

This is a tasty and colorful concoction that must be eaten soon after it is ready. I find that this sauce spoils easily. The beauty of this dish is that if you have unexpected guests you can always add a package of frozen peas and carrots and a peeled cubed potato, and that will be sufficient to serve at least four more people.

————☉————

8 to 10 servings

2 cut-up fryers, 2½ to 3 pounds each
1 quart water
1 bay leaf
2 garlic buds, peeled and crushed
    Few peppercorns
1 tablespoon salt
1 cup finely chopped white onion
¼ cup oil
1 28-ounce can Italian-style tomatoes or 4 ripe red tomatoes, peeled and chopped
2 4-ounce cans chopped mild green chiles
    Black pepper
½ teaspoon oregano
4 garlic buds, finely mashed

Poach chicken pieces until almost tender, about 15 minutes, in 1 quart of well-seasoned water, adding bay leaf, 2 garlic buds, peppercorns, and salt. Let chicken cool in broth.

Sauté onion until golden in hot oil in deep kettle or dutch oven. Add the tomatoes (do not blend tomatoes, just break them with your hands) and chiles. Season sauce with salt, black pepper, and oregano. Add 2 cups reserved chicken stock. Boil 5 minutes, add mashed garlic, and correct seasoning.

Place chicken in baking dish, pour all of the sauce over it, cover, and bake in 350° oven for 15 minutes, until bubbly. Serve with white rice and buttered green beans. A green onion, cucumber, and raw zucchini salad is wonderful with this dish.

————☉————

CHICKEN VALENTINA
Pollo a la Valentina

————⊙————

I think this recipe originated in Guadalajara. There are many versions of it and the purists might say this is not one of them, but I know I first tasted it in a small cafe in Guadalajara's Plaza del Sol. It is wonderful for a fast preparation, because you can poach the chicken, place it in the refrigerator covered with its own boiling liquid so that the pieces won't dry out, and then in the evening drain it and proceed with the instructions in the recipe. The potatoes may be boiled the day before with their jackets on. Be sure not to peel them until you are ready to fry them.

————⊙————

8 to 10 servings

2 cut-up fryers
6 red ancho chiles or New Mexico red chiles (mild)
4 garlic buds
2 tablespoons lard
1 cup canned tomatoes, puréed in blender and strained
1 teaspoon crushed oregano leaves
  Salt and pepper
1 tablespoon vinegar
  Oil for pan-frying
2 large boiled potatoes, peeled and cubed
  Fresh coriander leaves or fresh parsley for garnish

Poach chicken pieces in well-seasoned water to cover.

Boil red chiles after removing tops and seeds. Purée in blender with 3 garlic buds and strain.

In 2 tablespoons hot lard brown 1 garlic bud and remove. Add strained chile purée and tomatoes (it is best to blend and strain the tomatoes, as we need a clear thin sauce for coating the chicken). Add oregano, salt, pepper, and vinegar, and boil for 15 minutes until sauce is well seasoned. Cool and set aside.

Drain chicken and pat dry with paper towels. Have a large chicken-frying skillet ready with hot oil. Dip each chicken piece into sauce, then brown in thin layer of hot fat in skillet. Do this over very low heat. Red chile coating burns easily and becomes bitter. When part of the chicken pieces have been fried, check your pan; if you find too many overcooked bits of sauce adhering to the pan, then change pans, add more oil, and continue until all chicken has been fried.

Place 2 tablespoons hot oil in clean pan and fry your cubed potatoes. Brown lightly on both sides. Salt lightly.

Serve two chicken pieces to a plate with a generous garnish of the fried potatoes, half a seeded jalapeño pickled chile and a few lettuce leaves, a quarter of a peeled tomato, and cilantro or parsley sprigs. Serve with a casserole of corn tortilla strips, red chile sauce (same as that used for red enchiladas), and Jack cheese.

———⊙———

CHICKEN AND SPICES
Pollo al Jerez

———⊙———

This dish is not for anyone with ulcers, that's for sure! All those spices make it pungent but oh, so good. Scalloped potatoes are good with this, and do pass the pickled serrano peppers; they are not too hot and add a delightful touch. Most Mexicans eat these peppers as one would eat a dill pickle in the United States.

———⊙———

8 to 10 servings

2 2½-pound broiler-fryers,
     cut into serving pieces
4 tablespoons oil
1 onion, finely chopped
4 large ripe tomatoes, peeled and chopped
3 garlic buds, mashed
2 cups chicken stock
   Salt and pepper
¼ teaspoon ground cloves
½ teaspoon ground Mexican cinnamon (canela)
¼ teaspoon rosemary leaves
¼ cup breadcrumbs made from
     toasted sourdough bread
½ cup dry sherry
6 or 8 canned pickled serrano
     peppers for garnish

Poach chicken pieces in well-seasoned chicken broth. Cool in broth.

In oil fry onion, tomatoes, and mashed garlic, then add chicken stock and all the spices. Boil for 10 minutes. Be sure to add enough broth to have a sauce of medium-thick consistency. Add ¼ cup breadcrumbs to the sauce; this serves as a delicious thickening agent. Now add the sherry and correct seasoning.

In covered baking dish suitable for serving at table, place chicken pieces, pour sauce over them, and bake in moderate oven (350°) 15 minutes.

———⊙———

CHICKEN IN CHILE
AND CHOCOLATE SAUCE
Mole Poblano

—————⊙—————

8 to 10 servings

2 2½-pound broiler-fryers,
    cut into serving pieces
2 bay leaves
8 peppercorns
1 pint prepared mole poblano paste (page 14)
    dissolved in chicken broth
1 tablespoon Hershey's cocoa mixed with
    3 tablespoons hot water
1 tablespoon vinegar
6 garlic buds, peeled
2 tablespoons lard
2 tablespoons flour
    Salt and pepper
2 tablespoons sugar or according to taste
4 tablespoons sesame seeds, fried lightly in butter

Poach chicken with bay leaves and peppercorns in well-seasoned water to cover. Let cool in own broth.

Dissolve mole paste in 3 cups reserved strained chicken broth (easily done if you use a blender). While blending add cocoa paste, vinegar, and 6 peeled garlic buds. Add more chicken broth. Sauce must not be too thick to start with.

In 2 tablespoons lard brown 2 tablespoons flour until golden, add the mixture that's in the blender, rinse out the blender with 1 cup warm water, and add that to the sauce. Correct seasoning. Start adding sugar until sweetness is agreeable to you. I do not care for a sweet mole sauce but many people do.

Place warm chicken pieces in sauce and cook over very slow heat for 30 minutes. Keep kettle covered but stir often and check for sticking. Roux should give you a sauce of medium-thick consistency that holds together well. Grease tends to come to the surface. Unless you are calorie-counting do not remove, keep stirring it into the sauce.

Serve in a deep serving dish and sprinkle the toasted sesame seeds on top. It is a lovely sight to behold. A must—hot fresh corn tortillas, and a rice dish. I personally like a fresh cool lettuce salad and iced tea.

CHICKEN IN ALMOND SAUCE
Almendrado de Pollo

———⊙———

Almond sauces have become popular with the modern Mexican housewife mainly because they are easier to make, faster, and just as tasty as the old combinations of pumpkinseeds and sesame seeds. I will grant you that they are definitely more expensive but they are worth the price. By all means give your guests a soup spoon or teaspoon. I've never met anyone who could resist eating the almond sauce with a spoon.

———⊙———

8 to 10 servings

1 2½-pound broiler-fryer plus 2 chicken breasts
4 garlic cloves, peeled and finely mashed
1 tablespoon salt
2 ripe tomatoes, peeled and cut in fourths
6 cups of water
⅔ cup almond slivers
2 tablespoons pure pork lard
2 cups seasoned chicken broth
3 tablespoons salad oil
2 tablespoons all-purpose flour
   Salt and pepper
½ teaspoon ground cumin

Cook whole chicken and extra breasts with garlic, salt, and tomatoes in well-seasoned water, breast down, until tender. Allow to cool in its own broth. When cool enough to handle, cut the 2 extra breasts in half and cut the cooked chicken into serving pieces. Be sure not to overcook the chicken. Reserve broth and strain.

For sauce, lightly sauté the almond slivers in the 2 tablespoons pork lard. Place in the blender container. Add 2 cups of the chicken broth and purée until creamy.

Now heat the 3 tablespoons of oil in a dutch oven and brown the flour in oil until a light brown. Add the almond mixture and cook over medium heat until creamy and thick, stirring constantly. Taste for seasoning. Add the ground cumin and cover. Remove from heat.

Arrange chicken pieces in a casserole dish with a lid and cover with the almond sauce. Heat in a moderate oven and serve with a rice dish and a crisp salad.

Note: Sauce must be the consistency of heavy cream. If it becomes too thick, thin with some of the reserved chicken broth and cook, stirring, until of the right consistency. Almond sauces and moles are delightful ways to prepare game and poultry, adding either ripe red tomatoes and red chiles or tomatillos and red ancho chiles, and different herb combinations. If a recipe calls for either sesame seeds or pumpkinseeds, almonds may be used as a substitute. The idea of adding a small amount of roux helps to keep the sauce together and gives it a delightful earthy taste.

CHICKEN IN A PUEBLA-STYLE SAUCE
Tinga de Pollo
———⊙———

I think that the name of this dish has a lovely ring to it. Its origin in Mexico may be traced to the colonial period, when the Spanish way of cooking was being absorbed and merged with Mexican practices and becoming accepted by the nuns in the convents. (When important envoys from the Spanish courts arrived in Mexico they were probably boarded at the various convents where many of the now famous recipes were born.) Tinga uses a mixture of European and Mexican foods with a European cooking method.

———⊙———

Filling for at least
20 soft tacos

1 3-pound broiler-fryer
6 cups water
4 garlic cloves, peeled and bruised
1 teaspoon peppercorns
　Salt
4 tablespoons oil
2 cups sliced onions
2 cups Italian-style tomatoes, crushed (do not purée)
1 teaspoon mashed garlic
　Pepper
1 teaspoon ground canela (Mexican cinnamon)
½ teaspoon ground cloves
½ teaspoon ground cumin
1 tablespoon juice from canned chipotles
　Sugar (see below)

Place whole chicken, breast side down, in a dutch oven. Add water, bruised garlic cloves, peppercorns, and salt to taste. Cook, covered, over medium heat until tender. Remove from broth and cool. Strain broth and reserve. Skin the cooked chicken and shred the meat. Set aside.

Heat the oil in a dutch oven and sauté the onion slices. Do not brown. Add the crushed tomatoes and mashed garlic and season with salt and pepper. Add the spices and the chipotle juice. Add sugar to taste, 1 or 2 tablespoons to start with. Some cooks like it on the sweet side but I prefer it mildly sweetened. Simmer the sauce until thickened. Taste for seasoning and correct if needed.

Add the shredded chicken meat to the sauce. Cook about 5 minutes. Serve with hot corn tortillas. Tinga is mostly used as a filling for a soft unfried taco. Garnishes should be slices of ripe avocado and canned chipotle chiles.

———⊙———

MEXICAN CHICKEN FRICASSEE
Guisado de Pollo
———⊙———

I think chicken is great, and I never tire of it. This recipe is fine even as a leftover. Just shred the meat and mix again with the sauce, heat, and fill burritos with it.

———⊙———

8 servings

    2 cut-up fryers
    1 cup flour
      Salt and pepper
    ½ cup oil or shortening
    1 16-ounce can Italian-style canned tomatoes
    2 tablespoons tomato paste
    ½ teaspoon tarragon
    1 cup chopped onion
    1 cup sliced bell pepper
    2 sliced pickled jalapeño peppers

Roll pieces of chicken in seasoned flour, or salt and pepper chicken and roll in plain flour. Brown in thin layer of hot shortening in deep kettle. Drain off fat and save.

To kettle add 1 cup water and remaining ingredients, and correct seasoning. Cover tightly and cook slowly about 45 minutes. Add more water or chicken broth if needed. You do not want the sauce too thick.

May be served with peas and carrots and small boiled potatoes. Hot French bread is good, so that you can sop up the wonderful-tasting sauce.

CHICKEN FRICASSEE
WITH GREEN PUMPKINSEED SAUCE
Pipian Verde de Pollo

————⊙————

This is indeed a party dish. It takes time to prepare, but it is time well spent. It is a handsome concoction. If you have any leftovers, shred the chicken or simply remove it from the bone and heat with the leftover sauce and make burritos.

————⊙————

6 servings

1 2½- to 3-pound chicken,
   cut up into serving pieces
2 chicken breasts, cut in half
1 pound Mexican tomatillos (green tomatoes) or
   1 10-ounce can of tomatillos
1 large white onion, chopped
1 tablespoon mashed garlic
1 poblano chile and 1 fresh jalapeño chile,
   stems and seeds removed
1 cup fresh cilantro leaves (no stems)
1 teaspoon sugar
2 tablespoons butter
2 tablespoons salad oil
1 cup peeled pumpkinseeds (available in health food stores)
2 tablespoons pure pork lard (no substitutes)
   Salt and pepper
1 tablespoon instant chicken bouillon granules

Place chicken pieces in a large soup pot and barely cover with well-seasoned water. Poach chicken until almost tender, about 45 minutes. Allow to cool in its own broth. Set aside.

Boil tomatillos in 2 cups of water for 20 minutes. Be sure to remove the paperlike skin on the outside. Drain and purée in blender with ½ cup water and the chopped onion, garlic, both seeded green chiles, and cilantro leaves. Pour into a bowl. Add sugar.

In mixture of hot butter and oil lightly brown the pumpkinseeds in a medium-sized skillet, shaking pan often and stirring constantly to prevent pumpkinseeds from scorching. Do this cautiously over low heat. Place seeds in blender container and add 1 cup of the chicken stock. Purée until thick and creamy.

(Recipe continues)

Heat 2 tablespoons pure pork lard in a dutch oven and pour in the prepared tomatillo sauce. Stir in the pumpkinseed sauce and mix well. Cook at a simmer over medium heat for 3 minutes. Taste for seasoning. Add instant chicken bouillon and stir well. Cook 2 more minutes.

Arrange chicken pieces in a casserole with a lid. Pour the sauce over chicken and bake in a 325° oven, covered, until heated through.

Note: This dish is wonderful eating and holds up well. Assemble, cover, and place in the refrigerator until ready to heat. Serve with Mexican Red Rice (page 215), a green salad, and corn tortillas. May also be eaten with hot French rolls, as the sauce is delightful with either corn or wheat flour tortillas or bread.

————⊙————

BAKED CHICKEN WITH MEXICAN CORNBREAD DRESSING
Pollo al Horno con Relleno

————⊙————

Baked stuffed chicken would still be considered holiday fare in many Mexican homes. Be it Christmas or the celebration of an anniversary, christening, or birthday, stuffed chicken is wonderful, especially if you have guests. I urge you to try this stuffing because the flavors are so different, and then feel free to make all the other family dishes that you are accustomed to serve on Thanksgiving and Christmas.

Carving at table is definitely not an art in Mexico and most men prefer to have all that nonsense handled by the women and everything brought to the table or buffet ready to serve and eat. We always carved and served at the table but our meals were always rituals, prolonged and enjoyed.

————⊙————

8 to 10 servings

8 tablespoons unsalted butter
½ cup finely chopped onion
1 medium potato, peeled and diced
¼ cup chopped stuffed green olives
¼ cup raisins
1 unpeeled apple, diced
 Salt and pepper
½ teaspoon Mexican cinnamon (canela)
¼ teaspoon ground cloves
1 6-ounce bag unseasoned cornbread stuffing crumbs
3 cups chicken broth
1 teaspoon sugar
1 tablespoon vinegar
4 tablespoons dry sherry
2 2½- to 3-pound chickens suitable for baking

Melt butter in large pot on low heat. Sauté onion for 5 minutes. Combine potato, olives, raisins, apple, garlic, cinnamon, cloves, and salt and pepper, blend well, and add to onion. Watch your salt as stuffing crumbs tend to be salty. Add stuffing crumbs. Add broth, or if you do not have any chicken broth on hand you may use milk and one egg in substitution. Dissolve sugar in mixture of vinegar and sherry, and add. This makes stuffing for two chickens or one small turkey hen.

Have birds completely clean: Rinse with cold water, and pat dry with paper towels. Rub cavities of birds with pork lard mixed with 1 bud mashed garlic.

Fill birds with stuffing and truss. Place in roaster lined with heavy foil and rub outside of birds with melted butter. Add one cup water before closing foil wrap. Bake in a 375° oven 1½ to 2 hours. Baste after 30 minutes and check for doneness after 1 hour. Uncover for last 30 minutes so chicken browns. Remember, each bird is different.

In Mexico we are not able to get cranberries but we serve other stewed fruits, dried or fresh, with chicken, and applesauce enhanced with a little cinnamon and cloves is always a favorite.

———⊙———

OVEN-FRIED CHICKEN
WITH MEXICAN PAPRIKA
Pollo Frito al Horno

————⊙————

I don't think Mexican cooks could win a chicken-frying contest. Almost all American cooks are very good at frying chicken and I often think this recipe was invented just for that. It's foolproof.

————⊙————

8 servings

1 cup flour
2 teaspoons salt
½ teaspoon pepper
1 cup shortening (half butter)
2 cut-up frying chickens
2 tablespoons pimenton (Mexican paprika, a delightful spice similar
    in taste to New Mexico ground red mild chile peppers)

Heat oven to 425°. Mix flour, salt, and pepper in paper sack. Put shortening in a square or oblong pan. Pan must be 2 inches deep. Set pan in the oven for shortening to melt.

Shake 3 or 4 pieces of chicken at a time in flour in the paper bag to coat evenly. Place chicken skin side down in a single layer in hot shortening. Bake 30 minutes. Turn skin side up and bake another 30 minutes. You never know, you may have to lower the oven for last 30 minutes of oven-frying.

Remove from oven and sprinkle the Mexican paprika lightly over the cooked chicken, turning to coat evenly if necessary. Serve with a garlic-flavored salad with tarragon vinegar and olive oil, and cottage cheese and fruit.

————⊙————

SAUTÉED CHICKEN WITH BANANAS
Pollo con Salsa de Naranja y Platanos

———☉———

This is a delightful concoction and could be served with couscous and a salad of cucumbers and bell peppers. I first tasted it in a very modest hotel in Ixtapan de la Sal, prepared no doubt by a home cook with a wonderful imagination and leftover plantains and orange juice.

———☉———

6 servings

1 2½- to 3-pound chicken, cut into serving pieces
Salt and pepper
3 tablespoons butter
3 tablespoons corn oil
1 cup chopped onion
1 cup fresh or canned chicken broth
1 cup fresh orange juice
1 teaspoon chopped fresh ginger root
1 tablespoon finely mashed garlic
¼ cup white seedless raisins
¼ cup dry sherry
¼ cup orange liqueur or, if not available, 2 tablespoons sugar
1 large plantain or two firm bananas
¼ cup slivered almonds

Place the chicken pieces in a small kettle and add warm water to cover and salt and pepper to taste. Bring to the boil and partly cover. Simmer 30 minutes. Let cool in own broth. Drain, save broth, and pat chicken dry.

In dutch oven brown chicken in butter and corn oil mixture. As chicken pieces brown, remove with slotted spoon to an oven-proof casserole large enough to hold chicken and sauce.

In butter and oil mixture sauté onion for 1 minute and add chicken broth mixed with 1 cup fresh orange juice. Allow to come to a simmer and add ginger root and garlic. Soften raisins in sherry and add. Correct seasoning. Mix in orange liqueur or sugar. Cook over very low heat 1 minute, stirring constantly.

Pour sauce over chicken pieces, cover with foil, and heat in 400° oven for 15 minutes. Before bringing to table, cut bananas into fourths and sauté in butter for 1 minute, turning once. If plantains are used, fry for 5 minutes and sprinkle with sugar before serving. Add slivered almonds.

SMOTHERED CHICKEN
Tapado de Pollo

This is a dish without chile. It is important to dispel the myth that all Mexican cooking needs hot peppers to be Mexican. This is a fallacy. In fact it is not unusual to find a whole meal cooked without chiles either dried or green, but naturally the salsas will be on the table.

6 servings

6 tablespoons oil
  Salt and pepper
1 3½- or 4-pound chicken, cut into serving pieces
    (if chicken weighs less, buy two)
1 large onion, sliced
1 package frozen peas, parboiled 1 minute in
    salted water and drained
1 pound zucchini, quartered
6 carrots, peeled, sliced, and parboiled
    4 minutes in salted water
½ teaspoon nutmeg
1 16-ounce can Italian-style tomatoes
2 tablespoons tomato paste
2 bay leaves
4 garlic buds, mashed

Heat oil and brown salted and peppered chicken pieces, turning once only.

Arrange half of the chicken pieces on the bottom of a heavy ovenproof casserole that has a lid. Layer most of vegetables over the chicken and season with salt, pepper, and nutmeg.

To make sauce, mix tomatoes, tomato paste, bay leaves, and garlic. Add half to layers in casserole. Layer on remainder of chicken, add the remaining tomato mixture and remaining vegetables, if any, cover, and bake in moderate oven (350°) for 30 minutes. Serve with rice and pickled cauliflower.

Note: If a thin tomato sauce is desired you may purée the tomato mixture in blender and strain. I usually just mash it up with my hands, adding a little tomato juice if necessary.

CHICKEN BREASTS AND GREEN BEANS
Pollo con Ejotes

———⊙———

Celery is beginning to show its face in modern Mexican cooking, and so are bell peppers, mostly because the price of poblano chiles has gone up considerably and a bell pepper goes a long way. This recipe tends to have an Oriental flavor.

———⊙———

6 to 8 servings

Salt and pepper
4 chicken breasts, skinned, boned, and cut in bite-size pieces
4 tablespoons melted butter
½ cup green onions (tops and bulbs cut into ½-inch pieces)
4 tablespoons oil
1 cup sliced celery
1 cup sliced bell pepper
1 cup chicken broth
1 package frozen green beans
Chopped pimiento

Salt and pepper chicken pieces and brown lightly in butter. Set aside.

Sauté onions in hot oil for 2 minutes, then add celery and bell pepper, salt and pepper, and 1 cup chicken broth (canned chicken broth is fine). Cook for 5 minutes. Correct seasoning. Pour over chicken and stir.

In salted water cook beans for 5 minutes, drain, and stir into chicken mixture. Beans must retain their bright green color and be al dente. Heat the entire dish thoroughly, and garnish with chopped canned pimiento.

Serve with steamed rice and pass the soy sauce. Yes, we use a great deal of soy sauce in Mexico on occasion.

Note: If you like fiery jalapeños—by all means add one, seeded and sliced, to the sauce.

———⊙———

CHICKEN BREASTS VERACRUZ STYLE
Pechugas a la Veracruzana

————⊙————

This sauce is versatile. I think every cook has her or his own style of seasoning. The truth is that the classic recipe that calls for olives and capers is far beyond the reach of even middle class families. Try this sauce without the olives and I think you will agree that it is excellent. If I think the sauce is too thick, I add water with some chicken bouillon granules stirred in.

————⊙————

6 to 8 servings

4 chicken breasts, skinned and halved
Flour, seasoned with salt, pepper, and paprika
½ cup oil (half olive oil and half vegetable oil)
1 16-ounce can Italian-style canned tomatoes
2 tablespoons tomato paste
1 onion, thinly sliced
¼ teaspoon ground cloves
½ teaspoon ground Mexican cinnamon (canela)—
   if not available, use cloves only
2 bay leaves
Salt and pepper
1 teaspoon sugar
4 garlic buds, mashed
Strips of jalapeño chile
¼ cup stuffed green olives

Dust the chicken pieces with the seasoned flour, or better still, put flour in paper bag and shake chicken pieces in bag 3 or 4 at a time until evenly coated.

Heat half the oil mixture in a large skillet, and sauté the chicken pieces on both sides until golden. Set aside and keep warm.

Purée the tomatoes with the tomato paste in blender, and strain.

Add the remainder of the oil to the skillet, sauté the onion, and add the strained tomato mixture. Add the spices and bay leaves and cook, stirring, for about 5 minutes. Correct seasoning and add the sugar and mashed garlic buds.

Place chicken in baking dish and pour sauce over it. Add a few jalapeño strips and ¼ cup stuffed green olives and bake, covered, for 30 minutes in 325° oven. Remove bay leaves before serving. Serve with boiled small potatoes rolled in butter and chopped parsley, and garlic toast.

Note: This recipe may be doubled.

PICKLED CHICKEN AND VEGETABLE SALAD
Escabeche de Pollo y Verduras

———☉———

Escabeches are of Spanish extraction but the Mexican version can be made without the olive oil. I make a low-calorie version of this dish without the olive oil and it is light and just as tasty. The secret to the unique flavor is the Bay Leaf Tea.

———☉———

4–5 servings

2 chicken breasts, poached
½ cup vegetable oil
1 teaspoon finely mashed garlic
2 cups sliced zucchini
1 10-ounce package frozen peas and carrots
1 10-ounce package frozen cut green beans
  Salt and pepper
6 tablespoons white vinegar
1 cup sliced onion sautéed in ¼ cup olive oil
1 cup strong Bay Leaf Tea (page 11)
1 large garlic clove, thinly sliced
1 tablespoon crushed oregano
¼ cup red canned jalapeño strips

Poach chicken breasts in 4 cups of well-seasoned boiling water for 30 minutes. Drain. Cut up into bite-sized pieces. Combine ¼ cup olive oil with mashed garlic and pour over prepared chicken pieces. Set aside.

Poach zucchini in 2 cups boiling salted water for 1 minute just to blanch. Drain.

Cook peas and carrots in 1 cup salted boiling water for 2 minutes. Drain.

Cook green beans in salted water for 3 minutes and drain. All vegetables must be crisp tender.

When vegetables are cool, combine in large salad bowl and add salt and coarsely ground pepper to taste, 2 tablespoons vinegar, and 4 tablespoons vegetable oil. Add onions. Mix and set aside.

Mix bay leaf infusion with ¼ cup vinegar and add 1 sliced garlic clove and oregano.

Put a layer of chicken pieces in a large serving dish then cover with a layer of vegetables; repeat if you have enough ingredients for 2 layers, and be sure that top layer has a few pieces of chicken showing before adding the bay leaf mixture and the pickled jalapeño. Refrigerate for at least an hour before serving. Sprinkle oregano on top before serving.

————⊙————

BAKED DUCKLING
Pato al Horno

————⊙————

6 servings

1 4- to 5-pound ready-to-bake duckling
2 tablespoons softened butter
1 tablespoon salt
½ teaspoon black pepper
1 teaspoon ground coriander
2 unpeeled potatoes, cut into quarters
4 tablespoons melted butter for basting
   Sliced Cinnamon Apple Garnish (see below)

Preheat oven to 325°.

Wash duckling and dry with paper towels. Set aside. Mix softened butter with salt, pepper, and ground coriander, and rub all over duckling. Fill cavity of bird with the quartered unpeeled potatoes. Fasten the neck skin of the duckling to the back with skewers. Place duckling breast side up on rack in roaster. Pour 2 cups of water in bottom of roaster.

Roast in oven, covered, pricking skin with fork and brushing occasionally with the melted butter, about 2½ hours or a little more. Uncover after 2 hours and allow to roast last 30 minutes uncovered so duckling will brown evenly. If it becomes too brown, place a piece of aluminum foil lightly over the breast. Duckling is done when drumstick meat feels soft.

Remove duckling to cutting board and allow to rest 10 minutes. Remove potatoes before carving; I never use them—too greasy.

Pour off juices and place them in refrigerator to coagulate the fat. While juices are chilling, add 1 cup of water to roaster and scrape vigorously to release tasty particles that you will add to the sauce. Strain and taste (it must not taste scorched).

Now skim the chilled duck fat off the pan juices (save it if you might have a use for it in another dish). In a saucepan, dilute the pan juices with the pan scrapings, and thicken with 1 teaspoon cornstarch mixed with ¼ cup cold water. Boil until thick and season with ½ teaspoon dry tarragon leaves. Serve in gravy boat.

SLICED CINNAMON APPLE GARNISH
2 apples
½ cup sugar
½ teaspoon ground cinnamon

Halve the unpeeled apples, core, and slice thin. Parboil in ½ cup water until soft. Add sugar and cinnamon and allow to boil 1 full minute. Serve in a sauceboat as a sweet garnish for the duckling. Both flavors are great, the tarragon gravy and the apple slices.

Note: If you are an expert carver, by all means carve at table. I usually take the bird to the dining room already cut into serving pieces, the breast thinly sliced, and all presented on a heated platter.

———⊙———

ROAST GOOSE WITH CHERRY SAUCE
Ganzo al Horno con Salsa de Cerezas
———⊙———

6 servings

1 10- to 14-pound goose
Salt and pepper
1 lemon, cut in half and seeded
2 unpeeled large potatoes, cut into quarters
Sweet and Sour Cherry Sauce (see below)

Wash the goose and dry with paper towels. Rub the inside with the lemon halves. Rub the goose well with salt and pepper, fill the cavity with potato pieces, and truss. Place goose on a rack in a roasting pan and cover it with foil. Roast in a 375° oven about 2½ hours. Remove the foil after 2 hours and prick the skin of the goose with an ice pick to release the hot grease. Pour off the fat from the pan and reserve. Cover the goose again and continue cooking 30 minutes. Check once more. Remove cover and cook 15 or 20 minutes longer until skin is brown and crisp. I like to moisten a small piece of an old napkin in soy sauce and honey at this point and pat the goose with it. This renders the skin crisp and shiny and also imparts the perfect amount of saltiness—¼ cup of honey with 2 tablespoons of soy sauce is about right.

Serve the goose with the fabulous cherry sauce, and perhaps baked potatoes or a rice casserole and a spinach salad.

SWEET AND SOUR CHERRY SAUCE
About 3 cups

- 1 cup granulated sugar
- 1 cup water
- ¼ cup vinegar
- ½ teaspoon salt
- ½ teaspoon dry tarragon leaves (optional)
- 1 cup juice from cherries
- 2 teaspoons cornstarch dissolved in ¼ cup cold water
- 1 16-ounce can pitted sour cherries or dark sweet cherries

Caramelize sugar in a large skillet, stirring constantly. When a deep caramel color add the cup of water all at once. Melted sugar will puff up scandalously. Never you mind, just keep stirring and lifting up the big bubble the syrup turned into. You must cook, stirring occasionally, until all of the sugar is dissolved. Add the vinegar and salt and boil 2 minutes more. Now add half of the reserved liquid from the canned cherries and taste for tartness. When the taste suits you, add the cornstarch with the cold water. Boil 2 minutes, stirring often, and add the drained cherries. Lower heat and allow to simmer for 5 minutes. Flavors will meld and the liquid should thicken slightly. If you feel it is too thick, add the remaining ½ cup of juice.

This sauce keeps beautifully for a week or two in the refrigerator and freezes practically forever.

Note: I have specified that the tarragon is optional. Suit yourself, but it imparts a flavor all its own. If you decide to use it, stir it in with the vinegar and salt.

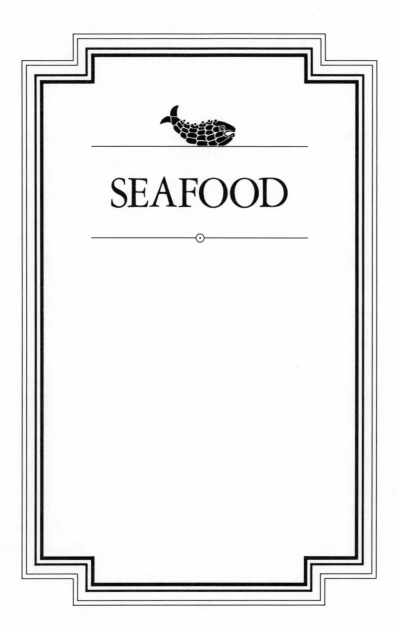

SEAFOOD

To one unfamiliar with Mexican food, the great variety of seafood dishes is a pleasant surprise. States situated on Mexico's extensive coastline and cities on its many rivers and lakes boast both very sophisticated preparations and some amazingly simple (and amazingly good) ones. For instance, a great favorite at Puerto Vallarta is freshly caught fish speared on a rough bamboo stick and charcoal-broiled on the beach. What a delight!

Picturesque Patzcuaro in the state of Michoacan is well known for its butterfly fishermen—the large "wings" dipping first on one side of the boat and then the other. The catch is their famed white fish, scaleless and buttery. This fish is usually simply prepared, broiled or pan-fried and served with fresh cut limes. The same succulent fish is also available in Lake Chapala, a retirement community near Guadalajara, Jalisco. But in the Chapala Beer Garden where every Sunday afternoon is fiesta time and whole families gather to eat to the strains of mariachi music, a new twist is added: The roe is sautéed with scallions and chile and served as an appetizer with tasty salsas and tiny, fresh-from-the-griddle corn tortillas. A flavor never to be forgotten and often to yearn for.

In addition to preserving traditional seafood recipes such as Fish Fillets Veracruz Style, Mexican housewives and restaurants are becoming adventuresome in their fish cookery. In recent years, the Mexican government has been heavily promoting the use of seafood over the radio and via pamphlets containing nutritional information and imaginative recipes. These booklets are generally distributed in Conasupo stores, grocery stores set up for government employees, and through schools and universities. Mexican housewives are becoming more aware of the importance of nutritionally balanced meals, and fish is in much demand. Imaginations are soaring and recipes are being born—with a Mexican flavor, of course.

FOIL-GRILLED FISH FILLETS
Pescado Enpapelado a la Brasa

This recipe calls for olive oil, but for weight-watchers I would suggest that you marinate the fish fillets in a Court Bouillon containing bottled clam juice, a small amount of vinegar, some dry sherry, and salt and pepper in small amounts. Now proceed with the recipe instructions and you will enjoy a delightful morsel, satisfying and low in calories.

4 servings

  Salt and pepper
4 fish fillets (sole, scrod, or cod) at least ½-inch thick, skinned
½ cup olive oil or Court Bouillon (page 170)
1 teaspoon finely mashed garlic
  Sauce (see below)

Salt and pepper the fish fillets generously and marinate them in oil combined with mashed garlic for 5 to 10 minutes.

While fish fillets are marinating, mix sauce ingredients.

Cut 4 pieces of heavy aluminum foil into 12 × 12-inch squares. Remove fish from marinade and place each fillet on a foil square. Use fish fillet to brush some marinade on the foil. Spoon enough sauce on each fillet to cover generously. If you wish, add 1 slice of chile to each fillet.

Wrap the fish in the foil squares and close the edges to seal tightly. Use any system you prefer; I like an envelope type of seal, but you suit yourself.

I use my oven broiler and I place the fish packages about 3 inches from the heat source. Do not overcook; grill 12 to 15 minutes and test if you're not too sure. (If you are using a barbecue grill, the fish packages should be about 4 or 5 inches from the source of heat.)

Unfold or cut the foil and serve, spooning any remaining sauce on fillets. Serve with freshly cut lime wedges.

SAUCE
2 cups chopped ripe tomatoes, peel left on.
1 cup green onions or scallions cut into ½-inch pieces
2 fresh serrano chiles or 1 large fresh green jalapeño, sliced
1 cup fresh cilantro leaves (no stems)
  Salt

BAKED FISH FILLETS
Filetes de Pescado al Horno

———⊙———

6 servings

2 pounds choice fish fillets (cod, scrod, or best of all, red snapper)
Juice of a green lime
Salt and pepper
½ cup vegetable oil
1 teaspoon mashed garlic

Marinate fish fillets in lime juice with salt and pepper for 15 minutes or more. Drain. Butter a 9 × 15-inch baking dish.

Dip marinated fish fillets in oil mixed with garlic. Arrange in buttered baking dish. Cover with a sheet of heavy aluminum foil and bake 15 minutes in a 350° oven.

Serve with tartar sauce and boiled parsleyed potatoes. A sliced zucchini salad would be terrific garnished with a few strips of pickled red jalapeño chiles.

———⊙———

BAKED FISH FILLETS SMOTHERED WITH VEGETABLES
Filetes de Pescado al Horno con Verduras

————⊙————

6 to 8 servings

2 pounds fish fillets (cod, scrod, red snapper, or other fish of your choice)
　Juice of one lemon
1 teaspoon mashed garlic
　Salt and pepper
　Crushed oregano
1 10-ounce package frozen peas and carrots
1 10-ounce package frozen cut green beans
1 cup sliced zucchini
½ cup melted butter
½ teaspoon ground cumin
　Vegetable oil

Marinate fish fillets in mixture of lemon juice, garlic, and salt and pepper for 15 minutes. Sprinkle crushed oregano leaves on top.

Cook frozen vegetables according to package instructions, and blanch zucchini slices. Drain and set aside. Mix all vegetables and fold in melted butter mixed with cumin. Set aside.

Butter a 9 × 13-inch Pyrex baking pan lavishly. Arrange fish fillets in bottom of pan. Dribble a few drops of oil on each fillet. Smother with buttered vegetables and bake in a 350° oven for 15 to 20 minutes. Test fish for doneness.

Serve from the baking dish and be generous with the pan juices.

Note: If possible undercook frozen vegetables so that they won't be overcooked when you take them out of the oven. It is also preferable to undercook the fish.

————⊙————

RANCH-STYLE FISH FILLETS
Pescado a la Ranchera

————⊙————

If unexpected guests arrive, you can stretch this dish by adding 1 large potato, peeled and cubed, and one small can drained peas and carrots to the sauce.

————⊙————

4 servings

    1 pound fish fillets (use any fresh, seasonal fish)
    2 cups Court Bouillon (see below)
      Sauce (see below)

Prepare Court Bouillon. Prepare sauce.

Poach fish in Court Bouillon for 3 minutes, and allow it to cool in the broth. Drain and break fish up into bite-sized pieces.

Arrange fish in baking dish and cover with sauce. Bake in moderate (350°) oven for 10 minutes, or heat on top of the stove. Serve over buttered steamed rice.

COURT BOUILLON
1 quart water
1 teaspoon salt
½ teaspoon peppercorns
2 bay leaves

SAUCE
½ cup chopped white onion
2 tablespoons oil
1 pound ripe tomatoes, peeled and chopped
1 fresh small green chile, seeded and chopped
Salt and pepper
½ teaspoon ground cumin, or more
1 teaspoon mashed garlic

In medium-sized saucepan, sauté onion in oil 1 minute and add tomatoes and chopped chile. Thin with ½ to 1 cup Court Bouillon. Season with salt and pepper, cumin, and mashed garlic. Simmer a minute or two and pour over fish.

LIGHT FISH FILLETS VERACRUZ STYLE
Pescado a la Veracruzana sin Grasa

———⊙———

Lovely Veracruz is tropical for the most part, marvelous for tourists though most of the accommodations are modest. But the tourist who does not require elegance will find some of the best seafood restaurants in Mexico. And, incidentally, the best coffee in Mexico —served at an old cafe called the Parish.

———⊙———

6 servings

    1½ pounds red snapper fillets
    1 quart Court Bouillon, (page 170) (or add 2 cups water
       to a small bottle of clam juice)
    Sauce (see below)

Prepare Court Bouillon. Prepare sauce.

Poach the fish fillets in the court bouillon or bottled clam juice and water for 2 minutes.

Smear bottom and sides of a 9 × 13-inch Pyrex baking dish with 1 teaspoon olive oil. Arrange poached fish fillets in pan. Cover with sauce and bake 10 minutes in a preheated 350° oven. Garnish with fresh lime slices.

SAUCE

    1 cup half-slices white onion
    Salt
    ½ teaspoon fresh ground pepper
    3 large ripe tomatoes, peeled and chopped
    1 4-ounce jar chopped pimientos
10 or 12 canned jalapeño chile strips
    1 bay leaf

Boil onion slices in half a cup of Court Bouillon in a large saucepan. Add salt to taste, and pepper. Stir in chopped tomatoes, pimientos, jalapeño strips, and bay leaf, and correct seasoning. Cook, covered, stirring often. (Note the absence of oil or butter.)

———⊙———

FISH FILLETS IN GARLIC SAUCE
Filetes de Pescado al Mojo de Ajo

————⊙————

For many people Mojo de Ajo, the Spanish name for garlic sauce, is an acquired taste. In Mexican restaurants it is often served in a side dish so that you can help yourself according to your garlic threshold. I for one am addicted to garlic in any size, shape, or form. Try it made this way but do not continue to cook once it has reached the degree of doneness you want, as it will continue to get darker and become somewhat bitter. Its origin is truly Spanish but it has been very popular in Mexico for many years.

————⊙————

4 servings

1 pound white fish fillets, such as haddock or sole
Juice of half a lemon
Salt and pepper
8 tablespoons margarine or butter
    mixed with 2 tablespoons vegetable oil
3 or 4 large garlic cloves, thinly sliced
¼ cup vegetable oil
¼ cup flour

Marinate fillets in lemon juice and sprinkle with salt and pepper to taste. Let stand while you prepare the garlic butter.

Heat butter or margarine and oil in a small skillet but do not allow to smoke or burn. Stir in the thinly sliced garlic over very low heat and keep stirring and watching over it carefully as garlic scorches easily. When it is a lovely light golden color remove from stove and immediately pour into a small sauceboat that can be kept warm.

Heat ¼ cup oil in a large skillet but do not let it smoke. Remove fish from marinade and roll in flour. Sauté in hot oil until fish flakes easily when tested with a fork, 7 to 10 minutes depending on the thickness of the fillets. Turn once only.

Divide fish into 4 serving portions and serve topped with the garlic butter. Good with steamed buttered small potatoes topped with parsley and a watercress salad enhanced with a few pine nuts and some Maggi sauce in the vinaigrette dressing. Or these fillets go beautifully with noodles or pasta cooked in your own special way.

FRIED FISH FILLETS
Filetes de Pescado (Empanizados)
———⊙———

6 servings

2 pounds fish fillets (sole if you feel extravagant,
  or any other firm-fleshed fish of your choice)
Juice of 1 lemon
Salt and pepper
½ cup seasoned flour
½ cup oil

Marinate fish fillets in strained lemon juice. Drain and add salt and pepper.
  Place fish in paper sack with seasoned flour and shake to coat.
  Pan-fry in large skillet in hot oil. Turn only once. Do not overcook. Fish
must be tender and juicy. Serve immediately.

———⊙———

RED SNAPPER VERACRUZ
Huachinango a la Veracruzana

————⊙————

Where did I taste Veracruz-style fish first? I believe it must have been during the time that a maternal grand-uncle of mine was collector of customs in the port of Veracruz. I remember that he had an excellent cook whose name was Ruperta. I would stand around the stove while she was cooking because the fact that she broiled everything on a clay griddle fascinated me. She would get all the fresh ingredients, onions, garlic cloves, tomatillos or tomatoes, and the fresh or dried peppers to be used and put them on the clay griddle, turning them as needed, never scorching them, and getting them all done in relays. Then she would sometimes peel and sometimes not and start mashing them and blending them in a *molcajete,* a gadget I had never used. She always cooked with pure pork lard and seasoned gloriously. She made this dish without the stuffed olives and the capers, adding potatoes to the sauce. It was always served with white rice on the side.

————⊙————

8 servings

Enough oil to sauté fish
2 pounds red snapper fillets or white fish fillets
Salt
Pepper
4 tablespoons vegetable oil
1 medium onion, thinly sliced in half-slices
1½ pounds red ripe tomatoes, peeled and finely chopped
1 cup water
8 or 10 peppercorns
2 bay leaves
2 garlic cloves finely mashed
About 2 pickled green jalapeño strips per person as garnish (optional)

Heat oil in large skillet and sauté the fillets after salting and peppering them lightly. Turn once only and do not overcook. Lay fillets in large oblong ovenproof dish and set aside.

In a large saucepan heat 4 tablespoons oil until hot but not smoking and sauté the sliced onion 1 minute, until limp but not brown, stirring constantly. Add peeled chopped tomatoes and water, season with salt, and add the peppercorns, the bay leaves, and finally the mashed garlic. Cook, covered, over medium heat 5 minutes.

Pour sauce over fish fillets and seal dish in foil. Heat a few minutes in a moderate oven before serving.

If you wish to splurge add 10 or 12 stuffed green olives to the fish and, even more daring, a few drained and rinsed capers. However if you don't have these on hand, add ½ to 1 cup frozen peas and carrots (cooked according to directions on package and drained well) and one cooked potato cut in thick slices and parboiled in salted water.

RED SNAPPER IN POBLANO CHILE CREAM SAUCE
Huachinango en Crema de Chile Poblano

———⊙———

It is well to note that poblano chiles are treacherous. You might pick a winner (a mild one, that is) and on the other hand, you might get a fiery one. So, a word of advice. Buy more than two or three, even though they may be expensive, because you should smell and try to taste them with the tip of your tongue. If you are daring you will go ahead with the fiery one, because the sauce will be great. Another word of warning: The milk may curdle. I always purée the chiles with one small can of evaporated milk, and you may prefer to do that, too, to be on the safe side.

———⊙———

6 to 8 servings

2 to 2½ pounds red snapper (whole fish or fillets)
      Salt and pepper
    2 tablespoons fresh lime juice
    1 large or 2 medium poblano chiles, tops cut off & seeded
   ½ cup chopped onion
    2 garlic cloves, peeled
    1 cup milk
    4 tablespoons butter plus 1 tablespoon vegetable oil
    1 cup sour cream

Prepare fish by sprinkling with salt and pepper and the lime juice. Set aside while preparing sauce.

In a blender, purée poblano pepper cut up in thick slices, seeds and all, the chopped onion, and the garlic cloves with the milk.

In large saucepan melt the butter and oil and strain the blended mixture into it. Cook, stirring constantly, over medium heat until sauce begins to thicken, about 3 minutes. Season with salt and pepper and blend in the sour cream.

Place whole fish or fish fillets in a baking dish large enough so that you will not crowd the whole fish or the fillets. Pour the sauce over fish and bake in a 350° oven, 20 minutes for whole fish, or 10 to 12 minutes for fillets. Serve with steamed rice and a crisp green salad.

Note: If using one large whole fish, poach it 5 minutes in boiling Court Bouillon before baking.

RED SNAPPER HASH
Salpicon de Huachinango

————⊙————

I started poaching fish a few years ago. I discovered this saved time, kept the fish from drying out, and facilitated the task of removing the skin and bones.

I first tasted Red Snapper Hash in Tampico. Feeling that my taste buds were at their peak, I told my hostess that I thought I could enumerate the ingredients that went into making that tasty dish. I started out and did beautifully but I kept insisting that there was a spice missing. She said no, that I had the recipe flavors down pat. We were staying at the former Holiday Inn and had asked her to come to breakfast the next morning. As she sat down at the table she said, "You were right, there was one ingredient missing. It was cumin, but ground cumin, and don't use it from a shaker or can that has been sitting too long on the shelf." Get ground cumin in small packages. The stale spice loses its aroma and pungent flavor.

This is one of my seafood favorites and may be made with any white fish also. Just as tasty and much more economical!

————⊙————

About 12 appetizers

Court Bouillon made with 2 cups water, salt, peppercorns, and a bay leaf
1 pound of red snapper fillets, to make 2 cups shredded fish
⅛ cup oil
½ cup finely chopped green onions
1 cup chopped ripe tomatoes
Salt and pepper
1 green serrano chile, sliced
1 tablespoon finely mashed garlic
8 tablespoons softened butter
½ teaspoon cumin
¼ teaspoon ground cloves
Canela (if not available, omit—do not use cinnamon)

In a large saucepan bring Court Bouillon ingredients to the boil. Poach fish fillets 5 minutes. Drain, remove skin, and shred.

Heat the oil in a large skillet and sauté the chopped green onions with the chopped tomatoes, adding salt and pepper to taste. Do not allow to brown. Add shredded fish and stir well over low heat. Push the chile slices into the mixture. Cover and remove from heat.

Mix garlic with softened butter. Over medium heat, cook half of this mixture in a large skillet; do not brown. When bubbly spoon in the snapper mixture, and push it down into the butter with the back of a large spoon. The idea is to lightly brown the shredded fish to resemble hash. While cooking, sprinkle with the cumin, the cloves, and the canela. (Use the canela sparingly.)

Heat the other half of the butter and garlic mixture in another skillet and flip the browned hash over into it to brown the top side. Take to the table in the skillet or serve in a round platter. Try not to disturb the hash circle. Serve with miniature flour tortillas and flavor with drops of fresh lime juice. If you wish, remove the chile slices. Did you count them?

———⊙———

TUNA VERACRUZ
Atun a la Veracruzana
———⊙———

6 servings

4 tablespoons oil (2 tablespoons salad oil and 2 tablespoons olive oil)
½ cup coarsely chopped onion
1 14½-ounce can Italian-style tomatoes, including their juice
4 garlic cloves, finely mashed
2 bay leaves
  Salt and pepper
1 potato, peeled and cubed
1 cup frozen peas and carrots
1 small zucchini, cut into thick slices and cubed
1 12½-ounce can oil-packed light tuna
¼ cup sliced stuffed green olives
1 2-ounce jar diced pimientos
10 or more canned pickled serrano chiles

Pour the oil mixture into large skillet and heat. Sauté chopped onion for 1 minute and then add the canned tomatoes, juice and all. They must be crushed by hand or potato masher; do not purée. Add garlic, bay leaves, and salt and pepper. Careful with the salt; remember canned tuna is salty. Cover and simmer over low heat for 10 minutes, stirring occasionally.

Blanch potato, peas and carrots, and zucchini separately in salted boiling water and then drain. Add to sauce and cook 5 minutes.

In an oblong baking dish that has a cover, spread out tuna, oil and all. (Best to use chunk light tuna and be sure to handle cautiously so that you can lift out the larger chunks without breaking them. They must give the impression that they are pieces of dry salt cod.) Place a few slices of stuffed green olives (or if you prefer use them whole) and a few pieces of the diced pimientos over the tuna and then smother with the sauce. Cover and bake until hot in a moderate oven. If you wish to splurge use more olives and more pimientos.

Garnish with the pickled seranno chiles, or you may use pickled jalapeños —whole, in slices, or in strips.

——————⊙——————

RANCH-STYLE SHRIMPS I
Camarones Rancheros I
——————⊙——————

Tampico, the principal port city of the state of Tamaulipas, is not too far from the Texas border city of Brownsville. They have a wonderful way of cooking seafood. After eating both versions of the Ranch-style Shrimp, I tested and tried to imitate the flavor and came up with this recipe. These shrimp are but one of the many appetizers served at the El Porvenir bar across the street from the cemetery. Their bar glasses have their motto stamped on them in red letters, something to the effect that "You rest better here than across the street."

——————⊙——————

4 servings

1 pound medium-sized shrimp, about 36
8 tablespoons butter
1 large garlic clove, finely mashed
  Salt and pepper
⅛ cup vegetable oil
1 cup thin half-slices onion
1 cup unpeeled finely chopped ripe tomatoes
¼ teaspoon ground cumin
  Slices of fresh jalapeño or serrano (optional)
4 sprigs cilantro

Wash the shrimp thoroughly. Shell and devein. Wash again and dry in paper towels. Stir-fry in the butter in a medium skillet, with the mashed garlic added, for 2 or 3 minutes. Add a little salt and pepper (careful if you are using salted butter). Set aside.

In a large skillet heat your oil and sauté the sliced onion. When it is limp add the chopped tomatoes, perhaps 3 or 4 tablespoons water, and season with salt and pepper to taste. Allow to cook over moderate heat, stirring occasionally. Correct seasoning, and add ground cumin and cilantro. Cook 3 minutes, covered. If sauce seems too dry, add a few more tablespoons water, or Court Bouillon if you have it on hand. Add the shrimp, stir well, and cover, but remove from heat. Let stand 5 minutes before serving.

Note: This dish should have one sliced hot chile added to the onion and tomato sauce; however this is optional. I usually count the slices of pepper, perhaps a serrano in thick slices or one or two slices of fresh green jalapeño, and later remove them before taking the dish to the table.

RANCH-STYLE SHRIMPS II
Camarones Rancheros II

4 servings

- 1 pound medium-sized shrimp, about 36
- 8 tablespoons butter
- 1 large garlic clove, finely mashed
- Salt and pepper
- ⅛ cup cooking oil
- 1 cup thin half-slices onion
- 2 cups finely chopped ripe tomatoes
- 1 teaspoon dry oregano leaves, crushed
- 1 green serrano chile or similar, cut into 5 slices

Wash the shrimp thoroughly. Shell and devein. Wash again and dry in paper towels. Stir-fry in the butter in a medium skillet, with the mashed garlic added, for 2 or 3 minutes. Add a little salt and pepper but be careful if you are using salted butter. Set aside.

In a large skillet heat your oil and sauté sliced onion, stirring constantly. When onion is limp, add the chopped tomatoes with perhaps 3 or 4 tablespoons water and season with salt and pepper to taste. Allow to cook over moderate heat, stirring occasionally, and correct seasoning before adding the crushed oregano. Cook 3 more minutes, covered, and add the shrimp and the chile slices.

Remove from heat and serve in the skillet or a heated serving dish. Remove the chile slices and save for the chile eaters. Serve with fresh lemon or lime slices and white rice.

---⊙---

BEACH PARTY SHRIMP SAUTÉ
Camarones en la Playa
---⊙---

6 to 8 servings

1 cup oil
2 pounds medium-sized shrimp, about 60
1 tablespoon salt
1 teaspoon coarse ground pepper
1 tablespoon crushed oregano leaves
1 cup thinly sliced white onion
1 tablespoon mashed garlic
2 fresh green jalapeños, sliced (seeds and all)
Juice of 2 lemons or 4 limes

In large pan or wok over a camp fire (if at the beach) heat oil. Add washed unshelled shrimps and stir-fry for 3 minutes. Add seasonings and remainder of ingredients. Just before serving add the freshly squeezed lemon or lime juice.

Note: This is also a great appetizer.

LAYERED SHRIMP AND ASPARAGUS CASSEROLE
Camarones y Esparragos

————⊙————

8 servings

2 pounds medium-sized shrimp, about 60
½ cup butter
¼ cup chopped onion
2 pounds fresh asparagus
1 cup White Sauce (see below)
1 4-ounce can pimientos
Salt
¼ teaspoon nutmeg
1 pound shredded longhorn cheese

Cook shrimp, cool, and peel. Sauté in butter with chopped onion.

Wash asparagus under running cold water and cut off tender tips. Reserve the stalks for soup. Cook tips in salted boiling water until crisp tender. Save some of the cooking liquid and set aside. Asparagus will be enough for 1 layer.

Prepare sauce.

Purée the canned pimientos with ½ cup asparagus broth. Season with salt and nutmeg. Add to cool white sauce.

To assemble: Arrange some shrimps in bottom of a generously buttered 9 × 13-inch dish. Cover shrimp with asparagus tips, then a handful or two of the shredded longhorn cheese. Cover with sauce, and add all the remaining shrimp. Top layer will be sauce and cheese. Bake in 350° oven for 15 minutes or until bubbly.

WHITE SAUCE
3 tablespoons butter
2 tablespoons flour
1 cup milk
Salt and white pepper

Melt butter and add flour. Cook, stirring often, for 1 minute. Do not allow flour to brown. Add the milk and cook until thick and smooth, stirring constantly. Season. If too thick, thin with 2 tablespoons of the reserved cool asparagus cooking liquid. Set aside to cool.

MEXICAN SCALLOPED OYSTERS
Ostiones con Crema al Horno

———⊙———

When I was a very small girl I thought the only way to eat oysters was from the half-shell. I was a grown-up young lady before I tasted fried oysters and scalloped oysters.

The truth of the matter is that I lived a considerable distance from any port. When my sisters and I were small tots we lived in a small town in Arizona with my grandmother and our servants and went to elementary school there. Our parents traveled to Mexico City often by train because during these years three presidents of Mexico came from our home state of Sonora and were very close to my grandfather. My grandfather belonged to two presidential cabinets at this time and at both inaugurations the presidential Pullmans were sent to the border to pick up members of my father's family.

So living that distance from the port of Guaymas, which was the nearest, meant that the oysters came to us in the shell in large gunny sacks—fresh, small, and with enough salt of their own so that you could actually eat them right from the shell without adding anything.

My father was a 100-oyster man. I remember I use to brag about this at school and no one would believe me, even when I mentioned that the oysters were very, very tiny. About ten or twelve years later I went to Guaymas to a Mardi Gras celebration as a young girl and found that I could eat fifty oysters and still ask for more. The oyster stalls along the waterfront were nothing fancy, just clean, and consisted of the oyster opener and the cashier. You ate right from the shell and were handed paper napkins to clean your chin. Best in the whole wide world, but New Orleans oysters run a close second! (By the way I now eat only one dozen, maybe two.)

———⊙———

4 servings

1 pint shelled oysters
2 cups medium-coarse cracker crumbs, freshly made
8 tablespoons melted butter
  Salt and pepper
1 cup heavy cream
2 tablespoons pickling liquid from a can of jalapeño chiles
8 strips canned red jalapeño chiles, rinsed and patted dry with paper
  towels (optional)

Drain oysters, reserving ⅓ cup of the liquid.

Combine crumbs and melted butter.

Use an 8-inch ovenproof pie pan suitable to take to the table, maybe about 1½ inches deep. Spread about ⅓ of the buttered cracker crumbs in the bottom of the pie pan, cover with half of the drained oysters, and sprinkle with salt and pepper (but go easy on the salt unless you are using unsalted crackers). Use another third of the crumbs and more oysters and then sprinkle with pepper.

Combine cream, reserved oyster liquid, salt, and jalapeño liquid. Pour over your oysters and top with the remaining third of the crumbs. If you want to be extravagant, dot with additional butter before baking. Garnish with jalapeño strips if you like. Bake in a preheated 350° oven for about 20 minutes or until done. This makes 4 servings but I usually double the recipe and use 2 pie pans. I like to bring this dish hot and bubbly to the table. Serve with lime wedges.

OYSTERS AMADA
Ostiones Amadita, Estilo Sinaloa

———⊙———

Oysters Amada was a cherished family recipe. A much loved foster aunt of mine passed it on to her daughters and they in turn gave it to me. It is a gala dish and in the state of Sinaloa, where oysters are plentiful, was probably used on all holidays and festive occasions.

———⊙———

4 servings as main course;
6 servings as appetizer

1 pint oysters (reserve some of the juice)
2 tablespoons vegetable oil
3 tablespoons finely minced green onions
1 cup peeled chopped ripe tomatoes
1 garlic clove, finely mashed
½ teaspoon crushed oregano leaves
Salt and pepper
½ cup fresh cracker crumbs
¼ cup hot vegetable oil

Pour oysters and juice into medium-sized saucepan and set over medium heat. Do not allow to boil, just heat until oysters curl. Drain and set aside.

In 2 tablespoons oil sauté onions until limp and add tomatoes, garlic, and oregano. Cook, stirring often, and add oyster liquid if necessary as sauce must not be too dry.

Place warm oysters in small baking dish and cover with the tomato sauce, then cover with fresh cracker crumbs.

Heat ¼ cup oil until it is sizzling. Spoon hot oil over cracker crumbs and bake in moderate oven until heated through. Serve with lemon slices. Do not overcook.

Note: Correct seasoning before layering ingredients. Be careful with the salt as the cracker crumbs tend to shed their salt into the sauce.

———⊙———

COLD MARINADE FOR FISH
Aderezo para Pescado

———☉———

About ½ cup

¼ cup fresh lemon juice or white vinegar
1 teaspoon salt
½ teaspoon white pepper
1 teaspoon finely mashed garlic

Mix all of the ingredients in a bowl and strain over the fish fillets to be marinated.

Note: White vinegar may be used in place of fresh lemon juice, but never substitute bottled lemon juice. It will completely distort the flavor of the marinade.

———☉———

THREE GARLIC SAUCES FOR FISH

———⊙———

These garlic sauces are much in evidence in Mexican home cooking as well as in authentic Mexican cafes and restaurants. You will very often find the phrase *al mojo de ajo* on a Mexican menu.

Garlic is sold in *ristras* during the peak of the garlic-harvesting season. They are beautifully braided and decorated with knick-knacks and colored ribbons—so pretty that you hate to cut into them. A *ristra* is a lovely gift, supposedly a good-luck charm. Believers say that lightning will not strike, your house will not burn, and all sorts of good things will happen if you keep a *ristra de ajos* in your kitchen.

———⊙———

I. GARLIC INFUSION
Mantequilla de Ajo

4 tablespoons unsalted butter
4 cloves garlic, crushed

Melt butter, add garlic and set aside.

Note: This is a garlic infusion and should be strained just before using, so that what is brushed onto the meat is actually a garlic-flavored butter.

II. GARLIC PASTE
Pasta de Ajo

6 tablespoons butter
2 tablespoons olive oil
6 cloves garlic, finely mashed

Melt butter with oil and add garlic. Cook over very low heat for 1 minute. Do not allow to brown. Brush on meat or fish before broiling.

III. GARLIC SLICES IN BUTTER
WITH HERBS
Mojo de Ajo con Hierbas Finas

10 garlic cloves
½ cup melted butter
3 tablespoons olive oil
Salt and white pepper
Finely chopped parsley or dried tarragon (optional)

Slice garlic cloves thinly. Melt the butter with the oil and add the sliced garlic cloves. Swirl the garlic around until it starts to change color and is slightly brown. Do not let the butter mixture burn. Stir in parsley or tarragon if you wish. Serve in sauceboat with fish fillets or shrimp.

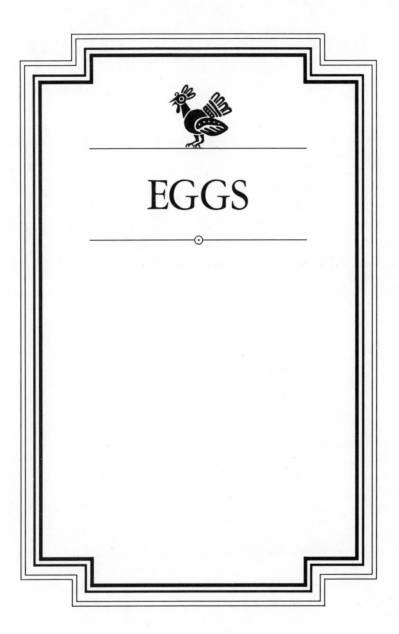

EGGS

O f all Mexican breakfast dishes, Huevos Rancheros (Ranch-style Eggs) have gained the most acceptance in the United States, and are served in thousands of restaurants across the country. Friends of mine crave them and enjoy even the facsimiles they sometimes get. The recipe is easy to make and the eggs are immensely satisfying. As a bonus, the ingredients are available almost everywhere.

Mexican breakfasts tend to be hearty. The customary lunch hour is from two to four in the afternoon and breakfast must sustain one until then. A typical breakfast menu might consist of Mexican Scrambled Eggs or Eggs with Mexican Sausage, Refried Beans, a slice of papaya, sweet bread, and coffee. (Start with papaya, of course.)

The Zucchini Omelet and the Potato Omelet are excellent brunch dishes and the potato omelet can even be served cold. Eggs with Green Beans can also be made with boiled cactus strips. This dish is served with Pico de Gallo Sauce and makes fine, light luncheon fare. It is traditional Lenten food.

Eggs are also often served for the lighter repasts of early evening. The noon meal in Mexico is more like dinner in the United States, perhaps consisting of even more courses. Obviously, then, the evening meal must be less hearty. I became very familiar with this in the state of Colima where I was invited as a guest teacher to offer a special advanced English course to an order of teaching nuns in a convent there.

I was given the royal treatment. Being housed with all these joyous young women, anxious to learn more, gracious in their hospitality and exuding contentment and happiness, was a revelation. The first meal of the day was an early breakfast consisting of freshly squeezed orange juice, a chile and corn tortilla casserole with either a red or green chile sauce and a garnish of fresh crumbled homemade cheese, and refried beans on the side. And always fruit, fruit, fruit. Sweet rolls, coffee or frothy Mexican hot chocolate, but *no eggs.* This astonished me until I was told that eggs were their standby for the evening meal. We had a heavy multicourse meal in midafternoon and then returned to our work. At eight in the evening we were called to the *merienda,* rather like British tea. We could have eggs prepared any way we pleased. The nuns obtained their eggs from a small farm they owned outside the city, so every egg was supremely fresh. I will never forget those *meriendas,* or those eggs.

MEXICAN SCRAMBLED EGGS I
Huevos a la Mexicana I

————⊙————

This recipe is a bit more substantial than the following one because it contains the fried tortilla strips. Somehow this marriage of the corn flavor with the eggs is unusually delicious—they just seem to go together. This is also a great way to use up leftover tortillas. I like to slice the chiles into a little thicker than usual slices because they tend to be hot and you may wish to remove them later. All you are looking for is flavor. Just that short time they were in the skillet with the other ingredients makes the difference and leaves a special taste in the eggs and tortilla strips.

————⊙————

4 servings

4 tablespoons vegetable oil
4 corn tortillas cut into strips with kitchen shears
4 eggs
1 cup shredded mozzarella cheese
¼ cup chopped onion
1 ripe tomato, peeled and chopped (if large, use only half)
½ 4-ounce can chopped green chiles
   Salt and pepper
1 fresh jalapeño chile, sliced (optional)

Heat oil in large skillet and sauté tortilla strips, stirring constantly; but do not allow to brown or turn crisp. Strips must remain soft and well coated with hot oil.

Beat eggs in bowl and add shredded cheese.

Add chopped onion and tomato to sautéed tortilla strips, stir-fry for a few seconds, and fold in chopped chiles. Pour in beaten eggs, season, and proceed as for scrambled eggs. Cook until done and serve with a tomato sauce similar to the topping on Chiles Rellenos.

————⊙————

MEXICAN SCRAMBLED EGGS II
Huevos a la Mexicana II
———⊙———

4 servings

4 tablespoons oil
¼ cup chopped green onion
½ cup chopped tomato
1 green serrano or jalapeño chile cut into thick slices
4 eggs, slightly beaten with salt added to taste

Heat oil in large skillet and sauté onion, tomato, and chile slices. Stir-fry 1 minute and pour in beaten eggs. Stir until set. Serve with garlic toast and Refried Beans, or with warmed fresh French rolls the Mexico City way.

Note: I like to cut the green chile into thick slices because it is easy to remove if you find the eggs too pungent.

———⊙———

MEXICAN SCRAMBLED EGGS III
Huevos a la Mexicana III
———⊙———

4 servings

6 tablespoons salad oil
4 corn tortillas, cut into small thin strips
½ cup chopped tomato
¼ cup chopped white onion
1 small green chile, seeded and chopped
4 eggs, beaten with salt until frothy

Heat half of the oil and sauté the tortilla strips. Drain.

Heat remaining oil in skillet and stir-fry the chopped tomato, onion, and green chile 30 seconds. Put tortilla strips back into the skillet.

Pour beaten eggs into the skillet over other ingredients and cook, stirring often, until mixture sets. Serve in warm plates with Refried Beans (page 236) and garlic toast.

RANCH-STYLE EGGS I
Huevos Rancheros I

———☉———

It is said that anything cooked up and served with a tomato, onions, and chile combination would be called ranchero style. I would think that it would be farm style, because there is many a ranch hidden away in the mountains of northern Mexico that does not have much fresh produce on the premises. Fresh tomatoes, fresh chiles, and salad makings are not always available.

Try both this and the following recipe—they are both very good. And then try the recipe called Ranch-style Eggs Another Way because this utilizes the same ingredients in a different fashion.

———☉———

6 servings

6 corn tortillas
6 tablespoons oil
6 eggs
¼ cup melted butter
2 cups heated Green Chile and
    Tomato Sauce (see below)

Basically all huevos rancheros recipes start the same. Fry the corn tortillas in the hot oil for 30 seconds or less. (The idea is to heat and soften the tortillas and flavor them with the hot oil). Drain tortillas on paper towels to get rid of the surplus oil, and immediately place on warm plates. Reserve the oil.

Gently fry the eggs, one at a time, in the melted butter. Place a fried tortilla on each warmed plate. Arrange a butter-fried egg on top and cover with the hot Green Chile and Tomato Sauce. Serve immediately.

GREEN CHILE AND TOMATO SAUCE
2 tablespoons oil that you fried the tortillas in
½ cup chopped onion
1 16-ounce can whole peeled tomatoes
1 fresh jalapeño chile, stemmed, seeded, and sliced thin
  Salt

Heat oil and sauté onion, stirring constantly, for 1 minute. Do not allow to brown. Chop tomatoes in blender. Do not allow to purée. Add to onion and stir in chile slices. Add salt and cook about 3 minutes until flavors meld. Remove from heat but keep warm, or heat up later to serve over the fried eggs. This sauce freezes well. Have some on hand always.

RANCH-STYLE EGGS II
Huevos Rancheros II

6 servings

2 cups canned Italian-style crushed tomatoes
1 teaspoon mashed garlic
1 (or perhaps 2) small dried red jap or arbol chile
6 tablespoons oil
½ cup sliced onion
   Salt
½ teaspoon crushed oregano leaves
6 tortillas
6 eggs
   Butter for frying eggs

Make sauce first. Place canned tomatoes, garlic, and dried red chile(s) in blender container. Purée until smooth and creamy.

Heat 2 tablespoons oil in medium saucepan and stir-fry the onion slices for 1 minute. Strain puréed sauce into the saucepan with the partially cooked onion slices. Season with salt and crushed oregano. Cook over medium heat for 3 minutes. Keep at a simmer until ready to use.

Have warm plates ready. Fry tortillas in remaining 4 tablespoons oil in medium skillet. Drain and place one on each plate.

Fry eggs in butter, one at a time.

Place an egg on each tortilla and cover with prepared sauce.

MILD RANCH-STYLE EGGS
Huevos Rancheros sin Chile

————⊙————

Wonderful for the children, and for adults who are not allowed chile in their food. It has the Mexican feeling without the pitfalls of hot sauces! Serve with Refried Beans.

————⊙————

4 servings

4 corn tortillas
6 tablespoons salad oil
¼ cup melted butter
4 eggs
1 cup tomato sauce (use recipe for
    sauce topping for Chiles Rellenos,
    page 308–9)

Have warm plates ready.

Fry tortillas in hot oil and drain on paper towels. Arrange one in each plate.

Heat sauce.

Heat butter in a small skillet and fry eggs, one at a time.

Place one egg carefully on each fried tortilla and spoon heated sauce over it.

Note: Even though the eggs are presented on tortillas, they are served with buttered toast at many Mexican cafes. If you would like to see a bit of green peeking through the red sauce, chopped bell pepper will do very well.

————⊙————

RANCH-STYLE EGGS ANOTHER WAY
Huevos Rancheros Sencillos

———⊙———

To some people (some of the members of my family included) the only way to eat an egg is scrambled. So I always fix Huevos Rancheros the classical way, and then do this dish the "scrambled way" for others, myself included. It is excellent as a brunch or luncheon dish with a breakfast meat added. Serve with Guacamole and corn chips and hot garlic toast sprinkled with Mexican paprika.

———⊙———

4 servings

4 corn tortillas
6 tablespoons oil
4 eggs
Salt and pepper
1 cup heated Chiles Rellenos Sauce, (page 303–4)
Half a jalapeño chile, seeded and chopped

Cut corn tortillas into strips with kitchen shears and sauté in 3 tablespoons oil until soft, not crisp.

Beat eggs until frothy and add salt and pepper to taste. Now pour eggs into skillet over the fried tortilla strips. Cook, stirring occasionally, until set. Have a medium-sized platter warmed and ready. Arrange egg and tortilla mixture in platter and pour heated sauce over mixture. Sprinkle with chopped green chile.

———⊙———

EGGS AND BLACK BEANS
Huevos con Frijoles Negros

————☉————

I have included this recipe because it's such an extra special combination. I still have to get used to black beans. In central Mexico and all the way south to the Guatemala border, black beans are the beans that are cooked almost daily in Mexican homes, no matter what the social or financial status is. They are just as tasty as pinto beans or pink beans, the beans more commonly used in my native area of northern Mexico.

————☉————

4 servings

4 slices French or sourdough bread or a split French roll
½ cup oil
4 eggs, poached
  Bean Purée (see below)
  Sour cream
  Mexican paprika
1 can pickled serrano chiles

Prepare Bean Purée first.

Deep-fry bread slices in oil. Drain on paper towels.

Place one poached egg on each slice of fried bread. Cover with Black Bean Purée. Garnish with a dollop of sour cream and sprinkle Mexican paprika on cream for taste and color.

Open up a can of pickled serrano chiles and serve juice and all in a sauce boat.

BEAN PURÉE
1 cup cooked black beans
¼ cup broth beans were cooked in
2 tablespoons oil
¼ cup chopped white onion
½ cup chopped tomato
  Salt and pepper

Purée cooked black beans in blender with about ¼ cup of own cooking broth. Heat 2 tablespoons oil in small saucepan and sauté chopped onion and tomato. Add salt and pepper to taste and stir in bean purée. Cook over low heat about 10 minutes, stirring often as beans tend to stick to bottom of pan.

EGGS AND SPINACH
Huevos con Espinacas

————⊙————

I like this vegetable and egg combination but somehow I fancy the creamed spinach spread evenly on the bottom of the baking dish and the eggs on top, then garnished with the cheese mixture!

————⊙————

4 servings

1 10-ounce package frozen chopped spinach
4 tablespoons butter
2 tablespoons heavy cream
¼ teaspoon nutmeg
4 eggs
   Butter for frying eggs
1 cup shredded mozzarella cheese mixed with
   2 tablespoons Parmesan cheese

Cook spinach in salted water according to package directions. Drain. Add the butter and cream and season with nutmeg.

Fry eggs in butter and arrange in a 2-quart baking dish. Cover eggs with the creamed spinach and sprinkle with the cheese mixture. Place under the broiler until cheese is melted.

Serve on buttered-toasted-English muffin halves.

————⊙————

EGGS WITH GREEN BEANS
Huevos con Ejotes

———⊙———

I tasted this combination of eggs and green beans about ten years ago in a bus depot restaurant—a regular stop for the bus that traveled between Mexico City and Juarez, Chihuahua, on the Texas border. I was on my way to San Luis Potosi to keep a teaching commitment. My car broke down and I went to the bus terminal to get on a bus traveling north.

It was around nine in the morning, way past my breakfast hour. The food was being served from a modern steam table and I served myself the scrambled eggs with these green bits barely showing. They asked if you wanted sauce on them (perfect fresh salsa with lots of cilantro) and you were offered hot corn tortillas or bread. I took the bread and, yes, the salsa, and glory be, what an encounter. Since then it has become one of my most often served egg dishes, but I serve it for lunch. (Oh yes, I went back for a second helping, this time with more salsa and hot corn tortillas—much better than bread!)

Prepare yourself for a delightful attack on your taste buds. Have enough eggs and green beans on hand, because you might have to fix a second batch.

———⊙———

6 servings

> 1 10-ounce package frozen cut green beans
> 6 tablespoons salad oil
> 6 eggs, beaten until frothy
>   Salt and pepper
> 2 cups Pico de Gallo fresh chile sauce (page 298)

Cook frozen green beans in salted water following package instructions. They must be crisp. Drain and cool. Set aside.

Heat oil in large skillet and stir-fry the beans 30 seconds.

Beat the eggs with salt and pepper, fold them into the beans, and cook mixture, stirring often, until set.

Serve in warm platter. Have a bowl of fresh Pico de Gallo sauce and fresh warm corn tortillas on the table.

———⊙———

SCRAMBLED EGGS WITH
A VEGETABLE MEDLEY
Revoltijo de Huevos con Verduras

———⊙———

This is ideal for vegetarians, near vegetarians, and as a Lenten dish.
But it is also wonderful served with some breakfast meat on the side.

———⊙———

6 servings

4 tablespoons oil
½ cup chopped green onion
1 cup chopped peeled tomatoes
½ cup cooked frozen peas
½ cup cooked frozen cut green beans
1 cold boiled potato, peeled and cubed
Salt and pepper
6 eggs
¼ cup melted butter
Mexican paprika

Heat 2 tablespoons oil in a dutch oven and stir-fry the onions and tomatoes
one minute. Add all the other vegetables. Season with salt and pepper.

Add remaining 2 tablespoons oil and stir in the beaten eggs. Cook as you
would scrambled eggs. Pour melted butter over all and sprinkle on some
Mexican paprika for flavor and color.

Note: Serve with garlic toast and a breakfast meat of your choice and pass a bowl
of freshly made Fresh Sauce (page 287).

———⊙———

EGGS WITH SHREDDED JERKY
Huevos con Machaca

———⊙———

A northern specialty, this is made from dehydrated meat strips or very thin cutlets. When I was a small girl, a cowboy looking for a job had to know many things before he was hired. Not least of these was how to butcher and how to cut meat into thin strips or cutlets so that they could be hung out in the sun to dry or dehydrate. The name for those strips of dried beef, so tasty and so good, is jerky. Baked in the oven, then soaked and shredded it becomes what is known as *machaca.* Try the recipe if you can find the ingredients. You will love it.

———⊙———

6 servings

4 tablespoons oil
1 cup shredded dry jerky
   (available in Mexican meat markets)
1 teaspoon mashed garlic
1 fresh serrano chile cut into thick slices,
   or half a sliced jalapeño chile
1 cup chopped tomatoes
¼ cup thin half-slices onion
6 eggs, slightly beaten

Heat oil and stir-fry the shredded meat in a large skillet over medium heat for about 1 minute. Add mashed garlic and stir often, pushing garlic into meat with the back of a large spoon. Add chile, tomatoes, and onion slices and keep cooking for 2 minutes, stirring often. If meat mixture is browning too fast, lower heat. Add beaten eggs and cook until set. Serve with flour tortillas and a fresh sauce of your choice.

Note: Shredded beef jerky is sold in Mexican meat markets in small 3- and 4-ounce sealed cellophane bags. Rather salty, so don't salt your egg mixture.

———⊙———

EGGS WITH MEXICAN SAUSAGE
Huevos con Chorizo

————⊙————

This recipe takes it for granted that you are using sausage links that you purchased in a supermarket. Fine! But I do hope that you will have read through my book and by this time you have already made some bulk Mexican sausage on your own. There is a world of difference. The homemade bulk sausage is infinitely better, so much so that I assure you that once you have tried it you will always have some of your very own either in the refrigerator or in the freezer.

————⊙————

6 servings

3 chorizo links or 1 cup homemade bulk sausage
5 tablespoons oil
6 eggs, beaten until frothy with a few grains of salt

Peel skin from sausage links and slice them. Cook in 2 tablespoons oil in a small skillet, stirring and pressing down with the back of a large spoon. This helps to crumble the chorizo and facilitates the draining of the fat later on. Cook over low heat, as the red chile powder in the sausage burns easily and turns your meat bitter. When cooked, drain and set aside in a small bowl.

In a larger skillet heat remaining 3 tablespoons of oil, stir in the beaten eggs and the reserved cooked chorizo and cook until eggs are set. Stir often to combine the eggs and sausage well.

Serve with flour tortillas by all means, and Refried Beans. If serving for lunch or brunch, then it would be well to add a crisp green salad with a mild vinegar and oil dressing. This is a glorious filling for burritos, too.

Note: Commercially sold chorizo is often very salty, so taste before adding salt to eggs.

————⊙————

EGGS WITH POTATOES AND MEXICAN SAUSAGE
Huevos con Papas y Chorizo

———⊙———

8 servings

2 Idaho potatoes
3 tablespoons vegetable oil
  Salt and pepper
1 cup cooked Mexican sausage
    (if in links, remove skins and mash first)
8 eggs

Peel the potatoes and slice them. Rinse and dry on paper towels. Heat a large nonstick skillet and add the oil. Add the potatoes and stir-fry for a minute or two, add salt and pepper, and cover. Cook, but stir occasionally. Brown on bottom side and turn over. Continue cooking about 1 minute. Remove from heat. Fold in the cooked Mexican sausage (chorizo).

Beat the eggs with a wire whisk. Pour the eggs over the mixture in skillet. Return to stove. Cook over high heat, stirring often. Serve when cooked to your taste.

Serve with toasted French rolls, split and buttered and placed under the broiler. Add some Refried Beans and a pungent fresh salsa for a more substantial breakfast or brunch. Also good for noon meal if you start with a tossed green salad.

Note of warning: Chorizo burns easily and the ground chile powder turns bitter. Always cook over mild heat, stirring constantly, and drain off all grease once it is cooked. Constant testing of recipes confirms my theory that the grease from chorizo is not suitable for cooking.

———⊙———

GOOD MORNING EGGS
Huevos "Buenos Dias"

————⊙————

I love this way of fixing eggs and think it's just as good if not better than the ever popular Huevos Rancheros. It is a lovely looking dish and very tasty, and even though it already has a corn tortilla on the bottom, and that should take care of the starch portion of the meal, I still like some buttered toast or a toasted flour tortilla on the side oozing with melted butter!

Whenever I fix this dish or any egg dish that might call for a corn tortilla base, I make the tortillas fresh—there is a great deal of difference between a day-old fried tortilla and a freshly made corn tortilla.

————⊙————

4 servings

1 cup Chiles Rellenos Quick Sauce, (page 320)
4 corn tortillas
6 tablespoons oil
4 eggs
  Butter
4 slices of Jack cheese or 8 tablespoons shredded mozzarella
  Jalapeño chile strips
1 ripe avocado, peeled and sliced

Prepare sauce and keep warm.

Deep-fry corn tortillas quickly in small skillet in small amount of oil. They must look glazed and be very soft. Drain on paper towels and place on warm plate. Reserve oil and refrigerate for future use.

Fry eggs in butter in small skillet.

Place one butter-fried egg on each fried tortilla, one to a plate. Cover each egg with a slice of Jack cheese or better still with 2 tablespoons of shredded mozzarella cheese. Spoon heated sauce on top of cheese and serve with a strip of canned jalapeño chile, Refried Beans (page 236), and avocado slices. Sliced avocado should be prepared just before serving and sprinkled with salt and a few drops of freshly squeezed lime juice.

————⊙————

BEAN-DIPPED TORTILLAS AND EGGS
Huevos Enfrijolados

————⊙————

This seems like an unusual combination indeed but I assure you that it is very good. That touch of cumin makes all the difference in the world.

————⊙————

4 servings

2 tablespoons pure pork lard
1 cup cooked beans
1 cup bean broth
  Salt
8 corn tortillas
6 tablespoons oil
½ cup chopped onion
1 cup chopped peeled tomatoes
1 4-ounce can chopped green chile
1 teaspoon ground cumin
4 eggs, beaten until frothy
  Butter
  Parmesan cheese, grated

Heat lard in medium saucepan and add beans. Cook for 1 minute and crush with back of spoon. Add bean broth gradually and stir often. Taste and season with a little salt. Cook over low heat 3 minutes. Mixture must be the consistency of a thick gravy.

Fry tortillas in hot oil. Drain on paper towels.

For sauce, heat 2 tablespoons oil in small saucepan and sauté chopped onion, chopped tomatoes, and canned chopped green chile. Season with salt and cumin.

Lightly scramble eggs in a small skillet in hot melted butter with a little salt added.

To assemble, spoon some scrambled eggs into each fried tortilla and top eggs with a teaspoon of sauce. Fold or roll and place in a small baking dish, folded side down. Cover with bean purée and sprinkle with grated Parmesan cheese. Heat in 350° oven for 5 minutes. Serve with extra sauce.

————⊙————

POTATO OMELET
Tortilla de Huevos con Papas
———⊙———

This is a modified version of the classic well-known Spanish omelet that always shows up on menus all over Spain and in many cities in Mexico.

———⊙———

4 servings

3 cups thinly sliced cooked potatoes
6 tablespoons oil
¼ cup chopped white onion
   Salt and pepper
4 eggs, beaten until frothy with 2 tablespoons evaporated milk or
   thick, fresh cream
4 tablespoons melted butter

Boil two large potatoes. Cool. Peel and slice as thin as possible.

Heat oil in large skillet. Fry the potatoes with the onion. Sprinkle with salt and pepper to taste. Pour in beaten egg mixture. Cover and cook over low heat for about 3 minutes.

Melt 4 tablespoons butter in another 10-inch skillet. Turn half-cooked omelet into buttered skillet and cook 1 minute. Loosen edges and serve cut in wedges.

Serve with a sauceboat filled with Spanish Sauce (page 300), and pass the garlic bread.

———⊙———

ZUCCHINI OMELET
Tortilla de Huevo con Calabacitas

———⊙———

6 servings

3 cups chopped raw unpeeled zucchini
6 tablespoons oil
½ cup chopped onions
1 cup peeled and finely chopped tomatoes
½ cup chopped fresh poblano or California green chile (canned will
     not do)
  Salt and pepper
6 eggs
2 tablespoons evaporated milk or heavy cream
1 tablespoon all-purpose flour
¼ teaspoon nutmeg
  Chopped parsley

Wash and chop zucchini. Cook in skillet with 2 tablespoons oil, adding onions, tomatoes, and chopped green chiles. Season with salt and pepper while cooking. Cover and simmer over low heat about 5 minutes. Set aside.

Beat eggs with milk or cream, flour, nutmeg, and salt and pepper to taste. Heat a 10-inch skillet and add 3 tablespoons oil. Pour in the beaten eggs and tilt pan to spread evenly. Reduce heat and cook slowly for 3 minutes. Flip over on another oiled hot skillet and cook 1 minute. Slide onto warm platter and fill one half with zucchini mixture. Fold over and sprinkle with chopped parsley leaves.

———⊙———

EGGS VINAIGRETTE
Huevos a la Vinagreta
———⊙———

6 servings

7 hard-boiled eggs
⅔ cup salad oil
⅓ cup vinegar
1 garlic clove, mashed
1 tablespoon finely chopped parsley leaves
2 tablespoons finely chopped onion
⅛ cup rinsed capers
¼ cup stuffed green olives, chopped
10 crisp lettuce leaves
10 ripe, firm, cherry tomatoes

Peel cold hard-boiled eggs and halve lengthwise. Cover and set aside, keeping one egg for sauce.

Scoop out yolk from reserved egg and mash it with a fork. Now whisk in the oil and vinegar. Add the garlic and parsley leaves and blend. Chop reserved egg white as fine as possible and stir into the vinaigrette, and lastly add the chopped onion, capers, and chopped olives. Place sauce in the refrigerator.

Line a chilled platter with lettuce leaves. Arrange egg halves on lettuce. Pour cold vinaigrette sauce over them and garnish platter with cherry tomatoes.

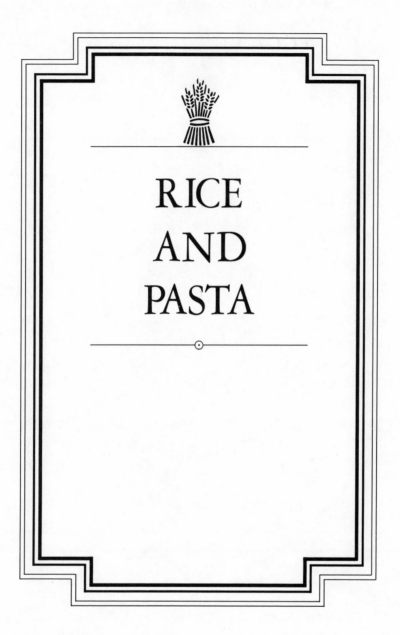

RICE
AND
PASTA

I t is a widely debated question how rice made its initial appearance in Mexico. Some historians credit the Spaniards with bringing it; others claim that it was introduced by the sailors who came on the Chinese merchant ship the *Nao* and had to remain in Mexico for months at a time while the ship was being loaded with supplies to return to China. Regardless of how it came to us, rice has become a staple of our diet.

Rice is featured in most merchant luncheon specials as a separate course after the soup and before the main course, and for this purpose it is usually prepared in the traditional Mexican Red Rice fashion (erroneously called Spanish Rice on some American menus). Rice is added to consommes but also to heartier vegetable soups. Housewives or their cooks do wonderful things with rice: They make casseroles with layers of kernel corn, sour cream, chile strips, and cheese; season it with puréed cilantro, romaine leaves, and poblano chiles; and mix it with mustard, which turns it yellow. Desserts and even beverages are made with rice—street vendors sell *horchata,* a refreshing drink made with rice water and canela sticks.

The pastas are easily traced to Italian immigrants who settled in Mexico and integrated their native cuisine with our repertoire. Many extremely poor people subsist on a diet of beans and pasta laced with a tasty salsa and sprinkled with cheese. The beans might boast a piece of pork rind (cuerito) or chorizo. All this is eaten with flour or corn tortillas and downed with copious amounts of cafe con leche, coffee with milk.

Speaking of pastas, some time ago I purchased a product that was new to me. The box read "substitute" linguine, no chemicals or preservatives had been added, and this additional note appeared on the box: "The word 'substitute' is used because our products contain the ingredient American jerusalem artichoke flour, which is not listed in the standards for macaroni products. . . . Our tubers are dehydrated into an artichoke powder that retains all of its natural ingredients." So the ingredients are semolina, soy flour, and jerusalem artichoke flour. The product? DeBole's Substitute Linguine. I know this is a strange insert in a Mexican cookbook, but I am so happy with this product that it is the only pasta I keep in my pantry.

MEXICAN RED RICE
Sopa de Arroz

————⊙————

Often inaccurately called Spanish rice on American restaurant menus, this is the old Mexican standby, fixed perhaps every other day in eighty percent of Mexican homes. It is an inexpensive dish and is good with some drained boiled beans stirred in. Serve this with good old-fashioned American fried chicken and hot corn tortillas spread with a little sour cream and freshly made salsa—the best combination you can find anywhere.

————⊙————

8 to 10 servings

¼ cup salad oil
2 cups long grain rice
4 cups chicken stock
3 garlic cloves, mashed
½ onion in thick slices
½ cup canned tomato sauce
Salt and pepper
1 cup frozen peas and carrots, parboiled in salted water 1 minute and drained

Heat the oil in a deep saucepan and sauté the rice until golden. Add chicken stock, garlic, onion, and tomato sauce. Season with salt and pepper. Bring to a boil; lower the heat, cover, and cook until almost all liquid has been absorbed. Uncover, fold in the peas and carrots carefully, cover again, and cook until all liquid has been absorbed.

Serve garnished with avocado slices and sliced ripe bananas.

————⊙————

GREEN RICE
Arroz Verde

————⊙————

This is one of my favorites. And I like it with any of the chile con carnes, be they green sauced or red. Green rice is handsome and awakens the taste buds on sight. If you bring it to the table with guacamole on the side and serve it with a platter of fried chicken and a bowl of fresh salsa and a salad you will have produced a fiesta menu with not too much effort. Try crisp corn chips instead of tortillas or bread.

————⊙————

4 to 6 servings

⅛ cup vegetable oil
1 cup rice
2 large poblano chiles, tops removed, seeded, and cut in fourths
1 cup fresh cilantro leaves
3 mashed garlic cloves
½ onion, sliced
2 tablespoons chicken bouillon granules
Salt and pepper
1 cup frozen peas and carrots
1 tablespoon butter

In a dutch oven with a tight-fitting lid, heat oil and sauté rice.

In blender purée chiles, cilantro leaves, garlic, and onion with 2 cups hot water. Strain over the sautéed rice. Add chicken bouillon granules and stir until dissolved. Add salt and pepper to taste. Cover and cook for 20 to 25 minutes until rice is tender.

In small saucepan cook frozen peas and carrots in slightly salted water for 1 minute. Drain. Add 1 tablespoon butter and garnish rice with them. Want more color? How about a few slices of canned pimientos?

Note: Should you feel that the poblano chiles you are using are too hot, look further for two milder ones. If you don't find a milder one, then use only one and perhaps add a drop or two of green food coloring to the blender mixture.

————⊙————

HOT GREEN RICE
Arroz Verde Picoso

————————☉————————

Cilantro is very special indeed. You can easily become addicted to the flavor, particularly when it is combined with hot green peppers and seasoned with salt and garlic. Be sure to use cilantro leaves only —no stems here. This recipe has the added touch of butter that plays down the pungency of the peppers. It is important that this rice dish be hot (picante) to serve with a blander dish like creamed cod or fish fillets or simply southern fried chicken.

————————☉————————

8 servings

6 poblano chiles, stems and seeds removed (if poblano chiles are not available, use 8 California peppers and add one fresh jalapeño)
1 cup chopped green onions (use both white and green part)
4 romaine lettuce leaves (outer leaves are greener)
2 cups cilantro leaves
4 cups water
    Salt and pepper
6 garlic cloves, finely mashed
¼ cup salad oil
2 cups long grain rice
¼ cup melted butter

In blender place half of the chiles, half the green onions, two or three lettuce leaves, and half the cilantro with 2 cups of water. Purée until almost liquefied. Empty blender contents into a bowl and repeat with remaining chiles, green onions, lettuce, cilantro, and 2 more cups of water. Mix all together and season with salt and pepper and the garlic. Strain.

Heat the oil and sauté the rice. Add the blended liquid mixture and cover. Cook for 30 minutes or until the liquid has almost been absorbed. Uncover and check. Add some melted butter, replace lid, and cook 5 or 10 minutes more until all liquid has been absorbed.

Serve in a white platter and garnish with a few slivers of canned pimiento.

Tip: Try not to brown the rice, as the green color will show only with white rice.

————————☉————————

CONFETTI RICE
Sopa de Arroz con Verduras

———⊙———

I am very fond of this rice dish. It is easy to make and would be ready in an hour. If you come home from work and need to fix a fancy meal in a hurry, prepare this rice dish and sautéed shrimps in garlic butter and lemon juice. Easy, delicious, and simple. A crisp green salad, would be lovely, and bread of your choice. Keep the dessert cool and simple. A chilled white wine would be delightful.

———⊙———

8 servings

2 cups long grain rice
¼ cup oil
4 cups chicken stock
4 tablespoons tomato paste
1 cup chopped green onions (green part included)
1 cup frozen peas and carrots, parboiled 2 minutes
1 5-ounce can yellow corn kernels, drained
1 3-ounce jar chopped pimientos
Salt and white pepper

In a dutch oven sauté the rice in hot oil until a light golden brown. Drain excess oil. Add the chicken stock mixed with the tomato paste. Add the chopped green onions and the rest of the vegetables and cook, covered, over medium heat for 30 minutes. Season with salt and pepper.

Wonderful with fried fish fillets and a green salad. As an added surprise garnish, why not stuff some pickled jalapeño chiles with softened cream cheese. Garlic toast would be better than tortillas.

Note: For stuffed jalapeños, halve the chiles from stem to tip. Scrape out seeds. Rinse and pat dry. Soften cream cheese with a little milk, season with salt, and fill jalapeño halves. Sprinkle with paprika—a delightful tidbit!

———⊙———

MUSTARD RICE
Arroz a la Mostaza

————⊙————

This is a daring combination of flavors. Furthermore it's a good-looking dish, great with fish or seafood. Salad mustard is not used much in Mexico's cuisine, though dry mustard is often called for.

————⊙————

4 to 6 servings

1 cup rice
4 tablespoons oil
2 cups chicken broth
1 tablespoon instant chicken bouillon granules
1 teaspoon mashed garlic
1 tablespoon prepared salad mustard
¼ cup sliced onion
½ teaspoon ground cumin
4 tablespoons butter
Parsley

Sauté rice in hot oil in dutch oven with a lid. Stir constantly and do not brown. Add remaining ingredients, except butter and parsley, cover, and cook at a simmer for 30 minutes. Remove lid and fluff out. Add 4 tablespoons fresh butter. Sprinkle snipped parsley on top before taking rice to the table.

————⊙————

RICE AND GREEN CHILE STRIPS
Arroz con Rajas

———⊙———

This was a favorite when our family lived on a remote cattle ranch in northern Mexico. I always had these ingredients in my pantry so it was easy to make up this casserole. Since we had our own milk cows we had fresh butter, buttermilk, fresh cream daily, and sour cream every other day, and fresh cold milk in the refrigerator every day, some skimmed and some whole. My daughters named the milk cows—Bossie, Babossie, and the third one Babosita. They were milked by hand and loved to be fondled. When it snowed I would have them brought into the blacksmith shop right in the house compound so that they would not stray and we could have our "dairy" on the premises.

———⊙———

4 to 6 servings

    1 cup long grain rice
    ¼ cup salad oil
    4 garlic buds, mashed
      Salt and pepper
    2 cans chopped mild green chiles
    2 cups grated Jack cheese or similar

SAUCE
    1 cup sour cream
    ¼ cup fresh milk
      Salt and pepper
    1 garlic clove, minced

Sauté rice in oil but do not brown. Add 2 cups water, garlic, salt, and pepper. Cover and cook over low heat until all liquid is absorbed, about 30 minutes. Turn into large bowl to cool.

While rice is cooling, prepare sauce. Dilute sour cream with milk and add salt and pepper to taste. Add finely mashed garlic clove.

Put a layer of cold cooked rice in a small baking dish. Then add a few chile strips or chopped pieces, a few handfuls of grated cheese, and some of the cream mixture. Repeat layers, ending with cream and cheese. Bake, uncovered, in a moderate oven for a few minutes, until cheese is melted.

Wonderful with poached fish and watercress salad.

RICE AND EGGPLANT CASSEROLE
Arroz con Berenjenas en Cazuela

———⊙———

I am very fond of eggplant but here in Mexico it is difficult to find young and tender ones. You have to be sure that the big ones are not bitter. I prefer the larger ones peeled and cut into 1-inch-thick slices, then the slices cut into large cubes. I parboil the eggplant cubes just to blanch. I find that sautéing in oil renders this type of dish much too greasy. The touch of cinnamon is delightful. A can of chopped mild green chiles (the California type) could be used instead of bell pepper but bell peppers have come into their own in my country and many Mexican housewives are beginning to depend on them instead of hot peppers. Use what you happen to have on hand. I am sure you will be happy with this dish.

———⊙———

6 to 8 servings

1 cup long grain rice
4 tablespoons salad oil
2 cups chicken broth, fresh or canned
6 garlic cloves, finely mashed
2 cups thinly sliced onions
1 cup chopped bell pepper
4 tablespoons butter
2 cups peeled eggplant, cubed and parboiled for 3 minutes
2 cups chopped peeled ripe tomatoes
½ teaspoon ground cinnamon
   Salt and pepper

Sauté rice in hot salad oil until golden in color. Transfer to baking dish. Add 2 cups of chicken broth and the garlic.

Sauté onions and bell pepper in butter; do not brown. Stir in drained cooked eggplant and tomatoes. Add ½ teaspoon ground cinnamon.

Spoon this vegetable mixture on top of rice. Correct seasoning. Cover and bake in moderate oven for 45 minutes.

Serve with Fancy Picadillo (page 131). Onion rolls are good with this rice dish and so is a sweet and sour cabbage salad.

———⊙———

RICE AND MUSHROOMS
Arroz con Champiñones

————⊙————

6 to 8 servings

2 cups sliced fresh mushrooms
2 tablespoons butter or 2 tablespoons olive oil
4 garlic cloves, finely marked
¼ cup finely chopped parsley
2 cups steamed rice, seasoned with salt and pepper to taste

Wash the mushrooms and remove the stems. (Save stems for future use.) Slice mushroom caps and sauté in butter mixed with garlic and parsley. When cooked but not too soft fold into steamed rice that has been kept hot.

Serve this in special rice bowls with strips of medium rare steaks on the side, and cold vine-ripened peeled tomatoes with lime juice, salt and pepper, and a few drained capers sprinkled on top for glamour.

Tip: I usually steam the rice in the top of my double boiler and leave it there over hot water while I prepare the rest of this dish. No need to reheat the rice, and it is at my fingertips when I need it.

Note: I have included olive oil in this recipe in case you should want a stronger flavor in your sautéed mushrooms. I prefer to use butter only.

————⊙————

RICE AND CHICKEN CASSEROLE
Cazuela de Arroz con Pollo

It is a well-known fact that Mexican cooks are experts at cooking rice. It matters not that they have very little to glorify the dish. As long as they have oil or shortening to brown their triple-washed rice, water, and salt, they find a way to do it just right and produce fluffy separate rice kernels lovely to look at and delightful to eat. When you combine the basics with chicken breasts the way we do in this recipe, you almost have a complete meal.

6–8 servings

2 cups long grain white rice, steamed in 4 cups lightly salted water
8 tablespoons butter, melted
¼ cup grated Parmesan cheese
¼ teaspoon crushed oregano leaves

FILLING

2 tablespoons salad oil
½ cup chopped onion
4 cups chopped ripe tomatoes
2 cans chopped mild green chiles
¼ cup chopped cilantro leaves
1 12-ounce can shoepeg corn kernels, drained (a 12-ounce can of golden whole corn kernels may be substituted)
Salt and pepper
2 chicken breasts, poached, cooled, and chopped

First, prepare filling. Sauté chopped onions in salad oil for 2 minutes, stirring constantly. Add tomatoes, chiles, cilantro leaves, drained corn kernels, and perhaps ½ cup water. Check seasoning and add salt and pepper if necessary. Cook for 2 minutes and then fold in the chopped cooked chicken breasts. The filling must not be too dry.

Cool rice after steaming. Add melted butter and Parmesan cheese mixed with the oregano.

Spread half the rice in a baking dish. Place all the chicken filling in the center. Cover with top layer of remaining rice. Put on lid or use heavy foil to seal baking dish, as casserole must not brown or crust. Bake 10 minutes in 325° oven.

This is an excellent luncheon dish, as all it needs is a tossed green salad and maybe buttered rye toast.

POOR MAN'S PAELLA
THE MEXICAN WAY
Paella Pobre a la Mexicana

―――⊙―――

I think this is a great recipe, a modified version of my mother-in-law's recipe. She added cumin to the reserved chicken broth. I do too sometimes and sometimes I just use the saffron. She was probably one of Mexico's best cooks, daring and versatile. And she cooked all of her food with *amor*. A great lady, my lovely mother-in-law.

―――⊙―――

8 servings

2 cups long grain white rice
½ cup oil (¼ cup olive oil and ¼ cup salad oil)
4 cups chicken stock
1 6½-ounce can minced or chopped clams
½ small (6-ounce) can tomato paste
½ teaspoon saffron threads dissolved in chicken broth
½ cup thick slices white onion
6 garlic cloves, mashed
　Salt and pepper
8 small pork chops
8 shrimp, shelled, cleaned, and butterflied (slash backs)
8 pieces cut-up chicken, poached (reserve broth)
1 cup frozen peas and carrots, parboiled 1 minute in salted water and
　　drained
1 can pimientos, in large pieces
4 links Texas-style chorizo, each cut in half and skinned

Sauté rice in hot oil until golden. Transfer to a large deep pan that will later hold all the ingredients. Pan must have a tight-fitting lid. Add the chicken stock mixed with the canned clams and their juice, the tomato paste, saffron, onion, and garlic. Correct seasoning.

　Parboil the pork chops in salted water for 15 minutes.

　Sauté the shrimp in some butter for 2 to 3 minutes.

　Let rice and broth cool a bit and then start adding the rest of the ingredients carefully, trying to follow a pattern: a piece of chicken, then a shrimp, then a pork chop, and a spoonful of peas and carrots, occasionally placing a piece of bright pimiento in a showoff spot. Cover and cook over low heat for 30 to 40 minutes. I prefer to place a griddle over my burner to solve the problem of sticking.

Fry the chorizos over very low heat, or better still cook them in a little pork lard in the top of a double boiler. When done set aside, drain on paper towels, and garnish each plate with a piece.

Ideally the hostess should serve this dish, so she is assured that everyone gets a sample of each major ingredient. Serve with Guacamole (page 49), garlic toast, a good cheese, and a good red wine.

————————⊙————————

RANCH-STYLE MACARONI
Macarronada Ranchera

————————⊙————————

This macaroni dish is great, simple to make and inexpensive. It is a good recipe for beginning cooks. I like to add two eggs to the milk and place it in the blender to meld. This turns the milk into a custardlike sauce, and is so nourishing and tasty. The bay leaf gives it a special tang, but should be removed before serving.

————————⊙————————

8 servings

8 ounces elbow macaroni
2 cups grated mild Cheddar cheese
½ teaspoon crushed oregano leaves
1 teaspoon salt
½ teaspoon pepper
2 garlic cloves, mashed
¼ cup melted butter
½ cup chopped onion
2 tablespoons salad oil
1 cup chopped tomatoes
1 bay leaf
1 cup milk

Heat oven to 325°.

Boil macaroni according to instructions on package. Drain. Combine hot boiled macaroni with butter mixed with oregano, salt, pepper, and garlic. Set aside. When cool, fold in cheese.

Sauté onion in oil and add tomatoes, ½ cup water, and bay leaf. Add salt and pepper to taste. Cook, covered, for 5 minutes. Spoon over macaroni mixture in baking dish. Remove bay leaf.

Pour milk over all and bake 15 minutes in 325° oven. Serve hot from baking dish.

JALAPEÑO MACARONI
Macarronada con Jalapeños

———⊙———

Macaroni has saved many a day for me. Living far from the city definitely makes a person a planner. You make lists and you date your lists. If you shop once a month for food you have to go into regular bookkeeping! Needless to say, I always had plenty of pasta on hand. Since there was no spoilage problem and very little storage problem, I was prepared if I stocked pastas and added rice and beans to my larder.

———⊙———

8 servings

8 ounces elbow macaroni
4 tablespoons butter, melted
2 cups milk
2 cups grated Cheddar cheese
2 cups soft rye bread crumbs
2 eggs, well beaten
2 tablespoons minced parsley
3 tablespoons minced onion
2 pickled jalapeño peppers, stemmed, seeded, and chopped
Salt and pepper to taste
1 teaspoon sweet paprika

Heat oven to 350°.

Cook macaroni according to instructions on package. Drain and add melted butter.

Combine all ingredients except paprika and pour into well-greased 3-quart Pyrex loaf pan. Set loaf pan in larger pan containing 1 inch of water. Bake 30 to 35 minutes, or until set. Sprinkle with paprika before serving.

———⊙———

SPAGHETTI IN RED CHILE SAUCE
Spaghetti Enchilado

───────☉───────

A wild combination but very Mexican and very good. Oh, how much can be done with that wonderful Red Enchilada Sauce! This excellent dish may be prepared ahead of time and kept covered in the refrigerator until ready to bake. I take it out well in advance so that it can more or less be at room temperature when I put it in the oven.

───────☉───────

8 servings

8 ounces spaghetti
½ cup melted butter
½ cup evaporated milk or heavy cream
1 garlic clove, finely mashed
2 cups Red Enchilada Sauce (see below)
  Salt and pepper
1 cup grated Jack cheese
3 tablespoons grated Parmesan cheese
1 teaspoon crumbled dry oregano leaves

Cook spaghetti according to package directions (add salt if none is called for). Drain. Add melted butter and evaporated milk or heavy cream mixed with garlic. Fold in warm Red Enchilada Sauce. Add salt and pepper to taste. Spoon into oblong baking dish. Sprinkle with mixed cheeses and oregano.

Bake, covered, in moderate oven until bubbling, about 15 minutes. Check often as red sauce tends to scorch easily.

Serve with cucumber, onion, and bell pepper salad, using a wine vinegar and olive oil dressing. Great with meat patties.

RED ENCHILADA SAUCE

3½ cups

8 red New Mexico chiles, tops and seeds removed
4 garlic cloves
2 tablespoons pork lard
2 tablespoons flour
1 tablespoon vinegar
1 teaspoon sugar
  Salt

(Recipe continues)

Wash, stem, and seed chiles. Boil red chiles in 1 quart water for 15 minutes. Let cool in their broth. Drain. Remove and purée chiles in blender with 3 cups cold water and garlic. Strain.

Heat lard and add flour. Cook to a golden colored roux and add strained red chile purée. Cook over low heat, stirring constantly, for 10 minutes. Add vinegar, sugar, and salt and cook over medium heat for 5 minutes.

Sauce keeps well in refrigerator for 2 weeks, or it may be frozen.

Tip: Use fresh water in thinning sauce instead of cooking water; this will help to lower hotness of sauce.

VERMICELLI CASSEROLE
Cazuela de Fideo

Pastas are popular in Mexico because they are inexpensive and filling. Many a large family will make a meal out of a simple vermicelli casserole composed of the pasta, a little oil, salt and pepper, water, and garlic and onion for flavoring. If lucky, the family may be able to afford some inexpensive canned tomato sauce, and of course a few crumbled oregano leaves will make all the difference in the world. This pasta casserole is just such a dish. Served with beans and fresh tortillas, it is a *peón* family's banquet.

Pastas made in Mexico have an extra special flavor because they are not made with bleached flour. Somehow or other this makes for a wheatier taste!

8 servings

4 tablespoons lard or salad oil
8 ounces thin noodles or vermicelli
1 onion, chopped
2 cups peeled and chopped tomatoes
4 garlic cloves, mashed
4 cups well-seasoned chicken stock
1 cup grated Jack cheese
2 tablespoons grated Parmesan cheese

Heat lard or salad oil and brown vermicelli coils lightly. Careful, they burn easily. Drain on paper towels. Put into a casserole with a tight-fitting lid.

Sauté onion in same oil and add chopped tomatoes and garlic. Cook for about 5 minutes, stirring constantly. Add stock and correct seasoning. Pour over noodles in casserole.

Cover and bake in moderate oven for about 30 minutes. Check and stir from time to time. Noodles will be done when all of the liquid has been absorbed. Before serving sprinkle with mixture of cheeses, or serve plain and pass cheese.

Note: If you prefer, preheat your oven to 400° and lay the vermicelli on a cookie sheet and brown it in the oven until golden. This is much easier and more frugal (you save on oil) and you avoid the problem of scorched pasta.

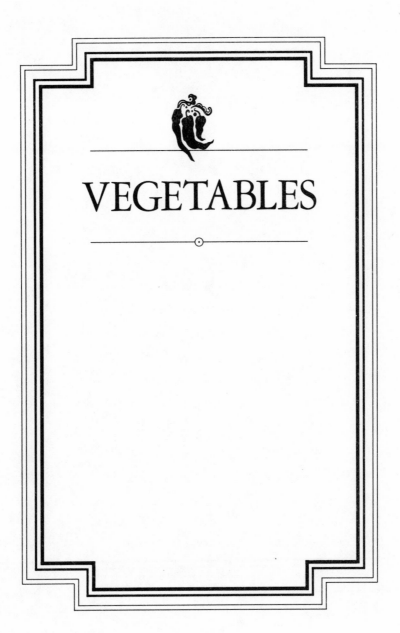

VEGETABLES

A visit to a Mexican *mercado,* or market, is a feast to the eyes—exotic fruits and vegetables are carefully arranged in neat pyramids of wildly exploding color. Red, juicy tomatoes, light green prickly chayotes, pale green cactus shoots, bright orange squash blossoms, green or satiny black avocados, and the endless carnival of chiles beckon. Produce is generally picked in its prime, and the taste will tell you. Due to the ever increasing popularity of Mexican cookery, much of this bounty is now available seasonally in major cities in the United States.

Vegetables are usually sautéed or sauced rather than merely steamed or boiled, and are often served as separate courses in merchants' luncheons or in the home. Ideally suited for this purpose are the many varieties of stuffed chiles.

The flavor of roasted, peeled chiles marries well with almost any meat, cheese, or vegetable, and the imagination can run wild. For a delightful summer dish, you might stuff green Anaheim chiles with chicken or seafood salad. A chile stuffed with red snapper hash would be a spectacular first course. By adjusting the portion size, any of these chiles can also serve as a main dish.

Beans are the principal staple in Mexico. Many years ago, in conjunction with research on polio, a study was made in Third World countries where, by medical standards, the nutrition is not what it should be. Mexico was a country that stumped these researchers—so little incidence of polio, never an epidemic per se, yet the vaccine was really not distributed nationally because it was not available on a wide scale. Eating habits and diet were discussed, and it was noted that Mexicans ate more protein, less fat, and less starch than many other countries. If diet was a factor, maybe beans were important. So versatile, affordable, tasty beans seem to have proved their worth. And a good thing, too, because few Mexican meals are served without a bean dish of some sort. Pinto beans are used mostly in the north and central parts of Mexico. They are served boiled with pork rind or ham hock, or mashed, fried in lard or bacon grease, refried, and presented plain or combined with Mexican sausage (chorizo) or stringy asadero cheese. Mozzarella is an acceptable substitute. In central and southern Mexico, black beans are usually served. Their earthy taste is appealing and satisfying.

Chile strips or bits can transform even the most mundane dish into a luscious taste sensation, and you will find several recipes here that use them.

BOILED BEANS
Frijoles Cocidos

───────○───────

In those awful days when we were plagued by foot-and-mouth disease in Mexico, the United States border was closed to the crossing of our cattle. Those were lean years and we made do with what we had. I remember ordering a sack of pink or pinto beans from a country store about forty-five miles from our ranch. The groceries arrived and we opened up the sack to find navy beans. There was no way of exchanging them, so navy beans it was for a little more than three weeks. I became an expert, fixing them a different way each day, but the first pot of good old boiled pinto beans that appeared on our table was greeted as if it were roast beef!

───────○───────

4 cups cooked beans
and 2 cups broth

2 cups pinto or pink beans
1 garlic clove, slightly crushed but not peeled
1 small chunk white onion
6 to 8 cups water
1 teaspoon salt

Clean the beans and rinse in cold water once or twice until water runs clear. Cover beans with cold water and soak overnight.

Place beans in deep kettle or saucepan that has a tight-fitting lid and add garlic clove, onion chunk, and 6 to 8 cups water. Bring to a boil and lower heat to medium, keeping contents at a simmer. Cook, covered, for 2 or 3 hours or until tender. If more water is needed always add boiling water, a cup or so at a time. Add salt midway through cooking time.

The normal yield should be about 4 cups cooked beans and about 2 cups broth.

───────○───────

STEAMING SOUPY BEANS
Frijoles Con Caldo

————⊙————

Eat with crisply toasted flour tortillas dripping with melted butter. *Delicioso!* Served with Quesadillas—a meal in itself. Add a green salad and a glass of beer—a banquet!

————⊙————

4 servings

4 cups Boiled Beans (preceding recipe) with all their broth
4 teaspoons finely chopped green onions
4 tablespoons oil
2 tablespoons apple cider vinegar
¼ teaspoon crushed oregano leaves per serving

Fill small heated soup bowls with hot steaming beans, broth and all (you want this to be soupy). Garnish with chopped green onions, oil, vinegar, and a sprinkling of crushed oregano leaves. May be served at table from a soup tureen. Mix all the ingredients in the tureen and serve.

————⊙————

REFRIED BEANS AND BEAN DIP
Frijoles Refritos

————⊙————

4 cups

4 cups Boiled Beans (page 235) with some of their broth
¼ cup lard, shortening, or oil (if beans are to be served cold, use oil)

Purée beans in a food mill, blender, or food processor a cup at a time with 2 or 3 tablespoons broth. In the meantime heat lard or other fat in a large skillet until smoking. Lower heat and cook puréed beans over medium heat, stirring constantly, until mixture begins to thicken. Cool, pack into containers, and freeze.

This is really the first frying. To refry beans, heat ¼ cup lard or shortening in medium-sized skillet and cook beans until thick and shiny. You may use thawed Refried Beans or beans that have been recently cooked and puréed. The amount of lard specified above may vary according to your preference.

When bean mixture is thick and bubbly, you may add grated Jack cheese and work it into the hot mixture with the back of a large spoon.

For bean dip it is best to use oil instead of lard or shortening. Heighten aroma and flavor by adding one chopped pickled jalapeño pepper, some of the pickling juice, and a sprinkling of grated Parmesan cheese. Serve cold, lukewarm, or hot.

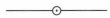

WHITE NAVY BEANS WITH BACON
Alubias con Tocino

As a strictly optional suggestion—2 or 3 sliced canned whole pimientos may be added for a tantalizing flavor and a touch of color. Serve with hot garlic toast and a salad as a snack or a light luncheon dish.

6 to 8 medium servings

1 pound dried navy or pea beans (In Mexico it is possible to get a large white bean about half the size of a large white dried lima bean called *alubias*. However, the American navy bean will do just fine.)
Salt and pepper
4 slices thick, choice bacon (each slice cut in quarters)
1 cup sliced onions
2 ripe tomatoes, peeled and diced
6 garlic buds, finely mashed
2 bay leaves

Place beans in cold water and soak overnight.

Rinse, place in large saucepan, cover with water, and heat to boiling. Reduce heat and simmer, uncovered, for 50 minutes or until tender. Do not boil or beans will burst. If too dry add hot water as they cook. Midway through cooking time add salt and pepper to taste.

In medium saucepan sauté bacon pieces until limp, but do not brown. Remove with slotted spoon and drain on paper towels. In bacon grease sauté chopped onions, stirring constantly, until soft but not brown. Add chopped tomatoes, garlic, and bay leaves. Cook over medium heat until mixture becomes mushy. Remove bay leaves.

Add sautéed mixture to cooked beans and add bacon pieces. Cover and cook until flavors combine thoroughly. Serve very hot.

TIPSY CARROTS
Zanahorias Borrachas

————⊙————

4 servings

1 pound carrots, peeled, sliced, and parboiled
8 tablespoons butter, melted
4 tablespoons brown sugar
½ teaspoon ground cinnamon
¼ teaspoon nutmeg
¼ teaspoon cloves
¼ cup rum or tequila

Arrange cooked carrot slices in a 1½-quart baking pan with a knob top lid. Mix the melted butter with the remainder of the ingredients. Pour over the carrots. Cover and bake for 15 minutes in a 325° oven.

————⊙————

STUFFED CAULIFLOWER FRITTERS
Coliflor Lampreada

——⊙——

About 16 to 20 fritters

    1 medium cauliflower
       Shredded mozzarella cheese (1 or 2 cups depending on size
         of cauliflower)
10 or 12 green chile strips (or 1 4-ounce can of chiles cut into strips)
    ½ cup seasoned flour
    4 eggs
       Salt and pepper
       Oil for deep-frying
    2 cups of Chile Relleno Sauce (page 303)

Wash cauliflower and remove outer leaves. Cut out core and wash head under cold running water. Parboil in salted boiling water for 15 or 20 minutes. Drain. Break up into large florets.

Cut down through center of each floret, starting at the top and cutting halfway down to the stem. Fill each floret, while still warm, with 1 teaspoon shredded cheese and 1 strip of green chile. Close tightly. The cheese will melt in the warm floret and bind all together.

Fill a large salt shaker with seasoned flour and shake over all filled florets.

Separate 2 eggs first. Beat egg whites until stiff, add 2 egg yolks and beat 1 minute more. Season foamy egg mixture with salt.

Holding them tightly, dip each filled floret in beaten egg mixture and deep-fry in hot oil until golden. Drain on paper towels. Serve with a bowl of hot Chile Relleno Sauce on the side. (By hot I don't mean pungent, I am referring to the temperature of the sauce.)

Note: If you run out of egg mixture, prepare the other 2 eggs the same way. Don't be stingy with the egg. Fritters should be plump and fluffy.

——⊙——

CHAYOTES AU GRATIN
Chayotes Gratinados

————⊙————

This is a vegetable dish that goes well with a traditional turkey dinner instead of creamed turnips or the like. Though bland by Mexican standards, it holds its own in "mixed company."

————⊙————

6 to 8 servings

4 large chayotes, boiled and peeled (save the cooking water)
1 4-ounce can green chiles, chopped
2 tablespoons butter or margarine
2 tablespoons flour
1 cup evaporated milk or heavy cream (do not use fresh milk; the sauce
    would be too thin)
1 cup water chayotes were cooked in
  Salt and pepper
1 cup shredded cheese (Jack, American Cheddar, or what's on hand)

Boil chayotes until tender in large saucepan in hot salted water to cover. Drain, but save 1 or 2 cups cooking liquid and set aside. Peel and slice chayotes. Stir in chopped green chiles.

Melt butter in a large saucepan over low heat. Stir in flour and cook as for a roux. Do not allow to brown. Add milk and water mixture, stirring constantly, until mixture is smooth and creamy. Remove from heat. Season with salt and pepper.

Stir sliced chayotes into sauce. Pour into buttered casserole. Cover with shredded cheese. Top with Crumb Topping (see below) if desired, and heat through in a 325° oven, 10 or 15 minutes at the most.

CRUMB TOPPING
½ cup dry bread crumbs (best to toast bread first)
2 tablespoons melted butter
¼ teaspoon ground nutmeg

Stir all ingredients together. Sprinkle over hot cooked or creamed vegetables.

————⊙————

GREEN CHILE STRIPS
Rajas

———⊙———

About 3 to 4 cups strips

2 tablespoons oil
1 large onion, peeled, quartered, and thinly sliced
10 garlic cloves, peeled and cut in half lengthwise
1 cup Bay Leaf Tea (page 11)
1 tablespoon peppercorns
¼ cup white vinegar
Salt
6 poblano chiles, broiled, peeled, deveined, and cut into strips
1 teaspoon crushed oregano leaves

In large skillet heat oil and sauté sliced onion for 1 minute, stirring constantly. Wilt only; do not allow to overcook or to brown. Add garlic cloves. Stir-fry garlic with onions 1 minute. Remove from heat.

In an oblong or square glass or ceramic dish, layer the chile strips, then the onions and garlic, sprinkle oregano leaves over all, and pour on the pickling liquid. Cover with foil or plastic wrap and refrigerate overnight so that flavors will meld.

Serve with sandwiches as you would pickle slices. Wonderful on Poor Boys, with corn chips spread with refried beans, and absolutely delicious on wieners.

Note: Bay Leaf Tea is an infusion, and with the addition of vinegar, oil, and peppercorns, it becomes a marvelous pickling and marinating liquid! The longer the bay leaves remain in the pickling liquid the better, but they may be removed at serving time.

———⊙———

MARINATED GREEN CHILES ANA LINDA
Rajas Ana Linda

———⊙———

I can't quite recall when my mother first started making these pickled chiles. Her name was Ana and all of her grandchildren called her Ana Linda, which means Lovely Ana. So this recipe was known as "Ana Linda's wonderful pickled green chile strips."

———⊙———

1 quart, or
10 to 12 single servings

Oil for frying the chiles
10 or 12 plump straight fresh green Anaheim chiles
1 cup vegetable oil plus 4 tablespoons olive oil
⅓ cup white vinegar
1 teaspoon salt
1 teaspoon coarsely ground black pepper
1 tablespoon crushed oregano leaves
1 tablespoon crushed garlic cloves
1 cup white onion in thin half slices

Pour about 1″ of oil in a large skillet and heat until almost smoking. Fry chiles, a few at a time, until blistered on all sides. You will need a cover for the skillet as the peppers sputter the oil dangerously. They will take on a lovely light brown color when correctly blistered.

Remove skins under cold running water. Make a slit on one side near the stem and wash the seeds out. Incidentally, do try to keep the peppers intact. Be especially careful not to disturb the stems. Arrange the prepared green chiles in an oblong glass dish about 12 × 9 × 2.

Make marinade by mixing all of the remaining ingredients except the onion slices. Cover chiles with all but 2 or 3 tablespoons of marinade and chill in the refrigerator.

Blanch onion slices by pouring boiling water over them and draining. Season onions with reserved marinade. Garnish the green chiles by sprinkling the onions over them, and serve with meat or fish.

———⊙———

GREEN CHILES STUFFED WITH CORN RELISH
Chiles Rellenos de Elote

———⊙———

8 single servings

8 canned whole green chiles prepared for stuffing, or 8 fresh green
    Anaheim chiles, the straightest and plumpest you can find
3 tablespoons vegetable oil
2 tablespoons vinegar
1 can shoepeg white whole kernel corn, drained
    Salt and pepper
2 tablespoons chopped chives
1 ripe tomato, peeled and chopped
2 tablespoons chopped cilantro leaves

Be sure the chiles are ready for stuffing, seeds removed and slit on one side.
Mix oil and vinegar and combine this dressing with a mixture of next 5
ingredients.

Stuff prepared chiles with corn mixture. Place on lettuce-lined serving platter and garnish with radishes and ripe olives.

Spoon garlic-flavored sour cream over chiles. I usually thin the cream with
a few spoonfuls of milk. Goes well with baked Virginia ham.

Note: Needless to say, if fresh corn is available it would do beautifully. So
would frozen corn kernels. Also, if you prefer, or do not have sour cream on
hand, serve with homemade mayonnaise.

Twisted or crooked fresh chiles are difficult to work with and impossible to
fill, so do heed my advice and choose the straight, plump Anaheims.

———⊙———

GREEN CHILES STUFFED WITH TUNA
Chiles Rellenos de Atun

————⊙————

Packing a picnic? Try this delightful "salad." Serve with crackers or cheese sandwiches, iced tea, and a homemade chocolate cake lavishly studded with chopped pecans.

————⊙————

8 single servings

8 canned whole green chiles prepared for stuffing, or 8 fresh green Anaheim chiles, as straight and plump as possible (see note, page 243)
  Marinade for chiles (recipe below)
1 6½-ounce can oil-packed tuna, drained
2 tablespoons chopped chives
2 tablespoons chopped pickled jalapeño chiles, seeded
1 hard-boiled egg, chopped
  Enough mayonnaise to hold filling together
  Grated longhorn cheese

Marinate chiles for at least 30 minutes. Drain marinade and reserve.

Stuff chiles with mixture of remaining ingredients except cheese and place in lettuce-lined platter. Spoon marinade over them and sprinkle with grated longhorn cheese. If you feel you need more color try the old standbys—ripe olives and pimientos.

MARINADE
1 cup salad oil
⅓ cup vinegar
  Salt and pepper to taste
1 garlic clove, finely mashed
½ teaspoon sweet paprika
1 teaspoon crushed dry oregano leaves

Thoroughly mix all ingredients, whisking until well combined.

————⊙————

DRIED RED CHILES IN RED SAUCE
Chiles Capones

This is an excellent meatless dish, and if served with Refried Beans and corn chips a positive delight. Good with a shredded cabbage salad with a vinegar and oil dressing, garnished with chopped green onions and sliced stuffed green olives.

8 single servings

8 ancho chiles
8 1½-inch-wide slices Monterey Jack cheese or
    white Cheddar, each ¼-inch thick
  Epazote
¼ cup oil
3 cups chopped onion
2 pounds ripe tomatoes or 1 large can Italian-style tomatoes
6 garlic cloves, finely mashed
  Salt and pepper
½ teaspoon crushed oregano leaves

Soften dry ancho peppers by soaking in hot water until soft enough to handle. Cut on the side and remove seeds and veins; if possible leave the stems on.

Fill each chile with a thick wide slice of cheese that will make the peppers regain their original shape, and put one epazote leaf in each chile. Set aside.

In large skillet heat oil and sauté chopped onions, but be sure you don't brown them. Add tomatoes (if you use fresh, peel and chop them; if canned, just mash with your hands and add to the onions, juice and all). Add mashed garlic, season with salt and pepper, and add the crushed oregano leaves. Simmer for 10 minutes.

Place the chiles in an oblong heatproof Pyrex dish and pour sauce over them. Cover with foil and bake in a 350° oven for 15 minutes. Watch carefully and check so that chiles do not overbrown on top or they will be bitter.

MEXICAN CORN PUDDING WITH GREEN CHILES
Torta de Elote con Rajas

———⊙———

Wonderful served with pan-fried thick pork chops flavored with a touch of garlic, and sliced tomatoes garnished with capers and served with a mild vinegar and oil dressing. Fresh rye bread is my choice as another accompaniment, but with all that starch it is not a must! This recipe would also make a marvelous addition to your Thanksgiving menu.

———⊙———

8 servings

    1 17-ounce can whole kernel corn or 2 12-ounce cans
        white shoepeg corn kernels, drained
    4 eggs
    2 tablespoons cornstarch
    ½ cup milk
      Salt and pepper
    1 tablespoon sugar or to taste
    1 teaspoon baking powder
    ½ cup (8 tablespoons) melted butter
    1 4-ounce can chopped green chiles
    1 cup shredded Monterey Jack cheese or white Cheddar

In a blender, lightly purée corn, eggs, cornstarch, and milk. Season with salt and pepper and add sugar to taste. Stir in the baking powder. Stir in melted butter by tablespoonfuls. Fold in chopped peppers, being careful to remove any pieces of scorched peels. Fold in shredded cheese.

Pour into a buttered 9 × 13-inch baking dish. Bake in a 350° oven for 45 minutes to 1 hour, until firm.

Note: If using salted butter, go easy on the salt.

———⊙———

GALA EGGPLANT FRICASSEE
Berenjenas de Gala

———⊙———

8 servings

1 large eggplant
2 or 3 zucchini squash, about 1 pound
2 California green chiles or 1 large poblano chile, cored and
    seeded
1 14½-ounce can Italian-style tomatoes
2 tablespoons olive oil mixed with 2 tablespoons salad oil
1 cup onion, coarsely chopped
    Salt and freshly ground pepper
1 teaspoon crushed oregano leaves
1 cup sliced fresh mushrooms
1 tablespoon finely mashed garlic

Peel the eggplant and slice it. Stack the slices and cut them into strips. Cube the strips. You should have about 4 cups. Cut the unpeeled zucchini into long strips lengthwise and cut them into ½-inch cubes (about 2 cups). Chop the chiles into ½-inch pieces (at least 1 cup).

Blanch the eggplant in salted boiling water for 1 minute and drain. Blanch the chopped zucchini in salted boiling water for 1 minute and drain. Parboil the chopped chiles in salted water for 2 minutes and drain. Mash the canned tomatoes by hand, juice and all, and set aside.

In a large saucepan heat the oil mixture and sauté the chopped onion for 2 minutes, stirring constantly. Add the parboiled chiles and stir-fry not more than 1 minute. Add the tomatoes and season with salt, pepper, and crushed oregano leaves. Stir in the mushroom slices and continue cooking until mushrooms are limp. Stir in the blanched eggplant and zucchini, correct seasoning, and remove from heat. Fold in mashed garlic. Cover closely. Let set 10 minutes before serving. Good cold also.

Note: Many a squash dish has been ruined by bitter zucchini. I always taste the heart of each squash—as I do with cucumbers—for bitterness, and discard the culprits. Many a culinary great has been guilty of presenting a bitter squash dish because he failed to taste beforehand.

———⊙———

POTATO SLICES
WITH BELL PEPPER SAUCE
Papas con Rajas

————⊙————

On my way to Chalma I stopped in at a drive-in fast-food stand and ate undoubtedly the best "quesadilla" I have ever had, filled with grated Jack cheese and pepper strips. I was pleasantly surprised to find that they were not poblano chile strips but a chopped bell pepper mixed in with the cheese. Delightful! I just garnished it with a teaspoon of hot sauce and proceeded to indulge.

————⊙————

Enough filling for 8 tacos,
quesadillas, or burritos

2 large Idaho potatoes
5 tablespoons corn oil
½ cup thin slices of white onion
1 cup peeled chopped ripe tomato
1 cup thinly sliced bell pepper
Salt and pepper
¼ cup heavy cream or evaporated milk
½ teaspoon ground cumin
Butter

Peel the potatoes and slice. Rinse and drain. Parboil in mildly salted water for 2 minutes and drain.

Heat 3 tablespoons oil in a medium skillet and sauté the potatoes for 2 minutes, turning carefully in order to keep slices whole.

To make sauce, heat remaining 2 tablespoons oil in small saucepan and sauté onions. Stir-fry 1 minute and add chopped tomato. Parboil bell pepper several minutes and drain. Add to onion and tomato mixture. Season with salt and pepper.

Add sauce to potatoes. Correct seasoning. Fold in heavy cream or evaporated milk carefully. Turn into small ovenproof casserole and sprinkle lavishly with ground cumin to suit your taste. Dot with butter and bake in a 375° oven for 10 minutes.

————⊙————

RANCH-STYLE POTATOES
Papas al Estilo Ranchero

———————☉———————

This is a great meatless dish, or if you have eaters with big appetites, garnish with chopped fried wieners. It's a wonderful combination.

———————☉———————

8 servings

4 Idaho potatoes, about 1½ pounds
3 tablespoons vegetable oil
  Salt and pepper
½ cup very thinly sliced onion, halved before slicing
1 cup chopped ripe tomato
1 4-ounce can chopped green chiles
1 cup coarsely grated or cubed Jack cheese or
  Wisconsin white Cheddar
1 teaspoon sweet paprika

Peel the potatoes and slice them as thinly as possible. Rinse and drain. Pat dry with paper towels.

Heat a deep skillet and add the oil. When it is very hot, add the potatoes. Sprinkle with salt and pepper. Cook and brown well, about 10 minutes, being careful not to cut into the slices.

Add the onion, tomato, and canned chopped green chiles (be mindful to remove any charred pieces of chile peeling visible). Add more salt and pepper, but do so sparingly. Continue cooking 1 minute, covered, to steam the contents.

Shake skillet and turn over potatoes in sauce. When well done, sprinkle cheese on top, cover one minute until cheese melts, sprinkle with sweet paprika, and serve from the skillet.

———————☉———————

TASTY SPINACH
Espinacas Sabrosas

————⊙————

I don't think my grandmother ever heard of Popeye, but the only way we would eat spinach was "her way." For the grown-ups she would set out a few fried dry red chiles and I can still hear the lovely crackling sound they made when they were bitten into. This is her recipe.

————⊙————

6 to 8 servings

3 or 4 10-ounce packages fresh spinach
Salt and freshly ground pepper
3 tablespoons vegetable oil
½ cup thinly sliced onion
2 ripe tomatoes, peeled and chopped
4 garlic buds, finely mashed

Pull away and discard any tough stems and discolored leaves from the spinach. Rinse at least twice and drain.

Pour 1 quart of water into a large kettle and bring to the boil. Add salt to taste and then the spinach. Stir down to wilt. Bring to the boil again, stirring occasionally, and cook about 5 minutes.

Empty the spinach into a colander and drain. Press with the back of a spoon to extract as much of the liquid as possible. I always save about ½ cup of liquid and set it aside for later use, as vegetables prepared this way often dry out and need a little freshening up. Set aside.

In a skillet heat the oil and stir-fry the onion slices for 1 minute. Add the chopped tomato and cook until soft and mushy, about 3 minutes. Season with salt and pepper to taste. Fold in cooked spinach and mashed garlic. Cover and cook over medium heat 2 or 3 minutes more. Uncover and correct seasoning. If too dry, add 1 or 2 tablespoons of reserved liquid.

————⊙————

GRANDMOTHER'S TASTY SPINACH
Espinacas al Estilo de la Abuela

————☉————

If a fresh pot of beans was boiling on the stove, a cupful was drained
in a colander and a few of the drained frijoles were scattered over
the spinach, with the red crispy chile slices showing their heads in
between. Glorious!

————☉————

8 servings

2 to 3 bunches fresh spinach (at least 10 ounces each)
    Salt and pepper
   3 tablespoons salad oil
   2 tablespoons all-purpose flour
   1 large garlic clove, peeled and crushed
  ½ cup thinly sliced onion
   1 cup chopped very ripe tomato
   4 tablespoons margarine or butter
   1 mild dry New Mexico red chile, seeded and cut into ½-inch
     slices with kitchen shears

Trim stems and roots from spinach before washing it in warm water. Rinse
leaves under cold water before cooking.

Pour 1 quart water into a large saucepan, add ½ teaspoon salt, and bring to
the boil. Add spinach and cook 5 minutes, stirring occasionally. Drain, but save
at least half of the spinach water. Set aside. Put the spinach in a large platter
and chop coarsely.

Heat oil in large skillet and brown the flour in it until it is a light golden
brown. Add peeled, slightly crushed garlic clove and stir 1 minute with the
roux. Add onion slices and chopped tomato and cook for 2 minutes, stirring
constantly. Add salt and pepper to taste. Then stir in the chopped cooked
spinach and ½ cup of the liquid. This dish should have the consistency of
creamed spinach.

Heat margarine or butter in a small skillet, remove from heat, and very
carefully toast the dry chile slices. Drain and garnish the spinach with them.

————☉————

SQUASH AND CHEESE CASSEROLE
Calabacitas con Queso

———⊙———

I had an aunt who used to serve this dish with fried chicken when she invited the whole family for an early lunch after church on Sunday. Cold beer is perfect with this combination. And small flour tortillas, of course. Any leftovers freeze well.

———⊙———

8 servings

2 pounds zucchini (about 6 medium)
  Salt and pepper
3 tablespoons shortening or cooking oil
¼ cup diced white onion
1 ripe tomato, peeled and chopped
1 4-ounce can diced mild green chiles
2 cups white kernel corn, either canned (well drained) or frozen
1 small can evaporated milk or 1 cup heavy cream
1 cup grated Wisconsin Cheddar or Monterey Jack cheese, or more
    if you wish

Wash the squash and pat dry. Trim off the ends but do not peel. Dice. Pour one quart of water into a kettle and bring to the boil. Add salt to taste and the zucchini, and cook for about 3 minutes. They should be al dente, by no means mushy. Empty into a colander and drain. Save one cup of the liquid. Set aside.

To a skillet add the cooking oil and heat. Sauté the diced white onion for 1 minute, stirring constantly. Now stir in the chopped tomato, the drained canned diced chiles (being sure to remove any pieces of skin visible), and the corn. If you use frozen shoepeg corn prepare as per package instructions, drain, and proceed as indicated above. Add salt and pepper to taste. Cook 3 minutes, stirring often. Fold in zucchini and evaporated milk or cream. Correct seasoning.

Pour into an ovenproof casserole and fold in the coarsely grated cheese. (If cheese is too soft you may cube it.) Bake in a 375° oven for 15 minutes or until bubbly. If too dry add some reserved liquid.

Note: If you wish to use fresh corn, of course you may do so. Carefully husk the ears, remove the silk, and boil corn in lightly salted water for 10 minutes. Drain, cool, and cut kernels off the cobs. Taste squash for bitterness before using.

MEXICAN RATATOUILLE
Chayotes Ratatouille

———⊙———

So good with pork chops and steamed rice. Tastes wonderful served cold as a relish with thick slices of baked ham.

———⊙———

6 to 8 servings

    4 large chayotes, cooked, peeled, and cubed
      Salt and pepper
    2 cups thickly sliced zucchini (about ½ pound)
    1 medium onion, finely chopped (about ½ cup)
    ¼ cup olive oil
    4 tomatoes, peeled and quartered
    1 4-ounce can chopped mild green chiles
    4 garlic cloves, finely chopped
    ½ teaspoon tarragon
    1 teaspoon coriander

Boil chayotes in 2 quarts boiling salted water (use about 4 teaspoons salt) until tender. Cool and peel. Cut in half lengthwise and scoop out heart seeds. Save for garnish. Cube chayotes and set aside.

Prepare zucchini and parboil in salted water for 1 minute. Drain.

Sauté onion in hot oil (be sure to use a deep saucepan). Do not brown. Add tomatoes and stir-cook 3 minutes. Stir in the chopped canned chiles and season with salt and pepper.

Mix garlic with ½ cup hot water and pour into mixture. Add tarragon and fold in prepared chayotes and zucchini. Cover and cook over medium heat, stirring occasionally, about 3 minutes. Vegetables should remain crisp-tender. Garnish with chayote heart seeds.

Note: No canned green chiles in the pantry? Parboiled bell pepper slices will do beautifully, plus a chopped jalapeño.

———⊙———

MEXICAN STIR-FRIED VEGETABLES
Revoltijo de Verduras

—⊙—

6 servings

½ cup salad oil
2 carrots, peeled and cut into thin sticks
½ head of cauliflower, parboiled in salted water and broken up
    into florets
1 chayote, parboiled, peeled, and cubed
½ pound fresh mushrooms, sliced
    Salt and pepper
1 tablespoon mashed garlic
6 or 8 dry epazote leaves boiled in ½ cup water
1 cup poblano chile strips (if not available use bell pepper slices,
    parboiled in salted water and drained)

Heat oil in wok until smoking. Stir-fry the carrots first, then the cauliflower, chayote, and mushrooms, frying each vegetable in order given for 2 minutes before adding the next. End by adding the sliced mushrooms and green onions. Season with salt, pepper, and garlic and then add the infusion of epazote leaves, leaves and all. Add chile strips on top as garnish.

SALADS,
RELISHES,
AND
SALAD
DRESSINGS

S alads as garniture have always been popular in Mexico. Guacamole, cacuts shoots, and chayote have been an integral part of our culinary heritage, and salads of these ingredients have been prepared for many years. (Guacamole especially has gained international acceptance and is widely featured on menus in the United States.) But recent years have seen the birth of exciting new alliances. Inventive housewives and restaurant chefs have developed recipes combining watercress and pine nuts, and spinach and jicama.

Green salads as they are known in the United States have not been as popular in Mexico but are rapidly gaining acceptance, especially where spinach is concerned. Weight-conscious housewives are adding salads to the noon meal with a view to calorie reduction. And it does work. Cabbage salad and cabbage relish are popular as garnishes on Mexican snacks, called *Antojitos.*

Our escabeches (pickled salads) and relishes are also very popular. A particular escabeche made with sliced zucchini, carrots, and jicama, a type of jardiniere, is offered by many restaurants as a complimentary appetizer.

Street vendors sell sliced jicama or jicama cut in intriguing flower shapes sprinkled with fresh lime juice and red chile powder. Oranges and mangos are also cut in fascinating shapes and sold in the same manner.

MIXED VEGETABLE SALAD
Ensalada de Verduras

——⊙——

This salad is one of my favorites, lovely looking and good with almost everything.

——⊙——

6 servings

1 cup thinly sliced peeled carrots
1 cup thinly sliced white onion
2 cups thinly sliced zucchini
1 10-ounce package frozen peas
1 10-ounce package frozen cut green beans or 1 pound fresh tender
    green beans
1 teaspoon crushed oregano leaves

Heat 4 cups well-salted water to boiling in a large saucepan. Add salt and blanch each vegetable separately. All must be crisp-tender.

Follow package directions for frozen peas and frozen green beans.

In a large platter or bowl, layer the blanched vegetables and spoon Simple Vinaigrette (page 274) over all. Place in the refrigerator until ready to serve. Sprinkle with crushed oregano.

Want a special Mexican touch? Cut some canned pickled jalapeños in half from stem to tip, scrape out the seeds, and fill the chiles with cream cheese. Line a chilled plate with romaine lettuce and fill with the salad. Garnish with the stuffed jalapeños, a few cherry tomatoes for color, and some mammoth size ripe olives that have been marinated in fresh squeezed lime juice. Superb!

——⊙——

WARM ZUCCHINI SALAD
Ensalada de Calabacitas

—————⊙—————

A lady whom I dearly loved taught me to make this salad. I used to call her my aunt Lupita, although she was no kin of mine. She was one of those people you wish were your real relatives. These are the ones we adopt as young children and who follow us into adulthood enjoying our triumphs and lamenting our sad moments. Such was this lady to me. Her children are my closest friends—a friendship that has endured for years.

This salad can be made in a few minutes, and it should be served warm. The idea is to serve it with a side dish of grated soft cheese, Jack or even mellow golden longhorn. The warmth of the slices of zucchini will slightly melt the cheese and make it stringy and out of this world.

—————⊙—————

6 servings

1½ pounds small firm fresh zucchini
½ cup thinly sliced purple onion
¼ cup vinegar
¾ cup vegetable oil
½ teaspoon salt
¼ teaspoon black pepper
1 teaspoon crushed oregano leaves

Thoroughly wash zucchini and cut off ends. Slice and cook 1 minute in salted boiling water. Drain and spread out in medium-sized platter.

Place onion slices in a small bowl and pour boiling water over them. Allow water to cool and then drain onion slices, and dry with paper towels. Place in a quart jar with a lid.

Mix vinegar, oil, and salt and pepper, stir well and pour over onion slices in jar. Shake well.

Spoon onions and dressing evenly over the warm zucchini slices in platter. Sprinkle with the crushed oregano leaves. Serve at once.

Note: Taste and discard any bitter zucchini before using in recipe. Leftover purple onion dressing keeps indefinitely. Use on another occasion on sliced peeled ripe tomatoes.

GUACAMOLE SALAD WITH ZUCCHINI
Guacamole con Calabacitas

————⊙————

There are many, many recipes for guacamole and they are all good. This particular version with zucchini added is an innovation and a welcome change. Use only young tender squash; older, bitter zucchini will ruin the taste of the dish. Like all guacamole recipes, it should be prepared at the last moment. This is an excellent way to make a few avocados go a long way and the flavor is milder, fresher, and delicious. Serve in a colorful bowl with corn chips.

————⊙————

8 to 10 small servings

2 small firm fresh zucchini
1 cup peeled and chopped tomatoes
¼ cup chopped green onions
½ cup roasted, seeded, chopped, green chile (optional)
¼ cup chopped cilantro leaves
3 ripe avocados
3 tablespoons oil
1 tablespoon freshly squeezed lime juice
Salt

Wash and stem the zucchini and grate coarsely on a cheese grater. Mix with tomatoes, onions, and chopped green chile. Add the cilantro.

Peel and seed the ripe avocados. In a large platter, mash them with a fork. Stir in the oil and vegetables and mix well. Add lime juice and season with salt.

All preparation should be done almost at serving time.

INSTANT AVOCADO
MADURAR AGUACATES VERDES AL INSTANTE

If you have a microwave oven, this is easy. Just put the avocados in the microwave in a plastic bag. Set at medium and leave for 2 minutes. Turn off microwave. Let avocados cool and they will be ready to eat and to cook with.

————⊙————

SPINACH SALAD
Ensalada de Espinacas

———⟨⟩———

This spinach salad is a delight to prepare and to eat. I usually wash the spinach a few hours before mealtime, drain and dry the leaves with paper towels, and reroll them in paper towels or a dry clean dish towel until they go into the salad bowl. Fix a big batch, as the men especially will come back for a second helping.

———⟨⟩———

6 to 8 servings

  3 10-ounce bunches fresh spinach
½ cup chopped green onion (use bulbs and tops)
  1 cup coriander leaves
½ cup Mexican-style Italian Dressing (page 276)
     Cherry tomatoes or sliced radishes for color and garnish

Wash spinach, discarding stems. Pat dry on paper towels and tear into chilled salad bowl. Chop green onions, including plenty of the green part, and add to spinach. Wash coriander and discard all stems. Pat dry between paper towels and place in salad bowl.

Toss spinach, green onions, and coriander leaves and add salad dressing. Garnish with cherry tomatoes or radishes. Serve immediately. A chopped hardboiled egg is great, sprinkled sparingly.

———⟨⟩———

SPINACH SALAD WITH JICAMA
Ensalada de Espinacas con Jicama

———⊙———

Spinach and jicama are great together, the perfect marriage of flavors. If you prefer a different dressing, use one of your own but do not add sugar. The pieces of jicama, you will note, have their own innate sweetness that does not need enhancing. I like this particular salad served with seafood of any kind fixed in any way. The freshness is perfect with fried fish, with baked fish, with shrimps, lobster—you name it. Try it, see if I'm not right.

———⊙———

6 to 8 servings

3 10-ounce bunches of fresh spinach
½ pound fresh mushrooms, sliced
1 cup thin slices of jicama
  Mexican-style Italian Dressing (page 276) to taste
2 tablespoons sesame seeds
2 tablespoons Maggi (optional)

Wash spinach, discarding stems. Pat dry on paper towels and tear into chilled salad bowl. Add sliced mushrooms.

Peel jicama and cut in half from top to bottom, then cut into quarters. Slice as thin as possible and wash in ice water. Dry with paper towels. Layer on top of the mushrooms.

Pour about ½ cup of the dressing over the salad and mix thoroughly, lifting the leaves from bottom to the top. Sprinkle with sesame seeds and serve with extra dressing in a sauceboat.

Note: The size of a jicama is often overwhelming, so they must be sliced to a manageable size.

———⊙———

MINTED SPINACH SALAD
Ensalada de Espinacas con Yerba Buena

A mint bed is a treasure indeed. When I was a little girl my grand-mother boasted of her mint bed because we lived in a desert town that had a copper smelter. The word "smog" had not been coined yet but the smoke from that smelter was murder to plants, flowers, and all growing matter. Later on they raised the height of the smokestacks and that helped a little, but it was hard even to raise a potted geranium in my home town. My grandmother's mint beds were actually not mint beds per se; the plants grew around the faucets for the water hose, and that trickle of water kept those mint plants green, lush, and lovely the year round.

6 servings

     1 pound fresh spinach
     ½ cup sliced green onion
     4 tablespoons snipped parsley
     6 tablespoons snipped mint leaves
     6 tablespoons olive oil and vegetable oil combined
     2 tablespoons wine vinegar
     1 tablespoon freshly squeezed lime juice
     ½ teaspoon salt
     3 tablespoons grated Parmesan cheese

Wash spinach and discard stems. Pat dry between paper towels. Tear into salad bowl, add sliced green onions, and mix in snipped parsley and fresh snipped mint. Combine well. Cover with plastic wrap and place in refrigerator until ready to mix.

Combine oils, wine vinegar, lime juice, and salt. Pour over salad, mix well, and sprinkle with grated Parmesan cheese just before serving. Garnish with wedges of 2 ripe tomatoes.

WATERCRESS AND PINE NUT SALAD
Ensalada de Berros

———⊙———

The mere writing of the word "watercress" fills me with a lovely glow. Our childhood is filled with such wonderful memories, at least mine was. My father was a family man in every sense of the word and, when we were spending our vacations on our cattle ranch his idea of enjoyment was unexpected outings.

One morning he would announce at the breakfast table that we were going down into a nearby canyon in search of watercress for our dinner that night. One of our cowboys had come across a patch of young tender cress in a rippling stream about five or six miles away. A lunch basket was packed, soft drinks were iced and placed in a portable ice box, and a proper container was carried to bring back the watercress. The driver was dispatched with all of this equipment in the pickup and we rode our horses down into the canyon. My mother was a good rider and so were my two sisters and I; my kid brother was a whiz though only three years old at the time. We had a log cabin down in the canyon with a picnic table and benches under these fabulous giant cottonwood trees. We would roll up our jeans above our knees, wade into the stream, and gather our watercress.

That night we had our salad, with a vinegar and oil dressing and broiled steaks.

———⊙———

8 servings

4 large bunches crisp watercress
1 clove garlic
2 tablespoons olive oil
⅛ cup wine vinegar
⅛ cup Maggi
  Fresh ground pepper
1 cup freshly shelled pine nuts (available in health food stores)

Wash the watercress, tear into bite-size sprigs, and drain. Wrap loosely in very wet paper towels and refrigerate until ready to assemble the salad.

Rub a large chilled salad bowl with a bruised garlic clove. Discard. Fill bowl with watercress, sprinkle with olive oil, and toss lightly. Now mix vinegar and Maggi sauce and pour over greens. Correct seasoning and grind black pepper over the salad. Garnish with the pine nuts.

CABBAGE SALAD
Ensalada de Repollo

———⊙———

So good, so economical, so fresh. You may purchase a large head of recently cut cabbage and carry it home with you, and if you store it in a cool place I can assure you it should keep every bit of two weeks.

———⊙———

8 servings

1 large green cabbage, about 1½ pounds
1 cup chopped fresh mint leaves
1 tablespoon chopped pickled canned green jalapeño strips
Zesty Dressing (page 279)

Cut off loose outer leaves of cabbage and remove any bruised spots. Wash cabbage thoroughly and cut in half. Cut out thick part of the core and wash cabbage halves under cold running water. Drain cut side down.

Shred or chop cabbage.

Place shredded cabbage in a large salad bowl and fold in mint leaves.

Shake dressing in bottle and remove garlic. Pour amount needed over shredded cabbage and mix. Garnish with pickled red chile pieces or 2 or 3 sliced radishes for color.

———⊙———

CACTUS SHOOTS SALAD
Ensalada de Nopalitos

———⊙———

Nopalitos are classified as a Lenten dish in all of Mexico. Years ago when the laws of the church were very strict the peons and the poor could go out into the fields and cut the amount they needed, for a meal or more. This salad is wonderful with fried chicken or pan-fried fish fillets, or add some fresh salsa and serve with steak strips or broiled meat patties. Serve it garnished with a few cubes of Monterey Jack cheese if you like.

———⊙———

4 servings

    1 pint jar of cactus shoots (nopalitos)
   ½ cup chopped green onions, tops and bulbs
    1 cup chopped peeled tomatoes
   ¼ cup chopped cilantro leaves
    1 chopped fresh green jalapeño chile, stem and seeds removed
      Salt and pepper
    3 tablespoons salad oil mixed with 1 mashed garlic clove
    2 tablespoons fresh lime juice

Drain the cactus shoots and rinse with cold running water. Drain in a colander and pat dry with paper towels.

Spoon into a small salad bowl, suitable for taking to table, and stir in the chopped green onions, tomatoes, cilantro leaves, and chopped jalapeño chile. Season with salt and pepper to taste.

Mix the oil and garlic infusion with the freshly squeezed lime juice.

Toss the vegetables with the dressing and place bowl in the refrigerator to chill. This keeps well, and can be used as a relish.

———⊙———

CHAYOTE SALAD
Ensalada de Chayotes

The chayote is quite bland, hence the use of more "spirited" ingredients for this salad. You might also try handling the chayote as you would potatoes. I have done so successfully and have produced the flavor of an everyday potato salad exactly, but do please omit hard-boiled eggs if you try this. They have much too strong a flavor for the bland chayote.

6 to 8 servings

3 chayotes
1 cup sliced purple onions
¼ cup vinegar
¾ cup oil
1 crushed garlic clove
Salt and pepper
1 teaspoon crushed oregano leaves
Pickled red jalapeño strips
Black olives

To cook chayotes, cut in half lengthwise and boil in 6 cups of water with 1 tablespoon salt added, until tender, about 1 hour. Drain and cool. Peel and slice in long thin slices.

Blanch sliced purple onions with 2 cups boiling water and drain. Marinate the onion slices in mixture of vinegar, oil, garlic clove, and salt and pepper, sprinkled with crushed oregano.

Arrange chayote slices on a large platter and spoon on onion slices to cover. Now spoon the marinade all over the salad. Garnish with strips of red jalapeño chiles and a few black olives.

Note: If red jalapeño strips are not available use a few green strips and a few crisp rings of bell pepper for garnish.

MUSHROOM SALAD
Ensalada de Hongos y Zanahorias

———⊙———

This is a surprise combination in that all the vegetables are prepared
in the raw state and do beautifully. You must remember, however
that the flavors must be given time to ripen. The salad may even be
made a day ahead. It is great for picnics because it may be tran-
sported in a covered glass jar or plastic container, but do keep it cool
or on ice. I like to add sliced green stuffed olives if I happen to have
any in my pantry.

———⊙———

6 to 8 servings

2 cups thinly sliced zucchini
2 cups sliced peeled carrots
2 cups sliced mushrooms
1 cup thinly sliced white onion
Mexican-style Italian Dressing with Oregano (page 277)

In medium-sized bowl, layer all the raw vegetable slices.
Spoon dressing over the vegetables, cover bowl with plastic wrap, and place
in refrigerator to ripen flavors. Serve as salad or vegetable dish.

———⊙———

SLICED TOMATOES AND CAPERS SALAD
Jitomates con Alcaparras

————⊙————

When in doubt, when in a hurry, when tired of the regular run of the mill salad, peel a few tomatoes—the large, ripe, luscious ones —and chill and slice them for this salad.

I once spent a vacation in La Paz in the famous "Baja" so popular now with American tourists. We drove to a tomato farm—rows and rows of plants, well planted and well tended, tied to four- or five-foot poles so the tomatoes never touched the soil. Beautiful and oh, so very, very large. In fact I've never seen tomatoes like those since. All the hotel restaurants and small cafes served them sliced with whatever you ordered from the menu, even for breakfast as a garnish for any egg dish. I first tasted this salad there at a Spaniard's small cafe. The olive oil was not of the best but regardless it did something for those capers. Try it with choice olive oil and wait for the compliments.

————⊙————

8 servings

4 large fancy ripe tomatoes, peeled
¼ cup thinly sliced white onion
¼ cup olive oil
   juice of half a lime
   Salt and coarsely ground black pepper
¼ teaspoon minced garlic
¼ cup ice water
   Romaine lettuce
¼ cup capers, rinsed

Peel tomatoes and chill. Place sliced onions in ice water for a few minutes. Drain.

Mix olive oil, lime juice, salt and pepper, and minced garlic, and add ¼ cup ice water.

Line a chilled platter with romaine lettuce leaves, using the heart of the lettuce head. We want the pale-colored leaves for color contrast.

Slice chilled tomatoes, arrange them on the lettuce, and spoon chilled onion slices on top. Garnish with capers and spoon the strained dressing over all.

POTATO SALAD
Ensalada de Papas

———⊙———

This was my grandmother's version of potato salad. For many years
this is what was eaten as a salad in my own home when I was a little
girl. Later on in my early teens when I went away to boarding school
I tasted the American version of the classic potato salad and I liked
it, but not as much as I liked the one served at home. The touch of
mustard made all the difference in the world.

You might sprinkle it with oregano leaves and garnish it with
chile strips—very good. It keeps beautifully in the refrigerator for
two or three days and may be served later with a garnish of cold
fresh deviled eggs.

———⊙———

8 servings

4 potatoes
¼ cup vinegar
½ cup salad oil
1 teaspoon prepared salad mustard
Salt and pepper
¼ cup minced green onion, tops and bulbs

Boil the unpeeled potatoes until tender but not too soft. Peel and slice them
when cool.

Place vinegar, oil, mustard, and salt and pepper in small jar and mix well
to blend mustard into oil and vinegar. Shake well and pour over sliced
potatoes. Mix well.

Arrange on platter and sprinkle with the chopped green onions. Cover with
plastic wrap and keep in refrigerator until ready to serve.

———⊙———

CABBAGE RELISH
Picado de Repollo

———⊙———

A delightful relish to serve with broiled steaks, hamburgers, and hot dogs. It ripens and keeps well.

———⊙———

About 2 quarts

    1 large green cabbage, about 1½ pounds
    1 cup white vinegar
    ¼ cup salad oil
    4 finely minced garlic cloves mixed with ½ cup ice water
    10 crushed chiltepins or 2 tablespoons dry red pepper flakes
    1 tablespoon salt or according to taste
      Coarse ground pepper to taste

Cut off loose outer leaves of cabbage and remove any bruised spots. Wash cabbage thoroughly and cut out thick part of core. Cut in half and wash under cold running water. Drain well.

Shred cabbage in processor or with a very sharp knife. Place in large bowl.

Add remainder of ingredients, mix well, cover, and place in the refrigerator.

———⊙———

FRESH MUSHROOM RELISH
Picado de Hongos

————⊙————

6–8 servings

1 pound mushrooms
1 carrot, peeled and cut into thin short strips
1 cup slices or strips of fresh Anaheim peppers
    (blistered in hot oil, peeled, and seeded)
1 cup peeled chopped ripe tomatoes
½ cup coarsely chopped green onions
1 cup salad oil
½ cup vinegar
    Salt and pepper

Quickly wipe mushrooms with damp paper towel or, if they are very dirty, remove stems and slice mushrooms and then wash slices quickly in warm water. Save stems for another use.

Combine mushroom slices, carrot strips, chile strips, tomatoes, and onions in medium-sized bowl and add the remaining ingredients. Marinate in refrigerator for 1 hour before serving.

————⊙————

FAST MARINATED ONIONS
Cebollas Curtidas

————⊙————

These onions are used as a garnish in many recipes from the state of Yucatán. They keep well in a covered container, are pleasant to look at, and a delight to taste.

————⊙————

3 to 4 cups

4 red or purple onions, thinly sliced
1 cup Bay Leaf Tea (page 11)
¼ cup white vinegar
1 teaspoon whole peppercorns
1 serrano chile, sliced
Salt
Crushed oregano leaves

Place sliced onions in large strainer and pour boiling water over them slowly to blanch them. Place onions in bowl and add infusion of bay leaf tea combined with vinegar, peppercorns, sliced serrano chile, and salt. Sprinkle with small amount of crushed oregano leaves. Allow to ripen a few hours or overnight.

Note: If purple onions are not available, use white or yellow and pour juice from a small can of beets to color—drain—then proceed with recipe.

————⊙————

PIQUANT SPREAD FOR SANDWICHES
Salsa para Tortas

———⊙———

This is good with all sandwich fillings but especially with a fish sandwich.

———⊙———

About 3 cups

1 pint mayonnaise
1 cup chopped dill pickles, well drained
½ cup chopped white onion
1 teaspoon mashed garlic
½ teaspoon pepper

Mix all ingredients and place in a large jar. Cover and keep in refrigerator. May be used as a sandwich spread or as a sauce to accompany fish. Keeps indefinitely.

———⊙———

SIMPLE VINAIGRETTE
Vinagreta Sencilla

———⊙———

1 cup

¼ cup vinegar
¾ cup oil
½ teaspoon salt and coarsely ground pepper to taste
1 garlic clove, bruised (optional)

Mix vinegar, oil, salt and pepper in a pint jar, adding a bruised garlic clove if you like. Remove the garlic before serving.

———⊙———

CLASSIC VINAIGRETTE
Vinagreta

————⊙————

This is the good old standby. I like to make some up fresh every Monday morning because it's handy to have all week long—ready and at your fingertips. I personally like to add about ¼ cup of cold water to this amount because it seems leaner and is better. Be sure to remove the garlic before using, and do shake the dressing well every time you use it.

————⊙————

About 1¼ cups

1 cup oil
¼ cup vinegar
1 teaspoon salt
1 teaspoon Mexican paprika
1 bruised garlic clove

Combine all ingredients in large jar with a lid. Place in refrigerator. Shake and strain before using.

————⊙————

GARLIC VINAIGRETTE
Vinagreta al Ajo

————⊙————

This is definitely my favorite. But then I am an inveterate garlic eater! This is a great way to enhance the salads that are to be served with a freshly made pasta. A modified Caesar salad (modified because I omit the anchovies and use only the yolk of the coddled egg) is great with this garlic dressing.

————⊙————

1⅓ cups

1 cup oil
⅓ cup white vinegar
1 tablespoon mashed garlic
1 teaspoon salt
½ teaspoon pepper
½ teaspoon Mexican paprika

Place all ingredients in a small jar with a cover. Keep in refrigerator and shake well before using. Do not strain or discard the garlic. This dressing must taste heavily of garlic.

ROSEMARY VINAIGRETTE
Vinagreta con Romero

———⊙———

All homemade dressings have the cook's touch, of that there is no doubt. If two or three persons make this particular dressing it will taste different in each instance. I personally like to soak the rosemary in hot water for about 3 minutes and then drain it and place it in a jar before adding the rest of the ingredients. (I make up a pint or a quart at a time because it ripens beautifully and keeps well.)

This dressing is great with crisp lettuce (romaine is best) and nothing else added except some fresh croutons.

———⊙———

1¼ cups

1 cup oil
¼ cup vinegar
1 teaspoon rosemary
1 teaspoon salt
½ teaspoon Mexican paprika
1 bruised garlic clove

Combine all ingredients in a jar with a lid. Shake well and refrigerate. Strain before using.

———⊙———

MEXICAN-STYLE ITALIAN DRESSING
Vinagreta Tipo Italiano

———⊙———

About 1½ cups

½ cup olive oil
½ cup vegetable oil
⅓ cup wine vinegar
½ teaspoon salt
1 teaspoon mashed garlic
1 teaspoon rosemary
¼ cup ice water

Combine ingredients in jar; cover and shake. Allow to ripen in refrigerator for 4 to 6 hours or overnight, thus allowing rosemary to flavor the dressing. Strain over salads.

MEXICAN-STYLE ITALIAN DRESSING WITH OREGANO
Vinagreta con Oregano

———⊙———

About 1 cup

½ cup oil
¼ cup vinegar
¼ cup ice water
  Salt and coarsely ground pepper to taste
1 tablespoon crushed oregano leaves

Mix the oil, vinegar, ice water, salt and pepper, and oregano. Strain.

———⊙———

LEMON JUICE AND OIL DRESSING
Aderezo de Aceite y Jugo de Limon

———⊙———

Lemon juice is what gives this recipe its special flavor. Lime juice in this case would render it too tart and spoil the salad. This is a great dressing for salads that contain fresh mint and/or chopped fresh parsley.

———⊙———

About ¾ cup

¼ cup oil
¼ cup ice water
6 tablespoons freshly squeezed lemon juice
½ teaspoon salt
½ teaspoon black pepper
1 garlic clove, peeled and bruised

Place all ingredients in a jar with a lid. Cover and shake before using. Discard garlic clove.

SWEET AND SOUR DRESSING FOR SPINACH SALADS
Aderezo Agridulce

———⊙———

Sweet and sour combinations do not appear too often in cooking in Mexican homes. The home in which I first tasted this dressing served with a spinach salad belongs to a lady who travels extensively, especially in the United States, but she likes to add fresh mint leaves to her salad and that changes the flavor considerably. I love it on sliced oranges and some fresh fruit combinations. It is also a must on raw vegetable salad combinations, especially cauliflower, zucchini, cherry tomatoes, and broccoli.

Modern innovative Mexican women are into all that is new and not necessarily traditional, and a new Mexican cuisine is emerging. It will be a credit to all of us if they will hold on to the old family recipes handed down from generation to generation and add a dish or two here and there of the *nueva cocina Mexicana* to their daily menus.

———⊙———

About 5½ cups

½ cup apple cider vinegar
1 tablespoon salt
1 teaspoon pepper
2 tablespoons dry mustard
1 teaspoon dried basil
1 teaspoon crushed oregano leaves
4 bruised garlic cloves
5 ounces granulated sugar (about ½ cup)
1 tablespoon Mexican paprika
1 quart oil
½ cup red wine vinegar

Combine all ingredients except oil and vinegar in a large bowl. Add oil while you whisk mixture slowly. When mixed well add ½ cup red wine vinegar. Store in a large jar in the refrigerator. When ready to use, be sure to strain the amount needed over the salad before mixing.

———⊙———

ZESTY DRESSING
Aderezo con Mostaza

———⊙———

About 1 cup

⅔ cup oil
⅓ cup white vinegar
1 bruised garlic clove
Salt and pepper
½ teaspoon of Mexican paprika
1 teaspoon prepared salad mustard

Combine in a jar oil, vinegar, garlic, salt and pepper, Mexican paprika, and salad mustard. Shake well. Refrigerate until ready to use.

———⊙———

LOW-CALORIE SALAD DRESSING
Aderezo para Ensalada sin Aceite

———⊙———

This recipe is great for weight-watchers. If you feel you must, you may add 1 teaspoon olive oil to this low-calorie dressing.

———⊙———

About 2 cups

1 14½-ounce can Italian-style tomatoes, undrained
2 tablespoons fresh lime juice or lemon juice
2 tablespoons white vinegar
1 teaspoon rosemary
1 mashed garlic clove
½ teaspoon pepper
1 teaspoon salt
1 teaspoon Mexican paprika (pimienton) or sweet paprika

Put all the ingredients in a blender container and almost liquefy. Strain into a large jar and store, covered, in the refrigerator.

SAUCES

I n mastering the art of making Mexican salsas, or sauces, you hold the key to a myriad of culinary treasures. Most Mexican dishes have a sauce or are served with one and while many can be used interchangeably at the table, others are essential to a particular dish, to provide its special character.

Salsas using tomatillo, the green-tomato-like vegetable with its papery skin, are good examples. Nothing tastes quite like a tomatillo—tart, refreshing, intriguing. It goes spectacularly well with chicken and seafood and is a natural complement to corn tortillas. Red chile sauces are another category altogether. Red chiles and green chiles are very seldom used together, and you cannot substitute green chiles for the dried red chile pods with their earthy, sensual flavor. Occasionally in an ajillo sauce you will find a few strips of green chile, and they are frequently mixed in Tex-Mex cooking, but normally it is not done.

It is customary to place at least one salsa, but more often two or three, on the dining table to season the prepared dishes. They can make a dish as hot as fire or merely add a high note depending on the kind of sauce and the amount used. Salsas almost always transform a dish, in addition to making it hot. In the case of the raw sauces, such as the Salsa Fresca or Pico de Gallo, they can also contribute interesting textures. Any broiled, roasted, or boiled meat can become Mexican by the simple addition of a fresh or cooked sauce.

As an added bonus, many salsas can be used as dips for chips of all kinds, and sliced raw vegetables, which are becoming increasingly popular in Mexico.

It is interesting to note that many salsas have been passed on from generation to generation in their original form from the time of the Aztec civilization. Bernal del Castillo, a historian from the time of the Conquest, describes many sauces that he tasted at a banquet in Montezuma's palace—sauces still used today. Also interesting is the fact that in rural Mexico and even in the cities, sauces are still made in the same manner—by grinding or puréeing the ingredients in a molcajete, a mortar and pestle made of heavy, volcanic rock.

In the American kitchen, it is best to use the blender when a recipe calls for puréeing the ingredients. Even though the food processor can be used, keep in mind that very often the texture will be different.

BASIC BOILED RED CHILE SAUCE
Salsa de Chile Colorado
────────⊙────────

To prepare Mexican food without resorting to the ready-made canned varieties of sauces, it is essential that the new aficionado learn this sauce above all others so that he or she can produce an authentic northern enchilada.

Traditionally the red chiles are stemmed and seeded and pan-fried in hot pork lard before boiling. But if you and your guests are counting calories, then by all means omit the sautéing of the dry red peppers and simply boil them. *But boil them you must.* Boiling plumps the chiles and restores the original flavor.

If the sauce seems too pungent once you have followed all the steps in the recipe, resort to an old family trick my grandmother used: Dissolve 1 teaspoon of sugar in 1 teaspoon of vinegar mixed with 2 tablespoons of cold water and stir this into the simmering sauce. Presto! Note the difference. Milder, and with a lovely flavor.

────────⊙────────

1 quart

10 to 12 New Mexico mild dry red chiles
4 cups cold water
4 garlic cloves
4 tablespoons vegetable oil
4 tablespoons all-purpose flour
Salt
1 tablespoon instant chicken bouillon granules
1 teaspoon vinegar
1 teaspoon sugar

Stem and seed the chiles. Wash. Boil in medium-sized saucepan in 1 quart hot water, stirring often. Be sure to push the chiles deep into the water, as they tend to rise. Cook, covered, over medium heat for 20 minutes. Allow to cool in water they were cooked in.

Drain chiles and purée in blender, 3 or 4 at a time, each batch with 1 cup cold water and 1 clove garlic. Strain into bowl. (Do the puréeing in four batches in order not to clog the blender blades.)

When all the chiles have been puréed and strained, heat 4 tablespoons oil in large skillet or dutch oven and brown the flour in the oil to a light golden color for a mild-tasting roux. Add the strained red chile mixture all at once and cook over low heat, stirring constantly, until thick and tasty. Add salt and chicken bouillon granules and boil 2 minutes. Correct seasoning. Now add the vinegar and sugar and stir well. Remove from heat. This sauce is now ready for enchiladas or to blend in with cooked meat for a tasty tamal filling. Freezes beautifully. One cup is enough for 6 enchiladas.

————⊙————

BASIC RED CHILE SAUCE WITH TOMATILLOS
Salsa de Chile Ancho con Tomatillo

————⊙————

This is a different-tasting red sauce because the tomatillo is tart and has seeds. The combination of the flavors is delightful and the addition of the sugar modifies the tartness of the green tomatoes.

————⊙————

3 cups

> 6 ancho chiles
> 1 teaspoon mashed garlic
> 1 cup canned tomatillos or 1 7-ounce can tomatillo sauce
> 1 teaspoon sugar
> 2 tablespoons lard or salad oil
> 1 teaspoon salt
> ½ teaspoon ground cumin

Wash dried ancho chiles and cook in 1 quart boiling water, well covered, until soft and puffy, about 30 minutes. Allow to cool in own cooking water. Drain. Remove stems.

Purée chiles in blender with garlic and 2 cups fresh water and strain into a bowl. Stir in the canned tomatillos or tomatillo sauce. Add sugar.

In large saucepan, heat lard or oil and add chile and tomatillo mixture. Cook over medium heat, stirring occasionally. Add salt to taste, and ground cumin, and stir well. Sauce is now ready for use. Excellent over poached chicken breasts and better still over pan-fried pork chops. I cook the meat with it in a standard pot roast recipe—the combination is great.

FRESH SAUCE
Salsa Fresca
————⊙————

There is a great deal of similarity between this sauce and Pico de Gallo (page 298). You will note that one is enhanced with fresh cilantro leaves and the other with oregano leaves. Both sauces are great and it stands to reason that if you do not have fresh cilantro on hand you use the oregano and get an excellent sauce just the same. This sauce may be made without the lime juice, but don't substitute lemon juice; use vinegar instead, or nothing at all.

If you find occasionally that you have a lot of Salsa Fresca left over, do not store it in its uncooked state. The flavor of that chopped tomato will turn into a spoiled flavor. Instead, put the leftover sauce in a small pan, add about ¼ or ½ cup of cold water, and let it come to a simmer over high heat. Then cover it, lower the heat, and let it cook for 3 to 5 minutes. Allow it to cool, place it in a covered jar, and use it the next day. It may also be frozen successfully.

————⊙————

2½ cups

  1 pound ripe tomatoes, skins left on
  ¼ cup chopped green onions, both white and green part
      Tips of 2 jalapeño chiles
  1 tablespoon freshly squeezed lime juice
  ½ cup ice water
      Salt
  1 teaspoon crushed oregano leaves

Chop tomatoes, onions, and tips of the jalapeño chiles. Combine in medium-sized bowl. Add remainder of ingredients and mix by hand, bruising the tomato pieces. Taste and correct seasoning. Serve at once—this sauce will not keep.

————⊙————

GRANDMOTHER'S FRESH CHILE SAUCE
Salsa de Chile Verde de Mi Abuelita

——⊙——

You will need a griddle or a heavy cast-iron skillet to broil the tomatoes and the green chiles. *This is a must.* This sauce is usually just mildly hot and very tasty. Simply folded into a hot flour or corn tortilla with a slice of soft cheese, it might serve as a snack or a light meal.

——⊙——

3 cups

1 pound ripe tomatoes
4 to 6 fresh green California chiles
1 teaspoon salt

Broil the tomatoes on top of the stove on a griddle or heavy cast-iron skillet over high heat. When tomatoes are done on one side, turn and continue broiling until skins are slightly charred. Have a bowl of cold water ready, and place broiled tomatoes in water carefully so that skins will not burst. We don't want the delicious juice to escape.

Now broil the green chiles the same way, but over medium heat. Skins may be charred or just blistered. Place chiles in a paper sack or a plastic bag, or better still wrap them in a damp dish towel. As the cooks of yore used to say, they must sweat. This softens the skins and facilitates the peeling of the chiles.

Have your sauce bowl ready. Skin the broiled tomatoes over the bowl to catch all the juice, and bruise and crush them by hand. This sauce is *never* puréed.

Clean the chiles, take the stems off, slit on one side, remove the seeds under cold running water, and cut into thin strips. (My granny used to crush and bruise them by hand if they weren't too hot.) Mix crushed tomatoes and chiles and add salt. Taste. Glorious in a hot flour tortilla the size you use for burritos.

——⊙——

COOKED SAUCE
Salsa Guizada

———⊙———

This is a wonderful sauce for people on a diet. Note, no oil—it is cooked with water only. It keeps indefinitely, freezes well, and may be served hot or cold. I like to serve this sauce as a modified topping for Huevos Rancheros.

———⊙———

3 to 4 cups

1 pound ripe tomatoes or
    1 28-ounce can Italian-style tomatoes
2 4-ounce cans chopped green chiles
½ cup chopped white onion
1 teaspoon salt
1 teaspoon mashed garlic
½ teaspoon crushed oregano leaves

If using fresh tomatoes, parboil them in ½ cup boiling water, peel, and chop. If using canned tomatoes, crush them.

Mix tomatoes, canned chiles, and chopped onion and cook, covered, for 3 minutes. Season with salt and add garlic and oregano leaves.

———⊙———

HOME-STYLE SAUCE
Salsa Casera

If you ask your restaurant waiter to bring some sauce, he will ask you if "salsa casera" is acceptable. That's a perfect title; it means what we mean when we ask for a "house" dressing for a salad. Each cafe has its own recipe, many more or less alike, but every once in a while you come across one with an unrecognizable ingredient that tickles your imagination. This happened to me the other day in a lovely little town in the state of Mexico, Tenancingo—a quaint town, so green, so lush, hilly with corn patches growing all the way up to the tops of the surrounding slopes, which were terraced to keep the seeds and water at the correct level. In the cafe in Tenancingo, the surprise ingredient was thyme—unusual and just great!

3 cups

1 pound ripe tomatoes, peeled and chopped
2 crisply fresh serrano chiles, stemmed, partially seeded, and chopped
½ cup chopped green onions (some of the green ends too, please)
½ cup chopped cilantro leaves, or more if you desire
¼ cup ice water
½ teaspoon salt
1 tablespoon freshly squeezed lime juice

Bruise ingredients by hand, and if too dry add more ice water. Combine all ingredients in a medium-sized bowl and allow flavors to ripen for 30 minutes before serving.

Do not substitute any ingredient, although fresh jalapeños will work in a pinch (but use just 1, not 2). Canned tomatoes will not do.

NEW SAUCE
Salsa Nueva

———⊙———

The addition of the chopped or thickly grated carrots to this sauce gives it a new flavor altogether, lowering the hotness of the chile and making Salsa Nueva almost like a relish. I've served this sauce at Thanksgiving and it was greeted with ohs and ahs—it is great with turkey.

———⊙———

3 cups

    1 pound ripe tomatoes, peeled and chopped
    2 carrots, parboiled, peeled, and finely chopped
      Salt
    2 canned pickled jalapeño chiles, minced (seeds and all)
    1 teaspoon oregano leaves
    2 tablespoons pickling liquid from canned chiles
    2 tablespoons salad oil
    1 teaspoon mashed garlic (optional)

Peel and chop the tomatoes and add to the diced carrots. Season with salt. Add jalapeños, oregano, pickling liquid, oil, and mashed garlic. Let sauce stand for at least 1 hour so that the flavors will blend.

———⊙———

SAUCE FOR FIRE-EATERS
Salsa para Comelumbres

There are two categories of champion chile eaters. First are those who can eat the stuff and really enjoy the heat of the sauce, and whose system can handle it with no repercussions. The second category includes those who delight in the great chile experience but have to cope with health problems that go with eating pungent salsas. Both groups are willing to embark on the great adventure no matter what. But the latter crowd carry the roll of Rolaids in their pockets! (Some old-timers in their seventies still swear by ½ teaspoon of baking soda swallowed with a little cool water.)

And so it goes, but once hooked there is no way out. I am often surprised by a gathering of my people and American friends partaking of a groaning board. You will always find Americans eating hotter chile and more of it than Mexicans. I consider it a compliment.

Wonderful for chile lovers and for champion chile sauce eaters. Good on and with almost everything—potatoes, meats, cheese, beans—you name it.

2½ to 3 cups

1 cup chopped fresh jalapeños, seeds and all
½ cup chopped onion
1 teaspoon crushed garlic
1 teaspoon salt
1 tablespoon vinegar
½ cup ice water
½ cup tomato juice

Stir in quart jar chopped jalapeño chiles, onion, and remainder of ingredients. Keep in refrigerator until ready to serve. Will keep for a week.

SAUCE FOR THE CHILDREN
Salsa para los Niños

————⊙————

This is a must in all homes where there are children, or adults with health problems. Because it is made with canned tomatoes, it will not sour or spoil quickly, and it is good with everything. It's a good dipping sauce, too, and if you're not too partial to onion you may omit it, but you can add garlic instead if you wish. Always use the oregano; that is essential.

————⊙————

3 cups

   1 28-ounce can Italian-style tomatoes, crushed
¼ cup finely chopped onions
½ cup ice water
   Salt
   1 tablespoon vinegar
   1 tablespoon salad oil
   1 teaspoon finely crushed oregano leaves

Crush tomatoes by hand. Add rest of ingredients. Serve in a pastel-hued bowl to denote mildness. Children love to say, "Please pass the sauce in the pink bowl—that's ours."

Wonderful on tacos, burritos, nachos (*sans* jalapeños), and corn chips.

————⊙————

LIQUID SAUCE
Salsa Liquida

———⊙———

Fast and simple to make and a delight to eat! Great with everything.

———⊙———

2½ cups

4 to 6 jap chiles
1 teaspoon finely minced garlic
½ cup boiling water
1 cup tomato juice
1 cup canned tomato sauce
1 tablespoon vinegar
Salt
1 teaspoon sugar
1 teaspoon crushed oregano leaves

Soak jap chiles in hot water, drain, and purée in blender with the garlic in ½ cup boiling water. Leave right in blender container and add the rest of the ingredients. Pour into a quart jar and leave in refrigerator until ready to serve. Stir with a wooden spoon and pour into a sauceboat.

Wonderful for dipping corn chips, over nachos, and for dipping miniature tacos.

———⊙———

I'M IN A HURRY SAUCE
Salsa Rapida

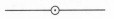

This is a modified northern *adobo* sauce using the same components with the exception of the red chile.

In Sonora we use the ground toasted red chiles, stemmed and seeded before being toasted and ground. The flavor of the gently toasted pepper is out of this world. It tastes mildly nutty and the earthy flavor of the raw chile disappears.

2 cups

½ cup pure ground red chile powder (no spices)
1 cup boiling water
¼ cup vinegar
1 teaspoon crushed oregano leaves
Salt
1 teaspoon sugar
1 tablespoon mashed garlic
1 tablespoon chile seeds for garnish

Soak chile powder in boiling water until doubled in bulk. Stir well and add vinegar, and if necessary more hot water until mixture is of the consistency of cream. Add oregano, salt, sugar, and mashed garlic. Allow to set a few minutes and serve in bowl, and *do* sprinkle the chile seeds on top.

Colorful and tasty. Good with broiled steaks and pan-fried pork chops, and let's not forget fresh boiled beans from the pot.

TIPSY SAUCE
Salsa Borracha

————⟨∘⟩————

I think that this is a sauce that must be experimented with. You can make it "tipsy" with the addition of spirits, that's easy to see, so why not do your own thing, as my grandchildren say. I've made it by adding 1 or 2 tablespoons of Tequila—not bad! But I have also used dry sherry only, adding and tasting, tasting and adding, until I like the end results. I have even tasted it doctored with bourbon, and it was a teaser but delightful. So make a batch up and use what you happen to have on hand.

————⟨∘⟩————

4 cups

4 tablespoons oil
8 ancho chiles, washed and dried with paper towels
1 tablespoon mashed garlic
1 cup cold water
1 tablespoon vinegar
1 cup stale lager beer
½ cup dry sherry
   Salt
1 teaspoon sugar
1 teaspoon oregano
½ cup grated Parmesan cheese
½ cup grated farmer's cheese
6 or more pickled canned serrano chiles

Heat oil in large skillet and pan-fry the ancho chiles over very low heat. Do this carefully, as chiles tend to scorch and give off a bitter taste.

Have 1 quart of water boiling in a deep pot. Boil the fried red chiles 20 to 30 minutes or until plump and soft. Allow to cool in own broth. Drain.

Remove ancho chile stems and place chiles in blender container with garlic and water. Purée and strain into a bowl. Add oil that the chiles were fried in, vinegar, beer and sherry, salt, sugar, and oregano. Place in refrigerator for 15 minutes.

Add cheeses, mixed, just before serving and fill a sauceboat with canned pickled serrano chiles as an accompaniment.

Note: This is modified because we have used the stale beer and the dry sherry instead of *pulque,* which is difficult to come by outside of Mexico. The substitution is fair and the flavor still comes through.

TOMATILLO CILANTRO SAUCE
Salsa de Tomatillo al Cilantro

This is a cooked salsa and very good indeed; furthermore it will keep indefinitely if cooked thoroughly. It's a handsome sauce; it appears on restaurant tables all over Mexico. If the tomatillos were not very green to begin with, it will take on a faded green color, which I remedy by adding a drop or two of green vegetable coloring.

This is a basic sauce and may be thickened in various ways. You can add 1 or 2 tablespoons of masa harina (corn flour) mixed with ¼ cup water; you can make a roux with 2 tablespoons of oil and 1 tablespoon of flour and pour the sauce into the lightly browned flour and oil mixture to thicken; or (this is my favorite) you can lightly brown ¼ cup slivered almonds till a pale gold in color, then purée them in the blender with a cup of water and 1 garlic clove, stir into the sauce, and cook until thick and creamy.

2½ cups

1 pound fresh tomatillos
1 cup cold water
4 garlic cloves
1 jalapeño chile, seeds and all
Half a medium-sized white onion
2 cups cilantro leaves
⅛ cup salad oil
2 teaspoons salt
1 teaspoon sugar

Remove outer paperlike skin from tomatillos and cook the tomatillos in 4 cups water for 20 minutes. Drain and place in blender container with 1 cup cold water, garlic, jalapeño, onion, and cilantro leaves. Purée until almost liquid.

Heat oil in a dutch oven and pour sauce from blender container directly into hot oil. Season with salt and sugar. Lower heat and simmer 5 minutes. If still too sour add another teaspoonful of sugar.

This sauce is excellent for crisp pork skins and for any stew with pork, chicken, or beef. Lovely to look at and delightful to eat.

TOMATILLOS AND CHIPOTLES IN AN UNCOOKED SAUCE
Salsa de Tomatillos y Chipotles

⎯⎯⊙⎯⎯

It's a good idea to have both this and Fresh Sauce (page 287) on the table in colorful pottery containers, and of course the pastel bowl of Sauce for the Children (page 293). It adds glamour and allows guests to experience another assault on their taste buds.

When you do not have the fresh ingredients, never you mind; go into your pantry and bring out a can of tomatillo sauce and one of pickled chipotle chiles, and you're in business. This keeps indefinitely in the refrigerator and will freeze well.

⎯⎯⊙⎯⎯

1½ cups

½ pound tomatillos
1 garlic clove
2 pickled canned chipotle chiles puréed in blender
    with ¼ cup ice water
Salt
½ to 1 teaspoon sugar

Discard outer dry skin from tomatillos. Place tomatilles in blender container and add garlic clove and puréed canned chipotle chiles. Purée but do not liquefy. Add salt to taste. Add ½ teaspoon sugar. Increase sugar to 1 teaspoon if sauce seems much too sour.

⎯⎯⊙⎯⎯

ROOSTER'S BEAK
Pico de Gallo

⎯⎯⊙⎯⎯

This is a literal translation of the name of this sauce. It has become popular and famous under this name so methinks it is well to keep it. However, the name is also given in some parts of Mexico to a fresh fruit medley sold in paper cones dusted with salt and ground red chile powder, slightly spiced and with a few drops of fresh lime juice added. Great and so very low in calories.

For small children and ulcer patients, make the sauce up with a tender crisp bell pepper, stemmed and seeded, in place of the serranos or jalapeños.

⎯⎯⊙⎯⎯

2½ cups

1 pound ripe tomatoes, peeled and chopped to a medium dice
½ cup chopped white onion
1 cup fresh cilantro leaves
4 crisply fresh serrano chiles or jalapeños, seeds and all, chopped
½ cup ice water
Salt
Freshly squeezed lime juice to taste

Mix chopped tomatoes, onion, cilantro, and chiles with water, then add salt and lime juice. Do not stir too much. This salsa is almost considered a relish and should be kept crisp and never mushy.

Good with everything.

————⊙————

GREEN GREEN SAUCE
Salsa Verde Verde

————⊙————

This is a quick sauce. I like it with a plump garlic clove puréed with the other ingredients in the blender, but if you are not too much into the flavor of raw garlic, do not use. It renders the sauce sharper and stronger in flavor. The addition of the sugar is a must because tomatillos are very tart and the sugar makes them just right.

————⊙————

2½ cups

1 pound tomatillos
2 fresh small chiles
¼ cup chopped green onions (including some of the green)
1 cup fresh cilantro leaves
Salt
1 teaspoon sugar

Remove dry paperlike skins from tomatillos. Coarsely purée uncooked tomatillos, chiles, green onions, and cilantro leaves in blender. Season with salt to taste and add 1 teaspoon sugar.

Serve with soft tacos or burritos and as a dip for corn chips. Also wonderful with fried chicken, pan-fried pork chops, and pan-fried potatoes.

Note: This sauce is also great with grilled tortillas filled with slices of Jack cheese, a few strips of green chiles, and a few epazote leaves (about two per serving). Heat griddle or heavy iron skillet. Put the filling on one corn tortilla, top with a second tortilla, and press down on the "package" (it will resemble two stacked hotcakes) with something heavy while grilling on top of the stove. To serve, set the cheese-filled tortillas flat on the plate, smother with this sauce, and eat with a fork. A great substitute for grilled cheese sandwiches!

———⊙———

SPANISH SAUCE
Salsa Española
———⊙———

I like to make up this sauce and keep it to serve with a breaded veal cutlet, with a Spanish omelet, or with a pasta cooked on the spur of the moment. It is a basic sauce and may be thinned with chicken broth, tomato juice, or simply hot water. It is great on miniature homemade pizzas if you sprinkle on a bit of oregano or sweet basil before putting in the oven. I often make those with split English muffins.

———⊙———

3 to 4 cups

    2 tablespoons olive oil plus 2 tablespoons vegetable oil
    ½ cup chopped onion
    1 28-ounce can Italian-style tomatoes, crushed
    1 cup tomato juice
    ½ small can tomato paste
      Salt and pepper
    1 teaspoon mashed garlic
    1 bay leaf

Heat oils in dutch oven and sauté chopped onion for 1 minute, stirring often. Add crushed tomatoes, tomato juice, and tomato paste. Mix to blend. Add salt and pepper to taste. Stir in mashed garlic and bay leaf. Cover and allow to simmer for 5 minutes. Remove bay leaf and store in refrigerator.

This sauce will keep 2 weeks and freezes well.

CAPER SAUCE
Salsa de Alcaparras

——⊙——

2 cups

6 tablespoons oil
½ cup chopped white onion
1 cup chopped peeled tomatoes
1 teaspoon mashed garlic
1 teaspoon dried tarragon leaves
  Salt and pepper
½ cup water
1 tablespoon instant chicken bouillon granules
1 teaspoon sugar
½ cup capers, washed and drained

Heat oil in dutch oven and sauté onion with tomatoes. Cook, stirring often, over low heat. Now add garlic and tarragon and season with salt and pepper. Add water and bouillon, sugar, and all but 2 tablespoons capers. Cook, covered, for 3 minutes. Cool.

Pour mixture into blender container and purée. Pour over prepared meat or chicken and heat in a 350° oven until bubbly. Arrange on a suitable platter, pour sauce over all, and garnish with reserved capers. This is also spectacular on cooked shrimp.

——⊙——

SAUCE FOR MOCK ENCHILADAS
Salsa para Entomatadas
————⊙————

When I find people who are hard to convince that Mexican food is not all fire and indigestible foods I invite them over and serve some baked mock enchiladas in a casserole. This is the sauce that I use. Mock enchiladas are so good, and all they need is a crisp green salad for a perfect luncheon menu. When I was a little girl they were fixed quite often on Fridays, always with shredded mild longhorn cheese.

————⊙————

3 cups

1 28-ounce can Italian-style tomatoes
4 tablespoons salad oil
3 tablespoons flour
   Salt and pepper
1 bay leaf
1 teaspoon mashed garlic (optional)

Purée canned tomatoes and strain. Make a roux with your oil and flour in a deep medium-sized saucepan. Brown flour lightly and add strained puréed tomatoes. Season with salt and pepper and add bay leaf. Allow to boil 5 minutes, stirring often. Cover, as this sauce often sputters. When slightly thick taste and correct seasoning. Remove bay leaf. The use of the mashed garlic is optional—it gives a delightful taste and if you use it, stir it in at this point. The sauce is now ready to use as you would enchilada sauce.

Freeze any leftover sauce. It may be used as a substitute for regular Chile Relleno Sauce.

————⊙————

SAUCE FOR CHILES RELLENOS I
Salsa para Chiles Rellenos I

To my mind a Chile Relleno that is not served swimming in this lovely sauce is like a hot cake without butter and syrup.

In the northern part of Mexico we simply call this a sauce but in central Mexico and further on south they call it a "caldillo" or a soupy salsa. It may be rendered thinner by the addition of tomato juice, chicken broth, or simply hot water with 1 tablespoon of instant chicken bouillon granules. The oregeno in this particular recipe is what gives it the special flavor, but you may use any other herb of your choice.

3 to 4 cups

    Half an onion, sliced
4 tablespoons salad oil
1 28-ounce can Italian-style tomatoes
1 teaspoon mashed garlic
    Salt and pepper
½ teaspoon crushed oregano
1 teaspoon sugar
1 cup chicken broth (if sauce is too thick)

Sauté onion slices in hot oil in medium-sized saucepan.

Purée canned tomatoes in blender with garlic. Strain. Add puréed tomatoes and garlic to sautéed onion slices. Season with salt and pepper and add oregano. Add sugar and correct seasoning. Cover and cook over medium heat for 5 minutes. If sauce thickens too much, add tomato juice and cook 2 minutes. Take to the table in a sauceboat. Should be served over Chiles Rellenos to cover.

SAUCE FOR CHILES RELLENOS II
Salsa para Chiles Rellenos II

—————⊙—————

3 to 4 cups

2 tablespoons salad oil
1 cup chopped onion
1 28-ounce can Italian-style tomatoes, crushed
2 tablespoons tomato paste
  Salt and pepper
1 teaspoon finely mashed garlic
1 bay leaf
1 teaspoon sugar
1 cup tomato juice (if sauce is too thick)

In medium saucepan heat oil and sauté chopped onion for 1 minute, stirring often, as onion must not brown. Add crushed tomatoes and tomato paste, salt and pepper, mashed garlic, bay leaf, and sugar, and cook, stirring, for 5 minutes. If too thick add 1 cup tomato juice and continue cooking for 3 minutes.

Spoon hot over Chiles Rellenos—wonderful.

FIESTA
DISHES

T he recipes in this chapter are my favorites—the ones I serve to my friends. Some I present at sit-down dinners, and others when I entertain informally and serve buffet-style. Please do not imagine that I offer them here as "official" Mexican fiesta dishes (if, indeed, there may be such things); they are simply the gala preparations dearest to my heart. Mind you, some of them take a great deal of time to prepare. Others are not so time-consuming. But every one is well worth the effort.

We love to party in Mexico, and most of our celebrations involve music, dance, drink, and especially food. Our major feast days are religious holidays, at which times certain foods are customary (special Lenten dishes are an example). During the Christmas season, friends and family may be invited to a tamalada; whole groups gather to make the tamales with their assorted fillings. The preparation itself becomes a party! The celebration of Christmas is lengthy, giving cooks a chance to show off for the better part of two weeks, and a daring few may even cook a turkey in addition to the traditional Mexican Christmas dishes.

A wedding reception at the bride's home might include a number of the dishes in this chapter, perhaps the Beef Tongue and Vegetable Salad and the Rice and Shrimp Salad, followed, of course, by wedding cake, a dessert wine, and *cafe de olla* or coffee in a clay pot.

On the other hand, Meatball Soup, the first recipe in this chapter, is most definitely not gala—yet it has a wonderful stick-to-your-ribs quality that can make a cold-weather gathering very festive.

I could go on and on, reviewing recipe after recipe, but I will instead urge you to try them out and discover for yourself how very special they are. I am sure you will adopt them as your "fiesta" dishes, too.

MEATBALL SOUP
Albondigas en Caldo

————⊙————

8 servings

2 pounds ground round or other lean ground beef
1 egg
½ cup Quaker dehydrated masa flour (masa harina) mixed with 4
     tablespoons warm water to make a small amount of dough
1 teaspoon salt
½ teaspoon pepper
2 tablespoons vinegar
2 tablespoons lard
2 tablespoons flour
1½ quarts well-seasoned chicken stock
2 green onions cut into ½-inch pieces
1 4-ounce can mild green California chiles
1 cup ripe unpeeled chopped tomatoes
¼ cup tomato sauce
4 garlic cloves, finely mashed
¼ cup fresh mint leaves or 1 tablespoon dry mint leaves
¼ cup fresh cilantro leaves and some stems

Mix meat, egg, masa harina dough, salt, pepper, and vinegar and knead to the consistency of soft dough. Make meatballs the size of a Ping-Pong ball and place on a cookie sheet. Set aside.

In a large kettle melt lard, add flour and brown lightly to make a roux. Now add the chicken stock, the green onions, chiles, chopped tomatoes, tomato sauce, garlic, mint leaves, and cilantro leaves and stems. Boil and then lower heat to a simmer. Correct seasoning.

While broth is simmering drop in meat balls carefully and poach for 30 minutes over low heat, covered.

Serve in soup bowls or soup plates with about a cupful of broth. These meatballs can be cooked in advance and stored in the refrigerator until ready to reheat. They freeze well.

Tip: To stretch the recipe, parboiled frozen peas and carrots, and a cubed potato may be added.

————⊙————

PORK RIBS AND HOMINY SOUP
Pozole

———⊙———

I would call this recipe a lazy housewife's recipe, or better still a working woman's quick recipe. It is so good, so easy, and such good eating. *Salud!*

———⊙———

8 servings

3 pounds pork loin back ribs, cut into single-rib portions
6 pieces pork neck bones
8 cups water
6 garlic cloves, finely mashed
   Salt and pepper
½ onion cut in thick slices
2 16-ounce cans white hominy

Place first 6 ingredients in large soup pot and cook for 45 minutes over high heat, partly covered. Test for doneness after 30 minutes and adjust heat accordingly. Best to simmer the last 15 or 20 minutes of cooking time. As soon as meat feels done but not falling off the bones, add two cans of white hominy, juice and all. Simmer for a few minutes more, and correct seasoning. Broth should be thin but very tasty.

Serve in large soup plates. Small plates should be set at each place setting for bone disposal. If your soup plates are big enough you may serve two ribs and one neck bone per person; otherwise second helpings are in order.

GARNISHES

In colorful condiment dishes or better still in a lazy susan, arrange chopped green onions, crushed dry oregano leaves, chopped fresh cilantro leaves, quartered green fresh limes, and crushed red pepper flakes. Serve with garlic toast or hot garlic bread. Pozole is definitely a one-dish meal, ideal for cold weather.

Note: If you feel you should have a thinner soup, add some canned chicken broth.

———⊙———

RICE CASSEROLE
Cazuela de Arroz al Horno

————☉————

8–10 servings

1 28-ounce can crushed Italian-style tomatoes
2 4-ounce cans chopped green chiles
½ cup chopped white onion sautéed in 2 tablespoons oil
  Salt and pepper
4 cups steamed rice, buttered lavishly
1 12-ounce can shoepeg whole-kernel white corn, drained
2 cups shredded mozzarella cheese
1 pint sour cream thinned with a little milk to spreading consistency

Prepare sauce. In medium saucepan, heat crushed canned tomatoes and canned green chiles and add sautéed onion. Salt and pepper to taste and cook 3 or 4 minutes over medium heat, stirring often. Your sauce is now ready.

Have steamed rice buttered and ready. Have rest of ingredients ready to assemble casserole.

In a 9 × 13-inch baking dish, suitable to take to the table, spread a layer of rice. Then spoon on some of the green chile sauce, sprinkle on a handful of corn kernels, and add some shredded cheese and a few tablespoonfuls of thinned cream. Continue to layer in this order, but be sure to top your casserole with a complete layer of thinned sour cream and cheese.

Bake in a 350° oven for 20 minutes until cheese melts and contents of casserole are hot and bubbly. This is delightful served with fried chicken and a tossed green salad.

Note: Yellow corn kernels may be substituted.

————☉————

AZTEC PIE
Budin Azteca

—⊙—

Cooks from all the regions of Mexico have their own versions of a corn tortilla casserole type of pie. Many use only green chile strips and tomatoes with cheese and sour cream, while others insist that the only way to make a tortilla pudding is with the regular green or red enchilada sauce. Still others use a chicken broth based sauce with the chile strips, cheese and cream. They are all super concoctions but I prefer one that I ate at my sister's home in Baja California. She and her husband have to be the world's best hosts! I have modified her recipe slightly, and added a different spice or two. It is delicious.

Speaking of sisters, my youngest is not a cook in the true sense of the word, but her table settings and decorations are contest winners. We call her the family Grandma Moses because she is a self-trained painter, who started painting after she became a grandmother.

—⊙—

8–12 servings

- 12 corn tortillas
- 1 cup cooking oil
- 4 tablespoons butter or margarine
- 1 cup chopped ripe peeled tomatoes
- ½ cup finely chopped scallions
- 1 teaspooon ground coriander seeds
- 4 cups shredded cooked chicken meat
- 4 cups easy Mole Sauce (page 14)
- 2 cups commercial sour cream
- 1 8-ounce package cream cheese
- ½ cup milk
- 1 garlic clove, mashed
  Salt
  Pepper
- 2 tablespoons instant chicken granules
- 2 cups shredded mozzarella cheese, or a bit more as needed

Cut tortillas in half with knife or kitchen shears and set aside to dry out slightly. Heat the oil in a large skillet and fry tortilla halves as quickly as possible, just to soften and moisten. Drain on paper towels.

In a small saucepan melt butter and sauté chopped onions and tomatoes for 2 minutes. Season with salt, pepper, instant chicken granules and ground coriander seeds. Add shredded chicken and set aside.

Cut the cream cheese into small cubes and puree in a blender with the sour cream and milk. Add the mashed garlic clove, and salt to taste. Set aside.

Prepare Mole Sauce (page 14) as directed in recipe. Add some to the chicken mixture if it seems too dry. Put the shredded cheese in a bowl and set aside.

To assemble: Line up all the ingredients in an assembly line fashion—first the fried tortillas, then the chicken mixture, Mole Sauce, sour cream mixture and shredded cheese.

Coat a 15-inch oblong Pyrex baking dish with a small amount of Mole Sauce. Place a layer of tortilla halves in the dish then a thin layer of the chicken mixture. Add a thin layer of Mole Sauce, followed by the sour cream mixture and a light sprinkling of shredded cheese. Repeat. Two layers is fine, but if you can make three layers it looks prettier. End with a layer of sour cream, more Mole Sauce and plenty of the cheese. (If you have ingredients left over assemble in a small dish, such as a glass pie plate.)

Bake in a 350° oven for 35 to 40 minutes or until the casserole is heated through and the sauce has begun to bubble.

This is great served with a crisp tossed salad, guacamole (page 49) and Refried Beans (page 236). Serve with garlic bread or sour dough bread— never more tortillas. If baked in an oblong dish serve 3 by 3 inch squares; if baked in a pie plate, serve in wedges.

———————⊙———————

ZUCCHINI AND CHEESE CRÊPES
Crepas de Calabacitas con Queso

Crêpes, the thin pancakes we customarily associate with French cooking, have grown in popularity in the last decade. Once considered complicated, they are actually quite easy to make and, since they freeze beautifully, are a great stand-by for use when unexpected guests arrive. These zucchini- and cheese-filled crêpes make a delightful luncheon dish. But crêpes can be filled with a variety of meat, fish, and seafood combinations to produce any effect you want. When covered with a sauce containing a touch of one of our famous chili sauces, crêpes offer color and spice in one stroke.

8 filled crêpes

8 crêpes (see below)
1 pound small tender fresh zucchini
2 tablespoons oil
½ cup finely chopped green onions (use both white and green parts)
   chopped
1 cup peeled chopped ripe tomatoes
1 4-ounce can chopped California green chiles
   Salt and pepper
3 cups commercial sour cream thinned with
   ½ cup milk and lightly salted
1 cup shredded mozzarella cheese mixed with 2 tablespoons
   grated Parmesan cheese

Prepare crêpes.

Wash zucchini, trim ends but do not peel. Chop fine and blanch with 2 cups boiling water. (I place the chopped zucchini in a large strainer and pour the boiling water over it.) Drain.

Heat oil in large skillet and sauté the onions, tomatoes, and canned green chiles, adding 1 or 2 tablespoons of water. Stir for 1 minute and mix in the zucchini. Season with salt and pepper, cook 2 minutes, and set aside.

Arrange crêpes and other ingredients in assembly-line fashion: crêpes, sour cream mixture, zucchini mixture, and cheese. Spread 1 tablespoon sour cream on open crêpe, sprinkle 1 heaping tablespoon zucchini mixture all over, sprinkle shredded cheese evenly over zucchini, and roll. Be stingy with the cheese; 1 tablespoon per crepe should be enough.

Spread a thin coating of sour cream on the bottom of an oblong Pyrex baking dish and place your rolled crêpes in seam side down and close together but not overlapping. Use only 1 layer. If they do not fit, use 2 baking dishes. Cover with remaining prepared sour cream and sprinkle with remaining cheese. Bake in a 350° oven until cheese is melted and crêpes are heated through. Do not allow to brown; they must remain moist and juicy.

Serve as a first course or as a luncheon dish with guacamole and a tossed green salad. These freeze well.

Note: If you have any zucchini mixture left over, sprinkle it on top of the cheese topping before baking.

NEVER-FAIL CRÊPES

20 to 22 8-inch crêpes

2 cups milk
2 large eggs
4 tablespoons melted butter or margarine
½ teaspoon salt
½ teaspoon baking powder
1¼ cups flour
1 stick (4 ounces) very cold margarine to use for coating crêpe pan

Put into blender milk, eggs, and melted butter. Whip for 1 minute. Sift together the dry ingredients. Remove lid from blender and at a very low speed add the dry ingredients by teaspoons. Then strain batter into a bowl.

Remove the top of the wrapper on the very cold margarine stick. Wrap the bottom of the stick with this extra paper to protect your hands while coating the hot crêpe pan. An 8-inch Teflon-coated skillet makes a perfect pan for this size crêpe. Heat the dry pan on a hot burner, coat with margarine, pour in a scant quarter cup of batter, and start tilting pan until bottom is covered with thin layer of batter. Cook until a pale brown, turn with a spatula, and cook 20 seconds. Fold in half and allow to cool on paper toweling.

I like to keep a supply of crêpes in my freezer. Stack them with wax paper between them, wrap the package securely in foil, mark the number of crêpes on top, and freeze.

Note: For a dessert crêpe, add 1 teaspoon vanilla and 2 tablespoons granulated sugar.

ROYAL CRÊPES WITH A TOUCH OF JALAPEÑOS
Crepas Jalapeñas Reales

————————⟨◊⟩————————

10 servings as first course or luncheon dish;
5 servings as dinner entree

10 crêpes from your favorite recipe, or see previous page
    Spinach Mixture (see below)
 1 cup deviled ham thinned with 2 tablespoons water
 ¼ cup pickling liquid from canned jalapeños (optional)
 3 cups sour cream thinned with ¼ cup milk
 1 teaspoon mashed garlic
 1 cup shredded mozzarella cheese
 ¼ cup grated Parmesan cheese
    Slices of mild canned jalapeños, or red strips, for garnish (optional)

Prepare crêpes. Prepare spinach.

Mash deviled ham, thin with 2 tablespoons water, and stir in 2 tablespoons pickling juice from canned jalapeños, if you like.

Thin sour cream with ¼ cup milk and season with mashed garlic.

Mix shredded mozzarella cheese with grated Parmesan.

Butter a baking dish large enough to hold 10 rolled crêpes in a single layer. Place prepared ingredients in bowls and arrange in assembly-line fashion on your work surface.

Place a crêpe on a plate. With a table knife or small spatula spread on a tablespoon of deviled ham, follow with a generous tablespoon of prepared spinach and a tablespoon of thinned sour cream, sprinkle on 1 tablespoon of cheese mixture and 3 or 4 drops of jalapeno juice. Roll crêpe and place seam side down in pan. Repeat with remaining crêpes until you have filled the pan with one layer only. Spread top with sour cream and sprinkle with cheese, garnish with jalapeño slices or strips if you wish, and bake in a 350° oven until crêpes are heated through and cheese is melted.

SPINACH MIXTURE
 1 10-ounce package frozen chopped spinach
 2 tablespoons oil
 ¼ cup finely chopped green onions (include some green)
 ½ cup chopped peeled tomatoes

Cook spinach according to package directions. (Do not use salt, as deviled ham is very salty.) Drain and press spinach in colander to get most of the liquid out.

Heat oil in saucepan and sauté chopped green onion with chopped tomatoes. Stir-fry for 1 minute and add prepared spinach. Set aside.

Note: The yield of the spinach is one cup, and with the addition of the onion and tomato it will be enough to fill 10 crêpes, using a generous tablespoon per crêpe.

————◦————

CANNED GREEN CHILES, STUFFED
Chiles Rellenos

————◦————

The pros and cons of the fresh green poblano chiles or the fresh California long green peppers versus the canned are quite a few. In favor of the fresh: looks, flavor, and authenticity. Arguments for using the canned chiles: ease, speed, accessibility, the saving, and the guarantee that all the chiles will be edible, if we are talking about "hot."

Mexicans today, living during an economic crisis, consider even dishes like Chiles Rellenos a luxury, as our fresh vegetables have soared sky-high in price. So my argument is, if you can afford the fresh, if they are available, and if you have the time to start from scratch, naturally choose the fresh (see page 319 for procedure). But if not, you will be serving a delightful substitute if you make your Chiles Rellenos with the canned whole chiles.

————◦————

20 small servings
10 generous servings

1 27-ounce can or 3 or 4 4-ounce cans whole green
    chiles (about 20 chiles)
1 pound Monterey Jack cheese (or a little more
    if you want to be generous)
  Salt and pepper
1 cup all-purpose flour
8 eggs
  Oil for frying

Make a slit in the side of each chile and remove the seeds. This step is easier done without a knife; canned chiles are so soft you will do better with your hands.

(Recipe continues)

Cut cheese into strips shorter than the chiles. Stuff chiles with cheese. Chiles will be too soft to stuff by pushing the cheese to their points so you will do best by wrapping chiles around the cheese sticks.

Dry the stuffed chiles with paper towels and sprinkle with salt and pepper. Roll in flour to cover thoroughly and set aside.

Separate 3 eggs (see note). In medium bowl beat the 3 egg whites until stiff and fold in the 3 corresponding lightly beaten egg yolks all at once. Mix lightly but thoroughly; egg mixture should not be streaked. Add about ¼ teaspoon salt and a pinch of pepper to the fluffy egg preparation.

In a medium skillet pour half an inch of oil to heat. Have hot, but lower the heat when you start cooking the chiles. Dip each flour-coated chile into the beaten eggs to coat, and fry in the hot oil until they are a light brown in color, as you would fry fritters. Turn with a pancake turner. I always have two on hand as I seem to do better at the turning and removing from the heat. Drain chiles well on a cookie sheet covered with a few paper towels. Serve with your Chile Relleno Sauce (pages 303–4). Be sure to be generous with the sauce, which you may thin with a can of undiluted chicken broth if you wish.

Note: I personally like to beat 3 eggs at a time because that way I always have an egg mixture that does not go flat on me. The moment I run out of egg I turn the heat off under the oil and check to see that it hasn't darkened. If it has, I drain the skillet, wipe it dry, add more clean oil, and then prepare another batch of beaten eggs with 3 more. This system will insure glorious looking stuffed peppers with plenty of egg and not a speck of skin peeking through. P.S. Reheat stuffed chiles in foil in a 350° oven for 15 minutes.

———⊙———

STUFFED GREEN CHILES
Chiles Rellenos

The creation of Chiles Rellenos entails a great deal of hard work, but it is one of those dishes that, once completed, gives you a glow and a sense of accomplishment. The lovely, golden, puffy peppers are an unforgettable experience for those who eat them the first time.

4 servings,
2 chiles to a guest

 8 green California chiles
   Oil for frying and oil for blistering the peppers
 1 pound Monterey Jack cheese
   Salt and pepper
 ½ cup all-purpose flour
 4 eggs, separated
   Quick Sauce (see below)

Wash and dry the green chiles. Dry them well; they will sputter in the oil while blistering. I use a large skillet that I can cover because even when carefully dried they sputter the oil and can burn you. Place chiles in hot oil and allow to fry about 1 to 2 minutes until a light brown color. You will see them blister as they cook. Fry on both sides and remove from oil. Peel under cold running water, trying to keep the stems on.

Cut a slit on one side and remove seeds as carefully as possible to avoid tearing the peppers.

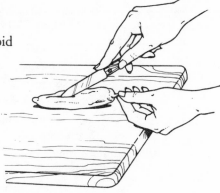

Cut cheese sticks to push in through the slits. They should measure about 4 inches long or be a little bit shorter than each chile. Stuff each chile with one cheese stick, dry with paper towels, sprinkle with salt and pepper, and roll in flour. Set aside and prepare egg mixture.

Beat egg whites in medium-sized bowl until stiff, as for meringue. Add beaten egg yolks, folding and mixing lightly so as not to disturb lightness of egg whites—but you do want a mixture that is not streaked by the yolks. Season egg mixture very lightly with salt and pepper.

Heat about half an inch of oil in a large skillet. Dip each floured chile in the egg mixture until well covered and fry in hot oil as you would fritters, turning once. They should be light golden in color.

Drain well on paper towels and serve immediately, with the sauce.

QUICK SAUCE

2 tablespoons oil
1 tablespoon flour
¼ cup chopped onion
  Salt and pepper
1 15-ounce can tomato sauce
1 bay leaf
½ cup tomato juice
1 garlic clove, mashed (optional)

Heat oil in medium-sized saucepan and brown flour in it lightly. Add onion, salt, and pepper and stir for 1 minute. Add tomato sauce, bay leaf, and tomato juice. Cook until sauce thickens. Remove bay leaf and pour into a sauceboat.

Note: If you use the garlic, mash well and stir it into sauce the last minute of cooking time.

———⊙———

STUFFED GREEN CHILES
WITH WALNUT SAUCE
Chiles en Nogada
———⊙———

6 servings

  6 tablespoons oil
  2 pounds ground meat (best to have 1 pound ground
      lean beef and 1 pound ground pork round)
½ cup chopped onion
  1 cup chopped peeled ripe tomatoes
  1 tablespoon finely mashed garlic
    Salt and pepper
½ teaspoon ground cloves
  1 teaspoon ground canela
½ teaspoon ground cumin
  1 tablespoon sugar
  1 teaspoon wine vinegar
  1 unpeeled cored apple, cubed
¼ cup slivered almonds
¼ cup raisins
½ cup sliced stuffed green olives
  6 poblano chiles
    Walnut Sauce (see below)

Heat oil in a dutch oven and add beef and pork. Cook until ground meat is no longer pink, stirring often. Add chopped onion, chopped tomatoes, and mashed garlic and season with salt and pepper, ground spices, sugar, and vinegar. Lower heat and cover. Cook for 2 minutes, stirring often, and pressing down on pieces of meat with back of spoon to keep mixture crumbly. Taste for seasoning. Add chopped apple, almonds, raisins, and sliced olives. Stir and cover. Set aside.

Heat ½ inch of oil in a large skillet and fry the chiles, blistering on both sides without burning or scorching skins (see Handling Fresh Chiles, page 18). If correctly blistered they will be a light golden color. Peel under cold running water and make a slit on the side to remove seeds and veins adhering to inside of the pepper. If chiles seem too pungent, place in well-salted cold water and soak for at least an hour. Remove from water and dry with paper towels.

If chiles are to be served cold, mix ¼ cup vinegar with ½ cup oil, add salt and crushed oregano, and brush this marinade on peppers before stuffing. Then stuff with filling and serve with walnut sauce. Or you can serve them hot, dipped in egg mixture and fried as you would regular Chiles Rellenos— definitely not traditional but common nowadays. In that case just dry peppers, stuff, fasten with a toothpick, and shake flour on them instead of rolling. Prepare beaten eggs as per Chiles Rellenos (page 320), dip, fry, drain, and serve with the walnut sauce. Sprinkle with pomegranate seeds, or if they are not available, garnish with cherry tomatoes, slices of radishes, or drained, sliced, bottled maraschino cherries.

WALNUT SAUCE

1 cup walnuts
1 8-ounce package cream cheese
1 cup half and half
  Salt
  Sugar (optional)
  Mexican cinnamon (canela) (optional)
¼ cup dry sherry (optional)

Place walnuts, cream cheese, half and half, and ½ teaspoon salt in blender container. Purée but do not overdo it; sauce should be consistency of thick mayonnaise. Add 1 tablespoon of sugar or a little less, according to taste, and flavor with dry sherry. Both sugar and dry sherry are optional and some cooks add ground canela. Suit yourself.

MEXICAN MOUSSAKA
Cazuela de Berenjena

————☉————

8 servings

1 large eggplant
4 cups boiling salted water
2 4-ounce cans chopped green chiles
8 tablespoons butter
6 tablespoons olive oil mixed with
    3 tablespoons vegetable oil
2 pounds lean ground beef round
1 cup finely chopped white onion
1 tablespoon finely mashed garlic
    Salt and pepper
½ teaspoon ground cloves
1 teaspoon canela
1 teaspoon ground cumin
1 28-ounce can Italian-style tomatoes
4 tablespoons tomato paste
    White Sauce (see below)
2 cups shredded mozzarella cheese mixed with
    4 tablespoons Parmesan cheese

Peel eggplant and cut into 1-inch cubes. Blanch in salted boiling water. Drain and mix with the chopped canned green chiles. Arrange in the bottom of a large baking dish, 9 × 12 × 2 inches or larger, buttered well with half the butter.

Heat 6 tablespoons oil mixture in a large heavy skillet and cook the ground beef until no longer pink. Stir often and press with back of spoon to keep crumbly. Add onion and garlic. Season with salt and pepper and add cloves, canela, and cumin. Cover, cook 3 minutes and remove from heat.

Purée canned tomatoes and tomato paste in blender. Heat remaining 3 tablespoons oil in small saucepan and cook puréed tomatoes and tomato paste at a low simmer for 5 minutes. Season with salt and pepper. Pour over cooked beef mixture and stir well. Set aside while you make the sauce.

(Recipe continues)

WHITE SAUCE

5 tablespoons butter
3 tablespoons all-purpose flour
1 cup evaporated milk
1 cup water
2 egg yolks mixed with ¼ cup water
Salt and pepper
4 tablespoons dry sherry

Melt the butter in a large skillet and stir in the flour. Cook until very light in color and add the milk mixed with the water all at once. Cook, stirring occasionally, until thick and creamy. Add salt and pepper. Mix the 2 egg yolks with ¼ cup cold water and stir into the cream sauce. Cook for 2 minutes, stirring constantly, and add dry sherry. Set aside.

To assemble: Pour meat sauce over the eggplant and green chile mixture. Smooth with back of large spoon. Cover meat mixture with the creamy white sauce and cover sauce with the cheese mixture. Dot with remaining 4 tablespoons butter. Bake in preheated 350° oven for 30 minutes.

BEEF TONGUE, VERACRUZ STYLE
Lengua a la Veracruzana
————⊙————

8 servings

1 fresh beef tongue
2 tablespoons salt
1 teaspoon peppercorns
2 bay leaves
¼ cup white vinegar
¼ cup salad oil
1 cup chopped white onion
1 28-ounce can peeled Italian-style tomatoes, crushed
1 tablespoon mashed garlic
1 bay leaf
1 cup broth tongue was cooked in
Salt and pepper
1 cup frozen peas and carrots, cooked
1 potato, peeled and cubed
6 to 8 pickled serrano chiles

Scrub tongue and simmer in 2 quarts water seasoned with 2 tablespoons salt, peppercorns, 2 bay leaves, and vinegar. Cooking time is normally 3 to 4 hours. Allow to cool in its own cooking liquid. Remove from broth, peel, and slice thinly. Reserve broth. Place sliced tongue in a bowl and pour 1 cup of its own cooking broth over it to keep it soft and moist.

In a dutch oven, heat oil and sauté chopped onion for 30 seconds. Add crushed tomatoes, garlic, 1 bay leaf, and the cup of tongue broth. Cook, covered, over medium heat for 10 minutes, stirring often. Season as needed.

Prepare vegetables. Parboil peas and carrots for 3 minutes in salted water and drain. Peel potatoes and cut into large cubes. Blanch potato cubes 3 to 4 minutes.

Arrange drained tongue slices in large oblong baking pan, spoon peas and carrots over tongue, add potato cubes, and cover with tomato sauce. Cover dish with thick foil and bake in a 325° oven for 20 minutes or until potatoes are done.

Serve with steamed, buttered white rice, a green salad, and hot French bread.

Note: The pickled serranos that this recipe calls for are best served in a small bowl with their own pickling liquid. It is not a good idea to cook the Veracruz sauce with chiles of any kind in it. Also, though many recipes call for stuffed green olives and capers in this sauce, these two ingredients are definitely classified as luxury items and are optional.

If you use a pressure cooker in your household, by all means choose it to cook the tongue and follow pressure cooker booklet instructions; perhaps the size of the tongue will decide the cooking time. Cool pressure cooker under cold running water and test tongue for doneness; if not ready, return to cooker and try 10 or 15 more minutes. I normally cook a 2½–3 pound tongue 45 minutes.

CHICKEN TABLECLOTH STAINER
Manchamanteles

————⊙————

This seems a homespun title for such a fancy dish, but I would say it's most appropriate. When I was a young girl, we were required in crafts class to produce gifts for our family members. The first choice among the grownups: an embroidered bib to wear when eating concoctions made with red chiles. Manchamanteles is even *more* ruinous to the wardrobe because it adds the menace of fruit and tomato stains to the red chiles.

I had never tasted chicken made this way until I encountered it at a dinner party at the home of friends. The hostess's mother, from Chiapas, was visiting, and helped her daughter with dinner preparations. I became immediately addicted to the recipe.

You can make it with whatever fruit you have on hand. I have done quite well with a can of sliced pineapple, an apple, some raisins, and a few prunes, with a few pecans thrown in for good measure. One time I had a few green tomatoes on hand. I stewed them with a cup of sugar and some ground cloves, boiled them down, cooled them, and used them as a garnish. What a master stroke! It was out of this world. So be inventive. Just keep the spices that might be considered American out of the sauce, and you're in business.

————⊙————

8 to 10 servings

2 broiler-fryers, cut up
6 New Mexico red chiles or ancho chiles
6 cloves garlic, finely mashed
4 tablespoons pork lard
2 16-ounce cans Italian-style tomatoes
½ small can tomato paste
2 tablespoons oil
1 onion, chopped
  Salt and pepper
1 bay leaf
½ teaspoon oregano leaves
1 teaspoon ground canela (Mexican cinnamon)
½ teaspoon ground cloves

½ teaspoon ground cumin

2 tablespoons sugar or to taste

1 tablespoon vinegar

½ cup sherry

3 tart cooking apples, cored, peeled, and cut into eighths

1 large can pineapple tidbits (save the juice, you may need it)

1 cup prunes

½ cup golden raisins

6 dried peach halves

10 dried apricot halves

6 dried pear halves cut into bite-sized pieces

1 cup blanched almonds

3 sweet potatoes, boiled, peeled, and cut into 1-inch pieces

3 not too ripe bananas, sautéed in butter and sprinkled with cinnamon sugar

Poach chicken pieces in well-seasoned hot water to cover. Drain and reserve broth.

Boil red chiles after removing tops and seeds. Place in blender with 2 cups reserved chicken stock and garlic cloves and purée. Strain. Heat lard and cook strained chile purée 5 minutes over low heat.

Mash tomatoes with hands, mix with tomato paste, and cook in 2 tablespoons oil with onion. Add salt and pepper and bay leaf. Cook over moderate heat for 5 minutes, add rest of spices, sugar, vinegar, and sherry and boil 10 more minutes. If sauce is too thick add pineapple juice. Add to chile purée.

In large turkey roaster layer your poached chicken pieces. Cover with a layer of the fruits (except bananas), then the almonds, and finally the tomato sauce that has been added to the chile purée.

Cover and bake in moderate oven for 30 minutes. Check a large chicken piece for doneness. Correct seasoning. Serve in large platter and garnish with pieces of sweet potato and sautéed bananas. I like steamed rice and a small salad of cucumbers and bell peppers with this. Serve with corn tortillas if you have them. And wine is the perfect complement.

———————⊙———————

NORTHERN TAMALES
Tamales Norteños

————⊙————

About 48 tamales

2 2½-pound chickens, to make 6 cups cooked chicken
  Salt and pepper
4 cloves garlic, mashed
1 quart chicken, pork, or beef stock, cooled and degreased
2 tablespoons vegetable oil
½ cup chopped onion
2 cups skinned and chopped ripe tomatoes
2 4-ounce cans green chiles, chopped or whole
½ teaspoon crushed oregano leaves
1 package corn husks (if skimpy better buy two)
5 cups Quaker masa harina (corn flour)
4 cups warm water
2½ cups pure pork lard or shortening

Make filling first. Cut up chickens and place in large kettle with lid. Add 6 cups water, salt and pepper to taste, and 4 mashed garlic cloves. Bring to the boil and partly cover. Simmer 30 minutes. Allow to cool in broth. Remove chicken from broth and remove skin. Place broth in refrigerator or freeze until grease solidifies so that it can be removed. Strain and measure and set aside. Four cups is more than enough. Shred chicken. Set aside.

In a large skillet heat 2 tablespoons of vegetable oil and sauté the chopped onion. Do not allow to brown. Add chopped tomatoes. Cook onions and tomatoes, stirring constantly. Add green chiles and ¼ cup stock that the chicken was cooked in. Add oregano. Taste and correct seasoning. Fold in shredded chicken. Mix well and set aside.

Now you must prepare the corn husks. Carefully shake out as much of the corn silk as possible; this is easily done when husks are dry and not so easily when they are wet. However, be careful not to open up the husks while dry, as they will split and break and be of no use to you. Once some of the corn silk has been disposed of, soak husks in hot water for about 15 minutes until they are soft and flexible. Wash them in warm water and drain. (I usually put an old wash cloth over the strainer in my sink to catch the debris and the corn silk.) Choose the larger husks for the tamales but hold on to the half pieces as they're very useful when you run short.

To make tamal dough, measure the corn flour (masa harina) into a bowl and add 4 cups of warm water to make a stiff dough. Set aside, covered with a damp cloth or piece of plastic wrap.

Cream shortening or lard, which has been softened at room temperature. I use my hand beater and my large mixer bowl. Whip until fluffy and creamy. Add the dough prepared from the corn flour. Then add the cool strained broth a cup or two at a time. Fold in by hand and *do not* revert to your beater or you will find the mixture all over the kitchen. Add salt to taste and beat until light and creamy. (Test by dropping a small piece into a cup of cold water; if the masa is ready it will float.) Now test your dough by heating a small skillet on top of the stove. Take a small corn husk and place a tablespoonful of dough in center, fold, and cook for 2 or 3 minutes on top of the stove in your hot skillet. When charred and blackened, open up and taste. If it comes off the husk it has the right amount of lard, and you will also find out if you put enough salt into the mixture. There is still time to correct the seasoning. *The consistency of the dough is about the same as for corn muffins.* This should serve as a guide to know how much broth to add to dough.

To make tamales: Spread 2 tablespoonfuls of dough on the wider end of a corn husk. Husks have a rough side and a smooth side. Place dough on the smooth side, spreading from left to right and only halfway down.

Place 1 heaping tablespoon of filling and—this is optional—one stuffed green olive and 2 or 3 white raisins on top of dough.

(Instructions continue)

Fold sides of husk toward center (left to center, right over left) so that they overlap.

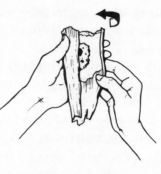

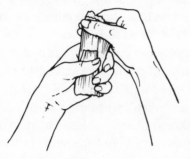

Fold the narrow pointed end toward the tamal and you're in business.

You have to do this about 48 more times. This is indeed a labor of love. The filling must be placed smack in the center of the dough-covered husk so that the sides will fold over and cover the filling completely.

How to steam: I like to steam my tamales in a large dutch oven (about 5 quarts). You may use a steaming rack if you have one or you may improvise, as I do, using aluminum foil. I crumble a large sheet of the heavy roasting aluminum foil and lay it on the bottom of the pan. Then I build a pyramid of tamales on top of the foil, open ends up (see illustration below). Then I pour water carefully around the sides just to the top of the foil. (Whether you are using a steaming rack or the foil method, the water should never touch the tamales). Dampen an old dish towel, squeeze and lay across the tamales. Cover tightly. Place over high heat until water starts to boil, then reduce heat to medium and steam for 45 minutes. Check the water after about 20 minutes and add more if necessary.

(Instructions continue)

Dip fingers in cold water before attempting to dislodge one from the stack, first lifting the dish cloth with some kitchen tongs. Let the tamal cool a bit before tasting. If it is not done you will detect a slight raw flavor; however, 45 minutes' cooking time is ample. Let stand at least 20 or 30 minutes before serving. If you don't, the dough, though cooked, will be too soft and difficult to scrape from the husks.

Serve these chicken tamales with additional green chile salsa (preferably cooked), Refried Beans (page 236) and a crisp salad with a garlic-flavored vinaigrette. Best served with coffee.

Note: Tamales freeze beautifully uncooked. When you are ready to use, simply steam them straight from the freezer for twice the normal cooking time. Do not thaw first.

TAMALE PIE
Tamal de Cazuela

12 slices

1 cup corn flour (masa harina)
1 cup all-purpose flour
1 teaspoon sugar
4 teaspoons baking powder
½ teaspoon salt
½ cup shortening
1 egg
1 cup milk or chicken broth

Filling: 2 cups shredded cooked chicken prepared with Basic Red Chile Sauce (page 285) boiled down to a thicker consistency, a few softened raisins, and some chopped or sliced stuffed green olives.

Mix all the dry ingredients in a large bowl. Cream shortening in a small bowl and add slightly beaten egg and milk or broth. Add dry ingredients by the spoonful and beat after each addition. If too dry, add some canned chicken broth slightly diluted with ¼ cup water. Masa must be of spreading consistency.

I prefer to use a 12 × 9 × 1-inch cookie tin. The tamale pie bakes faster and is much easier to cut and serve. Cover bottom of well-greased baking tin with a thin layer of prepared dough. Spread chicken filling evenly, sprinkle chopped stuffed olives and raisins over all, then cover with remainder of dough. Smooth with a rubber spatula.

Bake in a preheated 350° oven for 45 minutes. It must not be too dry to the touch. Serve in 3 × 3-inch squares with Refried Beans (page 236), extra red sauce, some salad, and a green vegetable.

---⊙---

PORK TAMALES
Tamales de Puerco
---⊙---

12 medium or
16 small tamales

2 pounds pork shoulder blade steaks or pork butt
6 cups of water
1 tablespoon mashed garlic
1 tablespoon salt for cooking meat
  Red Chile Sauce (see below)
2 cups instant corn flour (masa harina)
1¼ cups warm water
⅔ cup shortening or pork lard
1 cup reserved pork broth, cooled and well strained
1 teaspoon salt for the tamal dough
1 1-pound package corn husks, or perhaps 2 to be on the safe side
  Sliced stuffed green olives
  Raisins

For filling: Cut the pork meat up into large pieces and cook with 6 cups of water, mashed garlic, and salt. Cook until meat is very tender. Allow to cool in its own broth. Remove fat and shred the pork. Set aside. Cool.

While pork is cooling, prepare Red Chile Sauce. Stir 2 cups sauce into shredded pork.

For dough, moisten the instant corn flour with 1¼ cups warm water. Set aside. Beat the shortening or lard with a hand electric beater until creamy and fluffy. Fold in the corn flour dough lightly and add the cup of cool strained pork broth and salt. Dough should be of spreading consistency. If a small piece of dough dropped into a cup of cold water floats, the dough is ready.

Corn husks must be soaked in hot water for at least 20 minutes. Try to remove the inside husk without opening. The corn silk gets over all the husks and is tiresome to remove. Wash the soaked corn husks under warm running water and set in a colander to drain.

To assemble the tamales: Hold a corn husk in the palm of your hand with point resting on inner wrist. Place 1 heaping tablespoon of dough in the center and spread toward wide end. Fill with 1 tablespoon of meat, 1 slice of stuffed green olive, and 2 raisins. Fold sides of husk over the filling. Fold the pointed end of the husk over with seam on the outside. When steaming, stand the tamales on their folded ends in a steamer and place them in a deep covered pot with 2 cups of water. Steam, covered, 1 hour. If you do not have a steamer, crumple several pieces of thick foil in the bottom of a dutch oven, arrange the tamales in a pyramid on top of foil, cover with a damp napkin, and carefully pour water in around the sides. Cover with lid and steam.

RED CHILE SAUCE

12 mild New Mexico chile pods, stems and seeds removed
4 cups hot water
4 garlic cloves
2 to 4 tablespoons lard
3 tablespoons flour
Salt
¼ teaspoon oregano leaves

Remove stems and seeds from the red chile pods and cook in 4 cups of water until soft and plump. Drain. Place cooked chiles in the blender container and add 2 cups of cold water and the garlic. (If blender container seems crowded make sauce in 2 batches, each about 6 chiles, 2 garlic cloves, and 1 cup of cold water.) Purée until almost liquid. Strain in ricer or coarse strainer. The fine-textured strainer will not do.

Heat 2 to 4 tablespoons pure pork lard in a dutch oven and add 3 tablespoons flour. Brown lightly, stirring often, for a mild flavored roux. Add strained red chile mixture all at once and cook over medium heat until sauce thickens. Salt to taste and add the crushed oregano. Stir 2 cups of sauce into the shredded pork meat. Set aside for filling. Save leftover sauce for another use.

Note: If you prefer to make cocktail-size tamales, use 1 teaspoon of meat filling for each. The filling freezes beautifully.

MEXICAN SAUSAGE
Chorizo

————⊙————

Chorizo, that magical sounding word, is the appropriate singsong name for a unique flavor. Of course, not all chorizo is the same, and homemade chorizo without the casing, be it nature's own or a plastic casing, is most assuredly better, infinitely better. Making it with half pork and half beef renders this delectable dish superb in flavor, less greasy, and much easier on the digestive system.

It is important to note the word "pure" before the ingredient ground dry red chile. This means *no* additives of any kind, most especially spices. The reason for this underscored wording is that a certain type of "chili" (not chile) powder—with spices—is sold in the United States for use in Texas chili con carne recipes, delightful but not Mexican. Please follow this recipe step by step and use no substitutes if you wish to duplicate its unbelievable flavor.

Chorizo keeps well once it has been sautéed properly. It freezes beautifully and thaws like a dream in a microwave oven right in the small plastic bag it was frozen in. Use wherever chorizo is called for, but precook it very, very carefully over very low heat. If it scorches it will be bitter.

When packed in casings, each link would be called a chorizo. Hence use plural "chorizos."

————⊙————

8 to 10 servings

1 pound lean ground beef
1 pound ground round of pork
1 tablespoon finely crushed garlic (more if you like garlic)
1 tablespoon salt
¼ cup white vinegar
1 teaspoon black pepper
1 teaspoon ground canela (if not available,
    do not substitute cinnamon, simply omit)
½ teaspoon ground cloves
1 tablespoon crushed oregano leaves
¼ cup dry wine (any leftover wine except sparkling wine is fine)
1 teaspoon sugar
1 4-ounce package of pure ground dry red chile (use a 3-ounce
    package for a milder flavor)
1 cup boiling water

Place ground meats in a large bowl and add the crushed garlic and the salt. Add vinegar and mix well. Sprinkle pepper and ground spices over the mixture and blend. Sprinkle with crushed oregano, the red wine, and sugar. Mix well and knead lightly.

Place the ground red chile powder in a small bowl and add the boiling water all at once. Stir well to make into a paste. Work all of it into the meat mixture until well blended. The chorizo should now have a lovely red-orange color. Cover and set in refrigerator to ripen overnight.

Sauté the sausage in 1 cup pork lard in dutch oven over low heat until crumbly and partially cooked. Chorizo should always be cooked in pure pork lard, in a heavy skillet over medium heat, and should be stirred often. Cool. Pack in small plastic bags in 1-cup portions. Tie and freeze. Thaw and pan-fry like hash before using. Great with scrambled eggs.

————⊙————

BROILED WRAPPED OYSTERS
Ostiones Envueltos

————⊙————

Wrapped Oysters was an outstanding dish in the restaurant of the Chihuahua Hilton many years ago. It is such a tasty little tidbit that one becomes addicted the first time around. Beware.

————⊙————

6 servings as appetizer;
4 servings as entree

Sweet paprika or pure ground red chile powder
Flour
Salt and pepper
36 oysters
18 slices bacon

Mix sweet paprika or ground chile powder into the flour and add salt and pepper to taste. Drain oysters and roll in flour.

Cut bacon slices in half, wrap around the oysters tightly, and fasten with a toothpick. Broil in the oven until bacon is crisp, and drain on paper towels.

Serve in heated dish with sauce on the side. Use a spicy cocktail sauce with 2 tablespoons dry wine and some Tabasco sauce. If you are using this as a main course, serve saffron rice with it, and perhaps a light green salad.

SHRIMP IN CREAMED CHIPOTLE SAUCE
Camarones Enchipotlados

————⊙————

4 servings

1 pound medium-sized shrimp
4 tablespoons oil
¼ cup chopped onion
½ cup chopped peeled ripe tomatoes
½ cup heavy cream
1 cup mayonnaise
1 teaspoon pickling sauce from a can of chipotle chiles
   Salt and pepper
1 teaspoon ground cumin

Clean shrimp; leave tip of tail on. Heat 2 tablespoons oil in wok or large skillet or dutch oven and stir-fry 3 minutes. Add 2 tablespoons oil and onion and tomatoes and stir-fry 2 more minutes. Add cream. Mix mayonnaise with chipotle sauce and add to cooked shrimp. Sprinkle with cumin. Taste for seasoning. Serve. This concoction is great over steamed white rice, or with a hot, well-buttered pasta with Parmesan cheese sprinkled over the shrimp.

————⊙————

EXOTIC CRABMEAT HASH
Salpicon de Jaiba

———⊙———

This crabmeat delight is expensive and glorious. It is a Tampico dish, a favorite often prepared to be served at wedding receptions. In one of our popular restaurants it is served with a salad, au gratin potatoes, and hot fresh rolls and butter. I think it deserves to be served with Champagne or a choice Rhine wine! As an appetizer this hash would be a winner if served in hot miniature flour tortillas, but corn chips, melba toast, or toasted cocktail-size rye bread would do just as well.

———⊙———

about 2 cups

    1 pound fresh, frozen, or canned crabmeat (2 cups)
    ¼ cup oil
    ½ cup finely chopped green onions
    1 cup chopped peeled ripe tomatoes
      Salt and pepper
    1 green serrano chile, cut into slices (be sure to count them)
    1 tablespoon finely mashed garlic
    8 tablespoons softened butter
    ½ teaspoon ground cumin
      Cloves
      Canela

Thoroughly drain crabmeat and pick over to remove all the bits of shell and cartilage. Shred.

Heat the oil in a large skillet and sauté the chopped onions with the chopped tomatoes, adding salt and pepper to taste. Do not allow to brown. Add the shredded crabmeat and stir well. Push the chile slices into the mixture. Cover and remove from heat. Set aside.

Mix mashed garlic with the softened butter. Heat half of it in a large skillet; do not brown. When bubbly, spoon in the crabmeat mixture, pushing it down into the butter with the back of the spoon. The idea is to lightly brown the crabmeat to look like hash. While cooking, sprinkle with ground spices. First the cumin, and then the cloves and canela. Use ½ teaspoon cumin and sparingly sprinkle the other two spices. If canela is not available, omit—do not use cinnamon.

(Recipe continues)

Heat the rest of the butter in another skillet and flip the hash over into it to brown the other side. Serve in skillet (if it is shiny new and a lovely color) or in a round platter, but be sure not to disturb the hash circle.

Eat by spooning into fresh miniature flour tortillas, and flavoring with lime juice. These tidbits are called mulitas, cousins to burritos. Beware, it is easy to get addicted to them. Remove chile if too hot.

————⊙————

COMBINATION VEGETABLE SALAD WITH SHREDDED BEEF
Salpicon

————⊙————

8 servings

2 pounds lean, boneless top round steak
4 cups water
2 teaspoons salt
½ teaspoon peppercorns
2 bay leaves
2 medium potatoes, boiled
2 zucchini, parboiled crisp-tender
1 cup frozen peas
2 carrots, peeled and sliced
1 cup green beans
1 sliced onion
2 tablespoons oil
  Salt and pepper
2 teaspoons dried oregano leaves, crushed
1 garlic clove, finely mashed
⅓ cup vinegar
1 cup Monterey Jack or white Cheddar cheese cubes
1 poblano pepper, roasted, peeled, and seeded before chopping, or
    3 meaty canned pimientos cut into wide strips
1 recipe Onions Yucatán Style (page 340)

Cut steak in large pieces and place in a large saucepan. Add water, salt, peppercorns, and bay leaves. Cover and simmer until meat is tender, about 1½ hours. Allow to cool in its own broth. Drain and be sure to remove peppercorns and bay leaves. Shred meat. Set aside. Strain broth and refrigerate.

Boil the potatoes in their jackets as for potato salad. Plunge into cold water and peel. Do not slice until completely cool. Blanch sliced zucchini in boiling salted water 1 minute and drain. Cook frozen peas per package instructions. Do not overcook, as all vegetables must be crisp-tender. Carrots should be cut up into ¼-inch rounds and cooked in salted water. Green beans are best if fresh but frozen do well. Cook crisp-tender. Slices of onion should be rather thin and halved. (I usually cut the onion in half and then slice not too thin.)

Heat 2 tablespoons oil in medium-sized skillet and pan-fry the shredded meat, stirring often. Season with salt and pepper, sprinkle with 1 teaspoon crushed dry oregano leaves, and add ½ teaspoon of finely mashed garlic. Stir-fry 1 minute and place in a bowl in the refrigerator to cool. Be sure meat is cold before you assemble the salad.

For attractive service, a large fancy platter is a must. Layer your cooked vegetables from the rim of the platter inward, as follows:

1. Sliced potatoes seasoned with vinegar, oil, and salt and pepper
2. Carrot slices cooled and seasoned with lime juice
3. A band of green beans flavored with a little vinegar and mashed garlic, salt and pepper, and oregano
4. Peas
5. Sliced onions
6. Zucchini moistened with a tablespoon or more of vinaigrette

You may wish to make up a batch of Simple Vinaigrette (page 274) with which to season the vegetables.

This should cover the bottom of platter completely. Now sprinkle the prepared meat all over the vegetables and then layer with pickled slices of purple onion, Yucatán style, and garnish with very small cubes of Jack cheese and chopped poblano or pimiento. Since all ingredients should have been very cold, cheese will be tasty and cool and will not melt. Still want more color? Well, try a few cold ripe olives, drained and seasoned with freshly squeezed lime juice and sprinkled with salt. Add a few thick slices of canned pimientos plus choice whole cilantro leaves.

Note: This is a colorful cold dish. The platter could be larger and the recipe doubled. As to the meat, even leftover cold roast beef slices are great. Salpicon may be served with small hot biscuits, blueberry muffins, small corn bread muffins or sticks, whatever the hostess wishes in the line of hot homemade small breads. Guacamole and corn chips would be lovely. This is best as a luncheon dish, not an entree, unless your guests are light eaters.

ONIONS YUCATÁN STYLE
Cebollas Yucatecas

————⊙————

I always have some of this in a covered jar in the refrigerator. It keeps well. Naturally, I prefer red onions, but white onions taste just as good.

————⊙————

1⅔ cups

1 large purple or yellow onion
2 cups boiling water salted with 1 teaspoon salt
2 tablespoons white vinegar
½ cup Bay Leaf Tea
1 clove garlic (mashed)
1 teaspoon crushed oregano leaves
6 peppercorns
½ teaspoon salt

Peel onion. Cut in half through stem end and slice thinly into half-moon shaped slices. Place in a strainer and pour boiling water over them to blanch. Drain. Place in a small bowl and set aside. In a small saucepan boil the vinegar, bay leaf tea, garlic, oregano, peppercorns, and salt for 1 minute. Pour over blanched onions and let stand until cooled, stirring once or twice so that all of the onions get the benefit of the marinade. After using hold on to the liquid to make another recipe.

————⊙————

BEEF TONGUE AND VEGETABLE SALAD
Salpicon de Lengua

————⊙————

8 servings

 1 3-pound beef tongue, cooked in seasoned water
 2 medium-sized potatoes
 4 tablespoons oil
2⅓ tablespoons vinegar
 1 10-ounce package frozen peas and carrots, or frozen peas alone
 1 10-ounce package frozen green beans
 1 cup sliced onion
 ½ teaspoon crushed oregano
   Romaine lettuce leaves
   Canned red jalapeño strips
 2 fresh ripe tomatoes, peeled and cut into wedges
   Dressing (see below)

Scrub tongue and simmer in large soup pot in salted water to cover, adding 1 teaspoon whole peppercorns, 2 bay leaves, and ¼ cup white vinegar to pot. Cook until tongue is tender, about 3 to 4 hours, or 45 minutes in a pressure cooker. Allow to cool in its own broth. Remove skin and trim root. Slice with electric knife and place in bowl. Cover the slices with 1 cup of the strained liquid in which the tongue was cooked to keep meat from drying.

Boil potatoes in their skins until tender, and allow them to cool before peeling. When cool, peel, slice, and add 1 tablespoon oil and 1 teaspoon vinegar, sprinkle with salt and pepper, and set aside. Cook peas according to package instructions but allow less time: peas must be almost raw. Cook frozen green beans in salted water but do not overcook them. We need them crisp and green. If your frozen peas were not mixed with carrots, peel 2 carrots and slice thin. Parboil carrots in salted water for 5 minutes and drain. Blanch onion slices in boiling water for 1 minute, and cure by adding 2 tablespoons vinegar and 3 tablespoons oil, very little salt, and ½ teaspoon crushed oregano.

To assemble: Arrange romaine lettuce leaves all around the edge of a large chilled platter. Then continue circling platter from the outside in with potato slices, green beans, tongue slices, peas and carrots, more tongue slices, and so on. Spoon the dressing all over the salad and garnish with cured onion slices, red jalapeño chile strips, and tomato wedges.

DRESSING

¼ cup vinegar
¼ cup olive oil
¼ cup salad oil
½ cup Bay Leaf Tea (page 11)
1 teaspoon mashed garlic
1 teaspoon salt
½ teaspoon coarsely ground pepper

In a quart jar mix vinegar, mixture of oils, bay leaf tea, mashed garlic, and salt and pepper.

———⊙———

RICE AND SHRIMP SALAD
Ensalada de Arroz con Camarones

———⊙———

6 servings

1 cup long grain rice
1 pound medium-sized shrimp
2 cups frozen peas and carrots
1 cup chopped celery
¼ teaspoon chopped green onions
1 cup chopped dill pickles
2 cups mayonnaise
Strips of red jalapeño chiles

Cook rice according to package directions. Chill.

Place shrimp in 1 quart of water seasoned with ½ teaspoon peppercorns, bay leaf, and 2 tablespoons vinegar. Bring water to the boil and simmer for 2 to 3 minutes. Clean shrimp under cold running water. Remove vein that runs down their backs. Chop shrimp and chill.

Cook frozen peas and carrots only 2 or 3 minutes, as vegetables must be crisp-tender. Drain immediately and chill.

Mix all of the ingredients. Stir in mayonnaise. Fill a chilled bowl with salad and garnish with strips of red jalapeños.

———⊙———

SHRIMP, PINEAPPLE, AND JALAPEÑO SALAD
Ensalada de Camarones, Piña, y Jalapeños

8 servings

- 1 pound medium-sized shrimp in their shells
- 1 9-ounce can pineapple tidbits, or better still sliced pineapple
- ½ cup canned jalapeño chiles (labeled "nacho" slices—mild)
- 1 cup freshly made mayonnaise
- ½ cup sour cream

Combine 6 cups of water, 2 tablespoons salt, 2 bay leaves, 2 tablespoons vinegar, and 2 bruised garlic cloves. Add shrimp in the shells. Heat to boiling, then lower the heat and simmer for 3 minutes, or until shrimp turn pink. Drain. Peel the shrimp and remove the vein that runs down the back. Place in a bowl, cover with plastic wrap, and refrigerate.

Drain canned pineapple and cut each slice into 8 bite-sized pieces. Rinse nacho jalapeño slices or strips (if strips are long cut in half) and dry between paper towels.

Set aside 8 or 10 small shrimp for garnish and cut the rest of the shrimp in 2 or 3 pieces each.

Combine chopped shrimp, pineapple pieces, and jalapeños with mayonnaise and sour cream. Taste for seasoning. Add more mayonnaise if not creamy enough. Chill a bowl and fill with salad. Garnish with reserved whole shrimp.

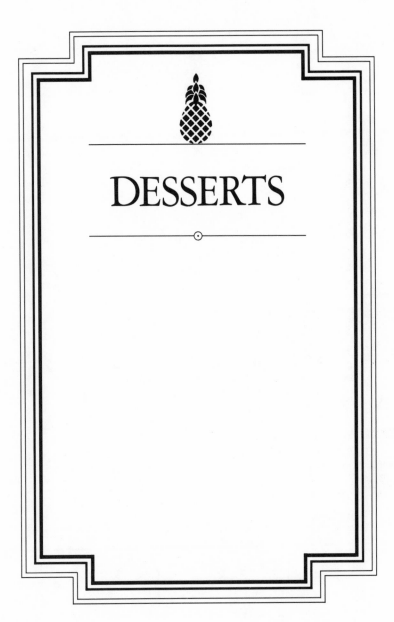

DESSERTS

M exican desserts are traditionally quite sweet and, to an American, might seem old-fashioned. However, they are delicious and eminently comforting, as they remind us of things Grandmother used to make.

Perhaps due to the lack of sophisticated cooking equipment, most Mexican desserts, other than fruit, are of the pudding, gelatine, or custard type. This can be a definite plus as they are usually very easy to prepare and hold quite well. The principal ingredients are milk, sugar, and eggs, and they take many guises. As a girl in boarding school, I kept the fixed calendar of dessert offerings in mind easily: Monday, rice pudding; Tuesday, Jello; Wednesday, vanilla pudding; Thursday, fruit compote; Friday, bread pudding made with all the leftover bread; Saturday, custard; and Sunday, ice cream. Pie seldom; cake on birthdays.

But this was better fare than I later offered my own little ones. They always had a choice: home-canned apples sprinkled with cinnamon sugar and doctored with fresh cream, or canned peaches either pickled whole or plain in slices. To this day I can hear the groans when they were asked which it would be, apples or peaches. The special dessert in those days was quince with homemade farmer's cheese. I would place an order for six crates of ripe quinces far ahead of time, and sure enough, around the first week in October I would see three or four donkeys coming down the mountain with their load of lovely yellow quinces.

The best known Mexican dessert is probably the flan, and it is wonderful. In the state of Jalisco, a layer of fruit such as cooked pineapple, or coconut, or nuts such as pine nuts or toasted almonds, is added to the pan after it has been coated with the caramelized sugar. Other times, ground pecans, almonds, or pine nuts are added to the milk, sugar, and egg mixture and then all is cooked. Delicious!

Capirotada, an interesting bread pudding, is the traditional Lenten dessert but is also served throughout the year. It is made by assembling layers of toasted or fried French bread that has been dipped in a syrup made by boiling sugar cones, water, chopped tomatoes, onions, and spices. The syrup-dipped bread is then covered with grated cheese, plump raisins, and nuts, and baked. The flavor combination is sensational and very unusual.

At the *merienda,* the Mexican evening repast somewhat similar to English high tea, one encounters pastries and luscious *pan dulce* and fruit, and sometimes mugs of a thin gruel flavored with cocoa, vanilla, or strawberries called *atole.* If you ever have a chance to taste it, do so. It's worth every fattening sip.

MILK AND EGG PUDDING
Leche con Huevo

———⊙———

This is a quick dessert similar to the old-fashioned vanilla pudding found in American cookbooks. I have included it because it was a favorite in my home when I was a small girl.

———⊙———

6 to 8 servings

¾ cup sugar
2 eggs, separated
¼ cup cornstarch
3 cups milk
1 teaspoon vanilla extract
⅛ teaspoon salt
Cinnamon sugar

In a small bowl mix ½ cup sugar, egg yolks, and cornstarch with ¼ cup cold milk. Stir into remainder of cold milk and cook, stirring constantly, in a large saucepan. Watch carefully as this mixture scorches easily. Bring to a boil over medium heat and boil 1 minute. Remove from heat. Stir in salt. Strain into large bowl.

Beat egg whites until frothy and gradually add ¼ cup granulated sugar while beating constantly until mixture is very stiff, as for meringue. Fold into warm pudding lightly. You must have a soft pudding but with a few meringue fluffs showing. Now sprinkle with cinnamon sugar and cool.

———⊙———

CREAMY PUDDING
Natillas

————⊙————

Natillas are very popular in restaurants in Mexico. I think that since many Mexican desserts are so sweet, restaurants always offer natillas for people who can't handle the gooey offerings. They are still made with too much sugar for my liking, but I have included a recipe here because it is also good as a pudding sauce and can be served with bread puddings.

Years ago vanilla beans were boiled right in the milk and later removed but now they are so terribly expensive (more than the whole dessert, I'll wager) that home cooks all use the vanilla extract instead.

This is good served with fruit—say strawberries or bananas, or better still a combination of both. Serve it after a heavy meal and in small portions, please.

————⊙————

6 to 8 servings

¾ cup sugar
2 eggs, separated
¼ cup cornstarch
¼ cup water
2¾ cups milk
1 teaspoon vanilla extract
¼ cup dry sherry
¼ teaspoon salt
¼ cup raisins

In a medium-sized saucepan, mix ½ cup sugar, egg yolks, cornstarch, and ¼ cup water. Stir in milk and continue to stir until all ingredients are combined. Bring to a boil over medium heat, stirring constantly. Boil 1 minute. Remove from heat. Stir in vanilla and dry sherry. Stir in a pinch of salt. Strain.

Beat egg whites until stiff, and add ¼ cup granulated sugar by teaspoons, beating after each addition. Fold into lukewarm pudding and sprinkle softened raisins on top.

Note: Soften raisins in dry sherry, and when they are plump and soft, dry between paper towels.

MILKLESS PUDDING
Budin sin Leche

———⊙———

Brown sugar was not a common item on grocery shelves in super-markets in Mexico until about ten years ago, and even now the maple taste of American brown sugar is missing.

This pudding was served at a ladies' luncheon that I was invited to, and I liked the flavor. When the hostess disclosed that it was a milkless pudding I was intrigued and tried it, but I added some evaporated milk to the boiling water and it made quite a difference. I have included it because it can be made with water and tastes very good.

———⊙———

6 servings

3 eggs, separated
⅓ cup cornstarch
1½ cups brown sugar
¼ cup cold water
2 cups boiling water
1 teaspoon vanilla
¼ teaspoon salt
2 tablespoons margarine (optional)
Chopped pecans

Mix egg yolks, cornstarch, and brown sugar with the cold water. Add 2 cups boiling water, stirring constantly. Cook until thickened and add vanilla and salt. Stir margarine into hot pudding. Strain into a large bowl.

Beat egg whites until stiff and fold into the pudding. Sprinkle with chopped pecans.

———⊙———

BUTTERSCOTCH PUDDING
Jericalla con Azucar Quemada

———⊙———

This is a long way from the taste of packaged butterscotch pudding —do try it and see for yourself. But this was the way it was made sixty years ago when puddings in boxes were not easily available, if they were available at all.

The caramelized sugar syrup should be made often and kept in the refrigerator to use in other dishes. It reminds me of one of my fondest memories, the little tin log cabin that Log Cabin syrup was sold in. Mother saved them for us; well washed and drained and dried in the sun, they made wonderful toys. We would make log cabin camps with them and play Indians—as you can see, I was a tomboy.

———⊙———

6 to 8 servings

⅓ cup granulated sugar
3 eggs, separated
¼ cup cornstarch
3 cups milk
8 tablespoons Caramelized Sugar Syrup (see below)
1 teaspoon vanilla extract
2 tablespoons margarine
¼ cup granulated sugar
Nutmeg

In a small bowl mix ⅓ cup granulated sugar, egg yolks, and cornstarch with ¼ cup cold milk. Stir into remainder of cold milk and add ½ cup Caramelized Sugar Syrup. Cook in a large saucepan and watch carefully, as it scorches easily. Bring to a boil over medium heat and boil 1 minute, stirring constantly. Remove from heat. Add vanilla and margarine. Pour into large bowl.

Beat egg whites until stiff and gradually add ¼ cup sugar to make meringue. Fold into warm pudding and sprinkle with nutmeg.

CARAMELIZED SUGAR SYRUP
1 cup granulated sugar
1 cup water

Place granulated sugar in a heavy saucepan and melt, stirring often, until a golden color. Add water and boil until all of the caramelized sugar dissolves. Cool and keep in a covered jar in the refrigerator. Will keep indefinitely.

SPECIAL CARAMEL PUDDING
Flan Especial

————⊙————

The flans I have eaten in my life would probably surround a state in the Union—not Texas of course, but maybe Rhode Island—and I still like it. It is a great dessert. This particular one is creamier than many, but sweeter, so serve very small pieces. It's wonderful. If you find you don't have enough syrup to coat or cover the portions you are serving, bring out the refrigerated Caramelized Sugar Syrup (page 352) you have stored away in your refrigerator, put it in a fancy pitcher, and bring it to the table.

This shows up best in a large dish instead of small individual dishes, so have your loveliest round platter ready and flip the baked flan onto it.

————⊙————

10 to 12 servings

⅔ cup sugar for caramel
1 can condensed milk
Equal amount fresh milk (pour into empty condensed milk can to measure)
4 eggs
½ teaspoon vanilla extract
½ teaspoon almond extract
¼ teaspoon salt
1 teaspoon Amaretto

To make the caramel, heat ⅔ cup sugar in a medium-sized skillet over medium heat. When sugar begins to melt, reduce heat to low and continue cooking until it has melted and browned. Spoon or pour over bottom and sides of a 1½-quart baking dish and tilt the dish so that caramel spreads evenly. Work quickly! The caramel hardens fast as it cools.

Fill blender container with all remaining ingredients and blend. Pour this mixture into cooled caramel-coated baking dish. Set in a larger pan of warm water (water must reach at least half the depth of the baking dish). Cover flan loosely with thick broiling foil to prevent it from overbrowning.

Bake in a preheated 325° oven for 1½ hours or until a knife inserted in the center comes out clean. Remove from larger baking pan and allow to cool. The flan tastes better when served chilled, so place in refrigerator for at least an hour before serving.

To serve, run a knife around the edge of the pudding and invert it on a round dessert platter. After syrup has settled around the pudding add a teaspoon of Amaretto liqueur and stir carefully so that all the syrup will be flavored.

————⊙————

AN OLD FLAN RECIPE
Receta de Flan Antigua

————⊙————

This is one of those recipes found in an old battered yellow-paged cookbook—caramel pudding the way it was made years and years ago. I thought it might be a nice addition to this cookbook.

————⊙————

6 to 8 servings

⅔ cup granulated sugar for caramel
5 eggs
2 egg yolks
4 cups half and half (half cream and half milk)
¼ teaspoon salt
1 cup sugar
1 tablespoon vanilla extract

Have a 2-quart pudding dish ready. Be sure it is dry. Melt and caramelize ⅔ cup sugar in a heavy skillet. When sugar melts and turns a light golden color, which usually takes about 5 minutes, pour into the pudding dish and tilt back and forth with a swirling motion to cover bottom and sides of dish. Set aside and allow to cool.

Beat eggs and yolks into the half and half and add salt and sugar. Stir until sugar dissolves. Add vanilla. Strain, and pour into prepared pudding dish. Set in a pan of hot water and bake covered with foil in a preheated 325° oven for 1½ hours or a little longer. Insert knife in center; if knife comes out clean flan is done. Remove from the oven and allow to cool slightly.

Place a round, rimmed platter over the flan and flip over slowly. Do this carefully, as the caramelized sugar syrup will pour out along with the flan. Cool. Serve in wedges with some of the syrup.

Note: A good variation is substituting almond extract for the vanilla extract and serving with extra Caramelized Sugar Syrup (page 352) with 1 or 2 ounces of dry sherry added. Superb!!

————⊙————

RICE CUSTARD
Jericalla de Arroz

————⊙————

Rice desserts are great if you have served a meal with little or no starches. That is the American way, and common sense dictates that it is the correct way. Mexican cooks even one generation back are not knowledgeable about balancing meals, so you are often astonished when you read that a restaurant will offer beans, rice, and potatoes or pasta all in one meal. Serve this lovely dessert after a light repast.

————⊙————

6 to 8 servings

6 eggs
3 cups milk
½ cup sugar
¼ teaspoon salt
1 teaspoon vanilla
1 cup cooked rice
⅓ cup sugar

Separate eggs. Beat egg yolks with milk. Stir in ½ cup sugar, salt, and vanilla, and add cooled cooked rice. Pour into baking dish. Place baking dish in a larger pan of hot water and bake in a moderate oven (350°) for 30 minutes or until a knife inserted in center of custard comes out clean. Remove from oven and set aside.

Beat egg whites until stiff and add ⅓ cup sugar gradually, by tablespoons. Continue beating until shiny. Top pudding with meringue and bake in 350° oven until golden brown, as you would a meringue pie.

OLD-FASHIONED RICE PUDDING
Arroz con Leche a la Antigua
————⊙————

When I was a small girl, my grandmother used to make an enormous bowl of this rice pudding with a thick sprinkling of cinnamon sugar on top. But she put a shaker of more cinnamon sugar on the table to take care of those of us who never got to taste the topping. If Dad was in the city, the choicest morsels were always set aside in small containers for him. Our enormous wood range had a shelf on top used as a food warmer so his food (well covered) was placed there and kept warm. When it came to the rice pudding, he was served the entire top with the delicious crust of cinnamon sugar. Then the cinnamon-sugar shaker went into action as another thick topping was sprinkled on the rice. When my girls were growing up they preferred this rice to oatmeal in the morning so I made it for them for breakfast once or twice a week.

————⊙————

8 servings

1 cup long grain rice
2½ cups hot water
¾ cup sugar
½ teaspoon salt
¼ cup cornstarch
3 eggs, separated
¼ cup cold water
3¼ cups milk
1 teaspoon vanilla
6 tablespoons sugar for meringue
Cinnamon sugar

Place rice, 2½ cups hot water, ¼ cup granulated sugar, and salt in top of double boiler and cook over boiling water until rice is cooked and all water is absorbed, 30 minutes. Place cooked rice in large bowl and allow to cool.

Mix ½ cup sugar, ¼ cup cornstarch, 3 egg yolks, and ¼ cup cold water. Pour into 3 cups of milk and whisk until all ingredients are combined. Cook in large saucepan, stirring often, until mixture comes to a boil. Cook 1 minute and strain over rice. Add vanilla.

Beat 3 egg whites until stiff, add 6 tablespoons sugar by tablespoons, beating after each addition. Fold meringue into warm pudding. Do not stir, as pudding should be soft and fluffy. Sprinkle with cinnamon sugar. May be served warm or chilled.

RICE PUDDING
WITH COCONUT TOPPING
Arroz de Leche

Rice pudding recipes abound in Mexican cookbooks. Years ago it was a very popular dessert. You will still find it on restaurant menus and on dessert carts. Sometimes it's good and other times not so good. I always ask for a cognac to have with my after-dinner coffee and save a teaspoonful to pour over my rice pudding. It gives it quite a lift as does any liqueur.

Serve this in sherbet glasses and pour on a little of whatever you happen to have handy and note the difference.

6 servings

1 cup long grain rice
½ teaspoon salt
¾ cup sugar
2 eggs, separated
¼ cup cornstarch
¼ cup cold water
2½ cups milk
½ teaspoon lemon extract
4 tablespoons sugar for meringue
1 tablespoon shredded coconut

Boil rice in 2 cups water with ¼ teaspoon salt and ¼ cup sugar. When cooked, drain and chill.

Mix ¼ cup sugar, 2 egg yolks, and cornstarch with ¼ cup cold water. Stir into cold milk and add salt. Cook in a medium saucepan until thick, stirring often. Strain into a large bowl and add lemon extract. Add rice.

Beat egg whites until stiff. Add 4 tablespoons of sugar gradually, beating constantly. Fold into warm pudding. Sprinkle with 1 tablespoon shredded coconut.

SYRUP-COATED BREAD PUDDING
Capirotada

———⊙———

This is a fantastic dessert and very Mexican. It is most often served
during the Lenten season, I suppose to make up for the absence of
meat. The idea of flavoring the syrup with tomatoes, cilantro, and
onions is brilliant. This departure from the normal molasses flavor
is unexpected and teases the taste buds. Combining cheese with the
syrup is also very Mexican.

———⊙———

10 to 12 servings

2 cups molasses-flavored Syrup I or II (see below)
Lard or oil for frying tortillas and roll slices
4 corn tortillas to line pudding dish
6 small stale French rolls, sliced
½ cup raisins
½ cup chopped pecans or walnuts
2 cups shredded mozzarella cheese

First, prepare syrup according to recipe and instructions below.

Heat lard or oil and deep-fry the corn tortillas first, dipping them into the
hot grease to soften them. Set aside. In the same hot lard or oil, deep-fry the
roll slices until slightly crisp and golden. Drain on paper towels. Set aside.

Have ready any vegetables you removed from syrup, along with raisins,
chopped nuts, and shredded cheese.

In a large baking dish at least 15×9×2, arrange the softened tortillas in
the bottom to line the dish. Layer the fried roll slices dipped into the syrup.
Top with bits of reserved vegetables, raisins, nuts, and shredded cheese. Repeat. Top layer must be cheese. Bake in a 350° oven until ingredients are
heated through and cheese has melted. If you have any syrup left, strain it into
a sauceboat and take it to the table to serve separately. Do not pour it over
the pudding before baking; the bread must not be too soggy.

MOLASSES-FLAVORED SYRUP I
2 cane sugar cones (piloncillo) (page 13)
2 cups water
2 ripe tomatoes
Peel from 1 orange, cut into strips

¼ cup 1-inch slices green onions
6 cloves
2 1-inch cinnamon sticks
½ cup fresh cilantro sprigs
¼ teaspoon salt

Place cane sugar cones in 2 cups water in large saucepan and add tomatoes cut in quarters, orange peel, green onion, cloves, cinnamon sticks, cilantro sprigs, and salt. Bring to the boil and lower heat. Watch carefully, since the syrup tends to boil over. Simmer over medium heat until cane sugar melts and syrup has thickened slightly. Strain into a bowl, pressing against bottom of strainer to catch flavors. Cool. If possible, reserve some of the orange strips and bits of cooked tomato to use in pudding layers.

MOLASSES-FLAVORED SYRUP II
1 12-ounce bottle natural light molasses
2 cups water
½ teaspoon salt
1 cup sugar
2 ripe tomatoes
    Peel from 1 orange, cut into strips
¼ cup 1-inch slices green onions
6 cloves
2 1-inch cinnamon sticks
½ cup cilantro sprigs

Place all ingredients in large, deep saucepan and boil over medium heat for 20 minutes, stirring occasionally. Watch carefully; syrup tends to boil over. Strain and set aside to cool. Try to save some of the bits of cooked tomato and the orange strips to use in the layers in the pudding dish.

Note: A lower calorie version would be to toast the bread slices in a moderate oven until golden and crisp. Spread with a small amount of lard or shortening as if it were butter and proceed with recipe instructions.

———⊙———

PINEAPPLE BREAD PUDDING
Budin de Pan con Piña

———⊙———

When I was a small girl this recipe was prepared often in my home to use up day-old bread. The crushed pineapple and the nuts made it special. It was so good warm or cold.

———⊙———

6 to 8 servings

1 cup sugar
3 cups milk
2 eggs, separated
¼ teaspoon salt
1 teaspoon lemon extract
4 cups leftover bread
¼ cup white raisins
1 7-ounce can crushed pineapple, well drained
½ cup chopped nuts
8 tablespoons butter
4 tablespoons sugar for meringue

Mix sugar, milk, egg yolks, salt, and lemon extract. Whisk until well mixed and sugar dissolves.

Butter a 9 × 13-inch oblong baking pan and arrange the broken slices of stale bread in bottom of dish. Cover with milk mixture. Sprinkle raisins on top and spoon drained crushed pineapple over all. Top with chopped nuts and dot with pieces of butter.

Set in a larger baking pan half-filled with water, and bake in a 350° oven until set. Remove from oven and set aside, but leave oven on, turning it up to 375°.

Beat egg whites until stiff and add 4 tablespoons sugar gradually, beating after each addition. Cover bread pudding with a thick coating of meringue and return to hot oven. Bake until topping browns to a soft golden color, about 30 minutes.

Serve with whipped cream flavored with vanilla.

———⊙———

POUND CAKE
Marquesote

————⊙————

Pound cake used to be the most expensive homemade cake ever. I remember listening to my mother's friends discussing the recipe, with one pound of butter and one dozen eggs, all the other ingredients, and always cognac for flavoring. This marquesote recipe is a far cry from those cakes and just as delicious. Bakeries in Mexico city now add a few floured nut chips and often times a few raisins that have been soaked in sherry. I prefer it plain or frosted. It also makes a perfect base for a strawberry shortcake.

————⊙————

6 to 8 servings

¾ cup butter
¾ cup sugar
3 eggs
½ teaspoon vanilla
½ teaspoon almond extract
1¼ cup sifted flour
1 teaspoon baking powder
¼ teaspoon salt

Cream butter and gradually add sugar, creaming until light, about 5 minutes if you are using your electric mixer. Add eggs, one at a time, beating well after each addition. Add vanilla and almond extracts.

Sift together dry ingredients and stir into the butter mixture with a folding motion. Mix well. Grease a 9×5×3-inch pan, flour lightly, and shake excess flour out. It's best to grease the bottom only. Spoon in the batter. Bake at 350° for 50 minutes or until done. Cool in pan. Sprinkle confectioner's sugar on top very lightly, using a strainer or flour sifter. Serve directly from baking dish if desired.

Note: This may also be baked in a tube pan—for 1 hour at 300°.

————⊙————

TURNOVERS
Empanadas

——⊙——

Empanadas are great favorites, perfect as a sweet tidbit when you have eaten a little too much. Fillings can vary in different regions. For example, in the fruit belt where almost all fruits except citrus fruits are harvested, any combination goes. When the Pachuca, Hidalgo mines became famous in Mexico, so did the pasties. It seems that several Scotsmen were hired to run the European-owned mines. From them came the recipes for these large empanadas. Tortillas, be they flour or corn, hardened, so these foreigners introduced the Hidalguenses to something that could be carried in the lunch pail and would be soft, tasty, and palatable.

——⊙——

24 empanadas

2 cups all-purpose flour
1 tablespoon sugar
½ teaspoon salt
1 teaspoon baking powder
½ cup margarine
1 egg yolk
 Ice water (enough to hold dough together)
 Preserves for filling

Sift dry ingredients. Add margarine to flour mixture with pastry blender. Add egg yolk mixed with 4 tablespoons ice water, adding a bit more water if needed to bind the dough. Place dough in a plastic bag and let stand 30 minutes.

Prepare baking tins. Have fillings ready. I like commercial marmalades. Pineapple, peach, and strawberry preserves are nice. (I pick out the whole berries and mash them with a fork.)

Pinch off pieces of dough the size of a walnut. Roll out on floured board to 3-inch circles. Place 1 teaspoon of filling on half of circle. Moisten edges and flip dough over to shape a turnover. Press edges together and prick top with a fork. Place on baking sheet and bake in a very hot (400°) oven about 12 minutes.

——⊙——

MANGO ICE CREAM
Helado de Mango

———⊙———

A desperate hostess with little time to spare (and not wanting to serve a bakery-bought cake) might do well with this lazy-day dessert. The secret is to drain the canned mango slices well. If possible drain them by placing them on double folds of paper towels. Place in a large platter and mash with a fork. You must not purée them even though it would be faster. The idea is to have a few pieces of canned mango slices visible. This is so good, and tastes different from the mango ice cream purchased in an ice cream shop.

———⊙———

6 to 8 servings

1 quart rich vanilla ice cream
1 16-ounce can of mango slices
  Food coloring (a drop or two of red and the same amount of yellow)

Soften vanilla ice cream. Drain canned mango slices and mash with a fork. Do not purée. Mix with ice cream. Color mixture with 2 drops red vegetable coloring and then add sufficient yellow to produce a soft peach color.

Repack in ice cream container and refreeze. Serve in dessert dishes and top with whipped cream flavored with almond extract. Save a few small bits of fruit and place them on top of the whipped cream.

———⊙———

CRÊPES
Crepas

———⊙———

20 6-inch crêpes

2¼ cups all-purpose flour
½ teaspoon baking powder
2 tablespoons sugar
½ teaspoon salt
2 cups milk
2 eggs
2 tablespoons melted butter
½ teaspoon vanilla

Mix flour, baking powder, sugar, and salt. Stir in remaining ingredients. Blend in blender for 1 minute. Strain. Set aside.

Heat a 6- to 8-inch skillet and smear the bottom with butter. (I keep a cold quarter-pound stick of butter nearby, but away from the heat of the stove, and use it to coat the bottom of the skillet. The heat melts the butter instantly.) Pour ¼ cup of batter into the skillet and quickly rotate the pan so the batter covers the bottom in a thin film. Return to heat and cook until light brown. Loosen with wide spatula, turn, and cook other side until light brown. Spread less attractive side of crêpe with soft butter, sprinkle with 1 teaspoon of sugar, fold, and set on wax paper. Keep covered.

SPECIAL FILLING
1 cup cajeta de leche (see note)
1 cup heavy cream
½ teaspoon vanilla
1 jigger tequila

Heat the cajeta de leche in the top of a double boiler. Whip the cream, flavor it with vanilla, and fold into the warm caramel sauce. Add tequila. Pour 2 tablespoonfuls over each folded crêpe.

Note: Cajeta de leche is a thick runny sauce like caramel, flavored with wine or vanilla. It is available in the Mexican section of American supermarkets in 16-ounce and quart containers.

MAIL ORDER SOURCES
FOR MEXICAN FOODS

ALBUQUERQUE
Bueno Mexican Foods
P.O. Box 293
Albuquerque, New Mexico 87103
(505) 243-2722

CHICAGO
Casa del Pueblo
1810 Blue Island
Chicago, Illinois 60608

Casa Esteiro
2719 West Division
Chicago, Illinois 60622
(312) 252-5432

Conte di Savoia
555 West Roosevelt Road
Chicago, Illinois 60607
(312) 666-3471

DALLAS
Adobe House
127 Payne Street
Dallas, Texas 75207
(214) 748-0983

DENVER
El Molino Foods, Inc.
1078 Santa Fe Drive
Denver, Colorado 80204
(303) 623-7870

EL PASO
Hilana Spice Company
7606 Boeing Drive
Suite H
El Paso, Texas 79925
(915) 779-5607

LOS ANGELES
El Mercado
First Avenue and Lorena
Los Angeles, California 90063

NEW YORK
Casa Moneo
210 West 14th Street
New York, New York 10014
(212) 929-1644

H. Roth and Son
1577 First Avenue, Box F
New York, New York 10028
(212) 734-1110

Pecos River Spice Company
186 Fifth Avenue
New York, New York 10010
(212) 620-7700

Trinacaria Importing Company
415 Third Avenue
New York, New York 10014
(212) 532-5567

SAN ANTONIO
Frank Pizzini
202 Produce Road
San Antonio, Texas 78207

SAN FRANCISCO
La Palma
2884 24th Street
San Francisco, California 94110
(415) 648-5500

SANTA FE
Theo Roybal Store
Rear 212–216 Galistero Street
Santa Fe, New Mexico 87501

SEATTLE
La Mexicana
10022 16th S.W.
Seattle, Washington 98146

Mexican Grocery
1914 Pike Place
Seattle, Washington 98101

**WASHINGTON, D.C.
AND VICINITY**
Casa Pena
1636 17th Street N.W.
Washington, D.C. 20009
(202) 632-6500

International Safeway
1330 Chain Bridge Road
McLean, Virginia 22101

INDEX

ABOUT THE AUTHOR

AÍDA GABILONDO is a well-known Mexican cook and teacher. She is the mother of four daughters, three of whom cook professionally. One of her daughers, Zarela Martinez, is the executive chef of Café Marimba on New York City's Upper East Side. Ms. Gabilondo and her husband have homes in Mexico City and Ixtapan de la Sal.